Pathways, Potholes, and the Persistence of Women in Science

Pathways, Potholes, and the Persistence of Women in Science

Reconsidering the Pipeline

Edited by Enobong Hannah Branch

LEXINGTON BOOKS
Lanham • Boulder • New York • London

Published by Lexington Books
An imprint of The Rowman & Littlefield Publishing Group, Inc.
4501 Forbes Boulevard, Suite 200, Lanham, Maryland 20706
www.rowman.com

Unit A, Whitacre Mews, 26-34 Stannary Street, London SE11 4AB

British Library Cataloguing in Publication Information Available

Library of Congress Cataloging-in-Publication Data

Names: Branch, Enobong Hannah, 1983- editor.
Title: Pathways, potholes, and the persistence of women in science :
    reconsidering the pipeline / edited by Enobong Hannah Branch.
Other titles: Women in science
Description: Lanham : Lexington Books, [2016] | Includes bibliographical
    references and index.
Identifiers: LCCN 2016013606 (print) | LCCN 2016015809 (ebook) | ISBN
    9781498516365 (cloth : alk. paper) | ISBN 9781498516372 (Electronic)
Subjects: LCSH: Women in science.
Classification: LCC Q130 .P384 2016 (print) | LCC Q130 (ebook) | DDC
    500.82—dc23
LC record available at https://lccn.loc.gov/2016013606

Contents

~

Figures

~

Tables

~

Introduction
Enobong Hannah Branch

What's wrong with the pipeline? Everything. The pipeline assumes a passive flow of women (and men) from one stage to the next culminating in a scientific career. Women's underrepresentation in science results then from their leakage from the pipeline, while men are more likely to persist. But this assumes equitable conditions for women along the way. Yet, we know men and women have different experiences in science. The battle seems to be over who can do science and who is rewarded. With the exception of fields that have tipped, or are tipping for women (e.g., biology and chemistry), men predominate. In both subtle and overt ways, the message is that women are outsiders in science.

Hence, if we focus on the pipeline, without acknowledging the battle women face to succeed and persist in science, we can actually facilitate a revolving door of women in science. Women, who perceived the challenge initially as one of entry but must engage continually in a struggle to demonstrate their belonging, are not served by interventions that simply help them get in the door. The assumption is untenable that simply moving women along from one stage to the next will solve the problems of underrepresentation and attrition. The pipeline metaphor does not engage the question of who leaks and why, more importantly, it does not ask who stays and how?

The choices women make to remain in or leave science are not "free" but are a response to conditions that are often unfavorable. What makes some women resilient, while others leave? An alternative model is needed that better articulates the ideas of agency, constraint, and variability along the path to scientific careers for women.

Imagine a Road

Envision for a moment the science pipeline. Is the pipeline the same for all groups? Is the entry point wider for men and narrower for women? Is the entry point wider for majority versus minority groups? Is there only one entry site or are there multiple sites? Where do sites of leakage appear? Why? Are the leakage sites wider for women and minority groups? How much does where you get on or off matter for success in the field? Are there bottlenecks? *Now imagine entry into scientific careers as a road with exits, pathways, and potholes: some people leave, some journey on, and some get stuck.*

This approach solves a few problems. First, the road offers us three vantage points to explore the experience of women once they enter science. What *pathways* facilitate women's success? What *potholes* impede women's progress? What contributes to the *exit* of women from science? Second, it highlights that the challenges faced on the road to scientific careers are not experienced uniformly. The first thing needed to navigate the road is a *car*. Even if the road were perfectly flat, with no imperfections, the difference between a new car with all the bells and whistles and an old jalopy would be appreciable. As the road conditions deteriorate, the conditions of the car become all the more important, directly impacting how, or whether, the driver can navigate the road ahead and certainly comfort along the way. If the road is bumpy, for instance, the driver of a car with good suspension can navigate it comfortably, since the car will absorb the shock of the bumps, whereas a car with bad suspension assures a rough ride for the driver, who will feel every bump in the road. *The car reflects the resources women have available to navigate the pursuit of scientific careers.*

Finally, the road and car draw attention to the driver. *Although the challenges to pursuing science appear universal, the challenge of a pothole is experienced individually.* Whether or not you hit a pothole, or are able to navigate around it, depends on the ability (agency) of the driver. Similarly, poor driving conditions (e.g., heavy rain) impact all drivers on the road. However, the ability of the driver to navigate it depends on their tools and the conditions of their wiper blades and tires, as well as driving ability. Likewise, *the presence or absence of tools and conditions will likely result in different outcomes for women compared to men on a scientific path.*

Imagining women navigating science as a driver navigating a road is also useful as it helps us to consider the roles of background and other character-istics. For example, we know the quality and age of a car matters, and can compare that to the economic and academic background of women. Horse-power could reflect a women's personal drive or commitment to the pursuit of science. Or the absence of passengers in the car could be compared to the relative isolation of women within their field. Familiarity with the local area would be similar to familial experience in or otherwise personal exposure to a scientific career. Women with a parent or cousin, for instance, employed in a scientific field have insider knowledge and a resource that can enable them to succeed despite challenges. Similarly, early exposure to scientific careers via science camps in middle school or robotics camps in high school can build the confidence and capacity of young women. Mentorship visits by underrepresented minority or women scientists can challenge the prevailing vision of who a scientist is (often presumed as white and male), what they do (work in a dark lab), showing them that another scientific world, in which they (and their interests) fit, exists.

Training for and pursuing a career in science can be treacherous for women; many more begin than ultimately complete at every stage. Charac-terizing this as a pipeline problem, however, leads to a focus on individual women instead of structural conditions. The metaphor of navigating a road refocuses our attention on challenges posed by and the conditions of scien-tific careers. Similarly, the car and driver draws our attention to the resources possessed by and the agency of women. It provides endless possibilities for analysis and evaluation that reflect different stages (entry, persistence, or exit) or levels (undergraduate or graduate students, academia vs. industry professionals).

The chapters in this volume apply the metaphor of the road to a variety of fields and moments that are characterized as exits, pathways, and potholes. They illustrate the importance of focusing on the choices, constraints, and agency of women in science to understand which women, under what con-ditions, with what tools, successfully manage to navigate science or leave. Collectively, the chapters exemplify the utility of this approach, provide useful tools, and suggest areas of exploration for those aiming to broaden the participation of women and minorities. Although this book focuses on gendered constraints, we are attentive to fact that gender intersects with other identities, such as race/ethnicity and nativity, both of which influence participation in science. Several chapters in the volume speak clearly to the experience of underrepresented minorities in science and others consider the circumstances and integration of non-U.S. born scientists, referred to in this volume as international scientists. Disaggregating gender deepens our understanding and illustrates how identity shapes the contours of the scientific road.

Chapter Previews

The twenty-one scholars featured in this edited volume engaged purposefully in translation of sociological scholarship on gender, work, and organizations. They focus on the themes that emerge from their scholarship that add to or build on our existing knowledge of scientific work, while identifying tools as well as challenges to diversifying science. This book contains a multitude of insights about navigating the road while training for and building a career in science. The chapters contain helpful data-driven advice for a dean of an engineering school or department chair who aims to increase the representation of women in science. They are equally useful for a woman in graduate school, or a junior faculty member of color, who is anticipating or responding to the challenges that lie ahead.

The book is organized into four sections. Part I, *Navigating the Scientific Path*, examines the contours of entry and consequences of scientific field choice. "Gendered Responses to Failure in Undergraduate Computing: Evidence, Contradictions, and New Directions" (chapter 1), by Enobong Hannah Branch and Sharla Alegria, focuses on students who demonstrate at least a minimal interest in science (by choosing to take at least two introductory computing classes) and examines the effects of early failure in these classes on their decision to pursue a major in computing. Gender, it seems, drives women away from science. Yet most of the literature on women in science examines women in isolation, while men leave science too. They argue that in order to better understand the role played by gender in the decision to persist or leave science, we need to examine *both* men and women who are at-risk for departure.

"Is College Enough? Gender Disparities in the Use of Science and Engineering Degrees in the Workforce" (chapter 2), by Margaret L. Usdansky and Rachel A. Gordon, asks, does studying science in college put women on equal footing with men in the workforce? The short answer is no. Even women who major in natural science or engineering fields remain less likely than men to hold STEM-related jobs after graduation. Using nationally representative data from the National Science Foundation, they reveal the size of the gender gap among college graduates holding science degrees, explore how this gap varies by race-ethnicity, and probe two key factors that contribute to this gap: differences in the fields of scientific study selected by men and women during college and gender differences in the impact of advanced degree attainment or its absence after college.

Part II, *Detours, Off-Ramps, and Gendered Roadblocks in Scientific Careers*, examines the road of women faculty in science and the off-ramps, roadblocks, and detours that leave many stuck at the rank of associate professor. "Women Faculty in Computing: A Key Case of Women in Science" (chapter 3), by Mary Frank Fox and Kathryn Kline, argues that women faculty in computing are a strategic case for the study of women in science because of the centrality of computing in modern life and the persistent challenges for women's participation in these fields. This chapter provides a nuanced profile of women, compared to men, faculty by rank in computing fields; illustrates the potential constraints and opportunities for women's transition to higher academic ranks; and depicts how institutional practices and policies to enhance women's rank and condition would vary depending on the perspectives of "pipelines" and "pathways."

"Does the Road Improve in the Land of the Tenured? Exploring Perceptions of Culture and Satisfaction by Rank and Gender" (chapter 4), by Julia McQuillan, Mary Anne Holmes, Patricia Wonch Hill, and Mindy Anderson-Knott, urges us to reconsider our assumptions about job satisfaction and rank. The assumption that tenure, and especially full professor, is the "promised land" is so ingrained that even asking whether higher rank results in more positive perceptions of department culture and higher satisfaction may seem superfluous. Yet their analysis of faculty satisfaction by gender and rank shows that many faculty at the level of associate professor, men and women, have lower satisfaction than assistant professors. This chapter explores six measures of department culture and satisfaction (general perception of positive culture, clarity of the tenure process, workload fairness, how much colleagues value one's research, family supportiveness, and intention to stay at the university). Insights from focus groups revealed some positive stories, but more evidence of heavier service loads, an undervaluation of service, more isolation, and less support among associate and full professors, compared to assistant professors that influenced satisfaction.

"Potholes and Detours on the Road to Full Professor: A Tale of STEM Faculty at Two Liberal Arts Colleges" (chapter 5), by Catherine White Berheide, focuses on promotion to full professor at two highly selective private liberal arts college. As women faculty go down the path toward becoming full professors, they encounter detours, especially administrative service, that delay their promotion and potholes, including chilly department climates, that leave them stuck as associate professors. Using data drawn from focus groups, a survey, as well as personnel records, Berheide shows that STEM women will be more successful in contexts in which they have positive relationships with their colleagues, and in which there is more than one pathway to promotion, especially one that values administrative service sufficiently. The chapter concludes with a call for colleges and universities to develop personnel procedures for providing feedback to associate professors about their progress toward meeting the standards for promotion to full professor.

Part III, *What the Pipeline Misses: Gender Performance at Work*, examines the interactive behavior of women in scientific environments reminding us that gender is an "accomplishment, an achieved property of situated conduct" with important implications for the scientific careers of women (West and Zimmerman 1987:126). "Crisis of Confidence: Young Women Doing Gender and Science" (chapter 6), by Laurel Smith-Doerr, Timothy Sacco, and Angela Stoutenburgh, asks, what does confidence look like in a lab presentation? They seek to uncover the social processes and contexts of scientists' confidence at the intersection of age and gender. Using observations from both academic and industrial weekly lab meetings, they compared performances of expertise by young women to young men and to their more experienced women and men colleagues. Their findings suggest the lab meeting presentation—as a performance space—seems particularly fraught for young women and thus is a uniquely rich location to observe the intersection of gender and age.

"Who's the Expert? Gendered Conceptions and Expressions of Expertise by Chemists-in-Training" (chapter 7), by Laura Hirshfield, explores men and women graduate students' and postdocs' expectations about and expressions of expertise. Drawing on a mixed-methods, qualitative study of five chemistry research groups at a research-intensive U.S. university, she argues that overall, men are more likely than their women peers to be seen as experts in chemistry broadly, while women's expertise is viewed as more local. As a result, men graduate students benefit from more practice with skills that are applicable to their future careers, applying scientific knowledge to relevant questions and communicating this information to others.

Part IV, *Differential On-Ramps? Historical Forces Shaping the Scientific Workforce*, focuses our attention on how the composition of the scientific workforce has shifted over time, drawing attention to who is integrated, who is underrepresented, and why. "The Postdoc Pothole: The Changing Segmentation of the Biomedical Research Workforce, 1993–2008" (chapter 8), by Lisa M. Frehill, examines the impact of the NIH funding expansion from 1998 and 2002 on who worked as a postdoc. Frehill used the Survey of Doctorate Recipients to examine how the postdoc workforce, segmented simultaneously by gender and nativity, changed in three key time periods relative to the NIH doubling period: 1993-1998 (pre-doubling); 1998–2003 (the doubling period); and 2003–2008 (post-doubling). This chapter shows that international postdocs' growth in the biomedical research workforce was due to "competitive advantage," with especially pronounced results for women. In contrast, U.S. men's postdoc growth was associated with the general growth of postdoc positions.

"The Long Shadow of Immigration Policy: 'Appropriate Work' and Wage Inequality in U.S. Tech Work" (chapter 9), by Sharla Alegria and Cassaundra Rodriguez, argues that contemporary debates about immigration ignore the legacy of past policies that selected for highly skilled Chinese immigrants and Mexican agricultural workers that have contributed to the human capital differences between these groups today. They find considerable wage discrepancies between Mexican and Chinese tech workers and argue that these discrepancies reflect the different legacies of immigration policies that shaped the paths into the United States for these two groups of workers. The chapter concludes that there is not one "science pipeline" that may contain blockages or leaks but multiple paths into tech work that are shaped by local, national, and transnational processes.

Part V, *Creating a Road Map: Strategies for Persistence*, concludes by charting a more inclusive path forward that recognizes the gendered constraints and offers agentic solutions. "Pathways for Women in Global Science" (chapter 10), by Kathrin Zippel, argues that global academia is the new frontier for scientists as international collaborations and mobility provide both challenges and opportunities especially for women and individuals from minority groups. While internationalization intensifies some gendered barriers, it also provides additional entry points or alternatives for career paths when opportunities are limited at home. The chapter concludes with a set of recommendations for policies and practices that will both promote international collaboration and level the playing field for women and minorities.

"Agency of Women of Color in STEM: Individual and Institutional Strategies for Persistence and Success" (chapter 11), by Maria Ong, Lily T. Ko, and Apriel Hodari, describes multiple ways in which women of color are active agents in their educational and career trajectories. Focusing on four disciplines in which they are most underrepresented—physics, astronomy, computer science, and engineering—the chapter illuminates how women of color are innovative agents in the strategies they utilize to navigate and persist in STEM. These strategies include: choosing to learn and work in

safe, welcoming places; participating in STEM diversity conferences; building alternative academic and professional networks; temporarily leaving the
STEM realm; and engaging in activism. This chapter concludes with a list of
actions for institutions to further promote the recruitment and retention of
women of color, which will lead to broadened participation in STEM.

"Smooth Roads to Promotion: Creating Data-Guided and Community-
Generated Changes for Eliminating Bumps and Potholes" (chapter 12),
by Julia McQuillan, Mary Anne Holmes, Patricia Wonch Hill, and Mindy
Anderson-Knott, explores what steps universities can take to improve the
roads, road signs, and maps to help recruit, retain, and promote women
in science, technology, engineering, and math (STEM) departments. The
chapter details the map-making process the University of Nebraska-Lincoln
(aided by a NSF ADVANCE-Institutional Transformation [IT] grant) used
to transform their STEM departments and institutional practices and policies to reduce the known barriers to success of STEM women faculty. Their
process involved self-study, an honest assessment of the study results, and
ongoing formative evaluation to adjust course on the road to an equitable,
enjoyable workplace.

Let the journey begin!

PART I

NAVIGATING THE SCIENTIFIC PATH

~

CHAPTER ONE

Gendered Responses to Failure in Undergraduate Computing

Evidence, Contradictions, and New Directions

Enobong Hannah Branch and Sharla Alegria

Among professional scientific fields computing is unique.[1] Women were early entrants into the field recruited from the mostly white and female ranks of keypunch operators who already possessed the skills needed for programming (Haigh 2010). Once it became clear that computing jobs would be good jobs, women were all but barred (Ensmenger 2010). Women's representation in computing peaked in the mid-1980s when they "earned 37 percent of all U.S. bachelor's degrees in computing," and "constituted fully 38% of the U.S. white-collar computing workforce" (Misa 2010:4). By the late 1980s, women had stopped entering the field in large numbers and their representation began falling and has fallen steadily to the present to about 17 percent. Misa (2010) notes, "No professional field has ever experienced such a decline in the proportion of women in its ranks." Yet, to define the challenges facing women in computing as simply a pipeline problem would be a mistake.

While women are underrepresented at all academic stages—bachelors, masters, and PhD—as well as in the workforce, simply increasing their representation at an earlier stage will not ensure steady growth at the end of the line. Attempts at "plugging the leaks," with support and mentoring, may help to increase participation for some groups of women, but these solutions are only part of an answer. They are based on assumptions about why women are underrepresented, assume passivity on the part of women who are encouraged to persist, and see their needs as uniform (Fox, Sonnert, and Nikiforova 2011).

Hence, despite concerted efforts to broaden participation, women remain underrepresented in computing. An extensive literature examines why women are more likely to leave a scientific or technical major or career after entering (Margolis and Fisher 2003; Cech, Rubineau, Silbey, and Seron 2011; Hanson, Shaub, and Baker 2006). However, by focusing on those who have traversed a pipeline by enrolling in a computing major or entering the professional field, we are missing an important early step that may filter out many undergraduate women, that is, the decision to enter the major. Most computing majors have minimum entry requirements based on performance in introductory courses, and introductory courses in computing often have higher than average failure rates, in part because the fast pace and heavy workload is more suited to students with pre-college computing experience (Barker, McDowell, and Kalahar 2009). As a result, entry into computing majors, for those without a technical background, likely reflects resilience to initial failure or poor performance in introductory courses. Gendered stereotypes about ability, however, shape how men and women perceive their performance feedback (Correll 2001; Nelson and Cooper 1997). This chapter explores resilience to failure in introductory computing courses and whether there are gender differences in the response to negative performance feedback.

Failure and Computing: Interpreting Performance Feedback

There is no shortage of messages to women that they do not belong in computing. Dasgupta (2011) and Cheryan, Drury, and Vichayapai (2013) show that subtle cues in achievement environments, such as only male professors or class examples that reference white male geek culture like World of Warcraft or Dungeons and Dragons, signal who naturally belongs there and is most likely to succeed as well as who does not fit. For undergraduate women in computing these cues signal that they do not belong, in many cases confirming earlier messages about math ability and the stereotypical computer scientist (Cheryan, Plaut, Handron, and Hudson 2013; Good, Rattan, and Dweck 2012). What role do these persistent exclusionary messages play in the resilience of women to withstand early failure in computing?

For many undergraduates early academic failure suggests they should pursue another field; however, computing has a success mythology personified by men including Bill Gates, Steve Jobs, and Mark Zuckerberg, who have infamous careers despite early academic failure. This alternative and masculine narrative may lead men to persist in computing despite failure, whereas the diverse and persistent exclusionary messages directed toward women might lead them to interpret failure as evidence of not belonging, and thus make them less likely to persevere.

In an experiment with ten year-old students, where students were randomly assigned to a group that would succeed with a computer task or a group that would fail, Nelson and Cooper (1997) find that even when girls succeed they are more likely to attribute their success to luck rather than ability, while the reverse is true for boys. When girls failed the computing task they were more likely to attribute their failure to inability whereas only a small portion of boys attributed failure to inability, even though success and failure were unrelated to anything the students did (Nelson and Cooper 1997). Following the computing task, Nelson and Cooper had students rate their computer ability. They found that girls who succeeded at the task rated their computer ability as average and girls who failed rated their ability significantly lower than average. Boys, however, tended to rate their computer ability higher than average regardless of failure or success.

In another experimental study, Cooper (2006) found that when girls' gender identity is salient to them they perform worse on a computer task than when their student identity is salient. Cooper's study confirms that stereotype threat, the phenomenon where people perform worse on tasks when they know that people "like them" are not expected to do well, regardless of the task or the group (Aronson, Lustina, Good, Keough, Steele, and Brown 1999), is an additional obstacle for women to enter computing.

Correll (2001) shows that in high school, women need to get higher grades than their male classmates to believe they are equally competent at math. However, when men and women think they are equally competent, they pursue calculus in college at the same rate. This research suggests that while girls tend to have lower assessments of their aptitude for math, they are just as likely as boys to pursue it when they assess their abilities similarly. Grades heavily shape students' assessment of their ability, but gender shapes how they interpret the grades.

Jagacinski, LeBold, and Salvendy (1988) found that men and women had different standards for satisfactory performance. While grades mattered for men and women, women left the major if their college computing grades did not compare favorably to the standard set by their high school achievement. Cohoon and Aspray (2006) conclude, after reviewing the existing research on the relationship between grades and persistence, "women might leave at disproportionate rates when their grades are depressed by inexperience—grades that may be satisfactory to a male classmate, but fail to meet a woman's personal standards" (153). Similarly, when examining the influence of grades on persistence over time in advanced courses in the computing major Katz, Allbritton, Aronis, Wilson, and Soffa (2006:47) found:

> Very few students of either sex who earned less than a C in CS401 continued to CS445 (8 percent overall; 10 percent of men who earned C or less and 0 percent of women). However, when we performed the same test using B as the performance cut-off, we found that men who earned less than B were more likely to continue to CS445 than were women who earned less than B.

Finally Strenta, Elliott, Adair, Matier, and Scott (1994) find that "even when their grades were the same as those of men, women in science and social science did feel less confident about their ability and more depressed about their progress than men" (531).

Persistence among Undergraduate Women in Computing: Agency and Constraint

The social psychological literature on women in computing and math suggests that women need more positive reinforcement to pursue computing than their male peers (Correll 2001; Frome and Eccles 1998; Bandura, Barbaranelli, Caprara, and Pastorelli 2001). But are all women the same? The extensive literature that attempts to explain why more women are not entering computing fields emphasizes *average* differences between men and women and does not examine how the women who pursue computing fields, despite gendered obstacles, may be different from the average women who do not. While women who chose to leave computing based on performance feedback are making an informed choice, Stout, Dasgupta, Hunsinger, and McManus (2011) question women's supposed "freedom" of choice and argue that choice is "constrained by gender stereotypes in academic cultures about who seems to naturally belong in which disciplines and professions and, by extension, who is likely to succeed" (1).

The existing scholarship points to important differences among middle and high school women, yet important differences among men and women emerge in postsecondary education. It may be a greater moment of experimentation. The decision to take a class versus declaring a major is significantly lower stakes and may encourage men and women to explore areas of interest but not certain competence. By focusing mainly on women who have entered and left the computing major, scholars have left the role of performance feedback on the decision to enter the major unexamined. Gendered response to early failure may be an undercurrent driving the underrepresentation of women in computing, while masquerading as women's choice.

What if we were able to capture both men and women in their early undergraduate academic encounters with computing and determine the influence of gender on their decision to persist or leave? Using data from the Northeast Public College and University IT Course database, on students' course taking and performance, we can do just that, and examine the effects of failing an introductory computing course on the decision to enter the major.

Gender, it seems, drives women away from computing. But most of the literature on women in computing focuses on why women leave; yet men leave computing too. In order to better understand the role played by gender in the decision to persist or leave computing, we need to examine *both* men and women who are at risk for departure. In this chapter, we focus on students who demonstrate at least a minimal interest in computer science (by choosing to take at least two computing classes) and examine the effects of early failure on their decision to pursue a major in computing. If gender is the driving force behind persistence, we expect men to be more likely to rebound and persist in computing compared to women. However, femininity is not monolithic, so we do not expect "all" women to respond similarly to failure in computing.

Summary and Hypotheses

The literature explaining why more women do not enter STEM fields makes broad claims about gendered obstacles. It suggests that women are more sensitive to grades generally and already have doubts about their competence in computing and will thus be less resilient to failure than comparable men. The largely quantitative and general focus in this literature means that the findings from these studies are most applicable to the "average" women at the center of the distribution. As Thorne (1993) found in her now classic study of children at play, when she focused her attention on the "popular kids" she found the children "doing gender" in more limited ways than when she refocused her attention to the more marginal students. It is possible that the academic choices of women who demonstrate more than a passing interest in computing, resemble those marginal students Thorne observed, that is, *they may be "doing gender" more broadly and differ from the "average" women in important ways.*

The biased self-assessments of women about their competence with math and computing may be a problem for women on average, but potentially less of a problem for those women who actually pursue computing, and are thus unlike most women in their willingness to enter a male-dominated field. Thus while the social psychological literature on stereotype threat would lead us to expect women to be less resilient to failure in introductory-level computing classes than men, this hypothesis reflects the behavior of the "average" woman. On the other hand, if we focus on differences among women, particularly atypical women who pursue computing at the outset, we would not expect them to be less resilient.

Data

Data for this study are drawn from the Northeast Public College and University IT Course database. This database combines institutional data compiled by SageFox Consultants from five schools across the Northeastern United States—three public (four-year) universities and two public (two-year) community colleges. Each school provided information on the demographic background, course taking, and academic performance of all students who took at least one IT class between fall 2000 and spring 2009. The complete dataset contains data on 29,292 students, 40 percent of whom are female. This unique data allows us to follow students longitudinally through their entire academic career, observing performance in IT classes, the order and quantity of these classes, as well as their entrance into and exit from academic majors.

Due to software and data storage issues, one of the universities was only able to provide data from 2006 to 2009, and one of the community colleges only provided data through spring 2008. Another university changed data management and storage programs mid-way through the observation period and merging records from the two programs resulted in missing data. Analysis of the missing data failed to uncover any patterns, thus we are comfortable regarding the missing data as missing at random and excluding it from analysis. The community colleges tended to have a higher proportion of women students, fewer students of color, and their students tended to be older on average.

Each school provided students' demographic information, grades obtained in IT and math classes, performance and major for each semester of enrollment, overall performance, and degree completion data. Schools received detailed instructions for formatting the information provided to ensure harmony of data across all institutions. In addition, we coded each class for math and computer science prerequisites and requirements based on descriptions available in each institution's course catalog. Ultimately these five institutional files (three universities and two community colleges) were merged together to produce an all-institution file that included harmonized data for all students with consistent achievement and course information measures.

The majority of students (67 percent) took only one IT class, possibly because IT courses satisfy a general education requirement at most institutions. Since we are interested in students who demonstrate more than a passing interest in IT we restricted our analysis to students who took at least two IT classes. Of the 9,592 students who took at least two IT classes, we excluded 826 students who declared an IT major before taking any IT courses, since their major decision would have come before they had an opportunity to fail an introductory-level course. It was possible at some institutions for students to enroll in their first IT course, decide they want to be IT majors, and declare their major in the same semester as their first course. Such students would have received performance feedback, which could have influenced their decision to enter the major, throughout the semester and thus remain in our analysis. Finally, we excluded an additional 266 students whose records were incomplete. The final dataset contains 8,500 students, 71 percent were men and 29 percent were women.

Dependent Variable

The dependent variable in our analysis is entering an IT major, which we define as any major where the primary focus of classes is mastering computing skills: building, designing, troubleshooting, or fixing computer hardware, software, components, or networks. At the four-year universities the range of majors that matched this description were quite small and consisted of computer science, electronic and computer engineering, and information technology. The community colleges offered a wider range of majors and certificate programs than were offered at the four-year universities, which included all of their majors as well as programs in computer game development, help desk and software support, webmaster, network technician, and office technology management.

Key Independent Variables

We are primarily interested in three independent variables, gender, early IT failure, and the interaction between gender and early IT failure. Gender is a dummy variable coded 1 for women and 0 for men. We define early IT failure as any grade below the minimum grade required to receive credit for the class toward a major in a 100-level class. At the four-year universities the minimum grade required for credit toward a major was a C or 2.0 and at the community colleges the minimum grade required was a D or 1.0. Early IT failure is a dummy variable coded 1 for students who experience failure in an introductory-level IT class and 0 for students who did not experience failure.

Other Variables

We also take into account the number of IT courses a student took in their first two semesters of IT course taking. This is the total number of classes a student took in the first two semesters during which they took at least one IT class. These classes need not be sequential. For example, if a student took an IT class in fall 2003 and did not take another IT class until fall 2004, fall 2003 and fall 2004 would be that student's first two IT semesters. This measure provides an indication of early IT interest. We also take into account each student's first semester IT GPA, which is the average grade he/she received in all IT courses taken during the first semester a student took any IT courses. Therefore a student's first IT semester may or may not be their first semester enrolled in the community college or university. This measure enables us to take into account first class performance.

Finally, we take into account institute type (four-year university or community college), age, and underrepresented minority status (URM). Institute type is a dummy variable coded 1 for community college and 0 for four-year universities. Age is measured at time of entry by subtracting students' year of entry at their institution from their year of birth. Underrepresented minority status (URM) is a dummy variable indicating status as a domestic minority student in IT. American students of color, except Asian American students, are coded 1, while Asian American, white, and foreign-born students are coded 0.

Descriptive Results

Table 1.1 summarizes the student characteristics of interests. Among students who took at least two IT classes, 45 percent of men and 19 percent of women became IT majors. Twenty-five percent of students experienced early IT failure, that is, failed at least one introductory-level IT class, however failure was more common for men than women. Twenty-one percent of women failed at least one introductory-level IT class, compared to 27 percent of their male classmates. Most students only took one IT course their first semester (85.4 percent), thus we consider students' first two semesters of IT classes (regression diagnostics show this provided for better model fit than first semester classes alone). Students tended not to take more than one IT

Table 1.1. Means and Standard Deviations of Characteristics of Students Who Took at least Two IT Classes, by Gender

Variable	Men (N=6016)		Women (N=2483)		All (N=8500)	
Entered an IT Major	0.45		0.19		0.38	
Early IT Failure	0.27		0.21		0.25	
Number of IT Courses taken in First Two Semesters	2.4	(0.89)	2.26	(0.72)	2.37	(.85)
First Semester IT GPA	2.31	(1.45)	2.45	(1.40)	2.35	(1.44)
Age	21.89	(6.32)	23.83	(7.15)	22.46	(6.63)
Underrepresented Minority (URM)	0.12		0.17		0.14	
Institute Type						
Four-year University[a]	0.81		0.80		0.81	
Community College	0.19		0.20		0.19	

Note: Numbers in parentheses are standard deviations.

[a] Omitted category

class per semester, on average men had taken 2.4 classes in their first two semesters and women had taken 2.26.

Women tended to have slightly higher grades on average. The average GPA for women was 2.45 and the average GPA for men was 2.31. The majority of students, 80 percent, in our dataset were at four-year universities. Men and women were equally represented at the two types of institutions, about 80 percent at four-year universities and 20 percent at community colleges. Women were slightly older than men on average, entering at ages 23.83 and 21.89, respectively. Slightly more women than men were underrepresented minorities, 17 percent and 12 percent, respectively.

Table 1.2 describes the relationships between early IT failure and entry into the IT major. More than half of men (51 percent) who pass all their introductory IT classes become an IT major compared to one-fifth (20 percent) of women. This substantial difference is important because these women have demonstrated ability in computing yet have resisted major entry. When we look at those who experienced early IT failure a more intriguing pattern emerges. For men there is a steep (20 percentage points) decline in entry into the major, now only 31 percent; whereas for women, the decline is comparatively miniscule, dropping only 4 percentage points, bringing the entry into the major to 16 percent. Hence, for women it would seem that early IT failure is less of a deterrent than it is for men before taking any related factors into account, although they are less likely to enter the major regardless of performance.

Table 1.2. Percentage of Students Who Passed and Failed Introductory-Level IT Classes and Became IT Majors, by Gender

	Failed Intro			Passed Intro		
	Became an IT Major	Did Not Become an IT Major	Total	Became an IT Major	Did Not Become an IT Major	Total
Men	495 (31%)	1,121 (69%)	1,616 (100%)	2,225 (51%)	2,176 (49%)	4,401 (100%)
Women	83 (16%)	430 (84%)	513 (100%)	399 (20%)	1,572 (80%)	1,917 (100%)
Total	578 (27%)	1,551 (73%)	2,129 (100%)	2,624 (41%)	3,748 (59%)	6,372 (100%)

Among Passing students $\chi^2=516.43$ P<.001

Among failing students $\chi^2=41.12$ P<.001

Multivariate Method

We use logistic regression to analyze the effects of gender, early IT failure, and their interaction on the likelihood that a student will enter an IT major. Logistic regression allows us to see the effect of early IT failure on the likelihood that a student will become an IT major, after taking into account age, underrepresented minority status (URM), the number of IT courses taken in the first two semesters, first semester IT GPA, and institute type. The key terms in our logistic regression models are a gender dummy, where woman is coded as 1, the early IT failure dummy, where failure is coded as 1, and the gender*early IT failure interaction. We use nested models to first see the baseline effects of gender, early IT failure, and the gender*early IT failure interaction before adding demographic characteristics (URM and age), student characteristics (number of IT courses taken in the first two semesters and first semester IT GPA), and finally institute type.

This approach allows us to isolate the effect of early IT failure on the likelihood that a student will become an IT major while allowing the effect of early IT failure to differ by gender. Taking the demographic characteristics into account first allows us to see if the gender and the early IT failure effects we initially observed reflect differences in the demographic characteristics of men and women. For example, women are slightly older on average and there are more women of color than men of color, thus the demographic controls allow us to ensure that the gender differences are not due to variation in these other characteristics. The student characteristics included allow us to account for differences in investment and performance in IT. Men took more classes on average than women but women received higher grades on average. Finally, structural differences in institution type may explain some of the gender and failure effects, as students are more likely to major in IT at a community college than at a four-year university.

Models 1 and 2 show the baseline effects of gender and early IT failure, respectively. Model 3 shows the main effects of gender and early IT failure together, while model 4 adds the conditional effect of the interaction between gender and early IT failure. Model 5 introduces controls for demographic characteristics, age, and underrepresented minority status. Model 6 adds the controls for student characteristics, number of IT classes taken in the first two semesters, and first semester IT GPA. Finally, model 7 introduces the institute type control where community colleges are coded as 1.

Multivariate Results

Table 1.3 presents odds ratios from the logistic regression models as opposed to coefficients for ease of interpretation. An odds ratio represents the probability of entering an IT major. To determine the percent change in the probability from the odds ratio we subtract 1 from odds ratios larger than 1 and subtract odds ratios less than 1 from 1. Odds ratios above 1 indicate an increase in probability, whereas odds ratios below 1 indicate a decrease in probability. For example, an odds ratio of 1.25 (1.25–1=0.25) would be a 25 percent increase in the probability of entering an IT major. On the other hand, an odds ratio of 0.75 (1–0.75=0.25) would indicate a 25 percent decrease in the probability of entering an IT major.

Our descriptive analysis (table 1.2) suggested that women are in fact less likely to major in IT if they experience early IT failure (16 percent of women compared to 31 percent of men subsequently enter the major) as the literature on women in science would suggest. Multivariate analysis, however, confirms that the negative effect of early IT failure for women is dwarfed by the strong negative effect of gender on all women's likelihood of majoring in IT, regardless of performance.

Gender has a strong, stable, and negative effect on women's likelihood of majoring in IT across all seven models, net of all controls. Women are 71 percent less likely in the baseline model (model 1) and 74 percent less likely in the full model (model 7) to major in IT than their male peers. The effect of early IT failure is also stable, strong, and negative for all students. In the baseline early IT failure model (model 2) students who fail are 47 percent less likely to declare an IT major than those who pass. Controlling for gender (model 3), students who experience early IT failure are 53 percent less likely to enter an IT major than those who pass, and the introduction of all the controls (model 7) does little to change this relationship. Students who experience early IT failure are still 54 percent less likely than their peers who do not fail to declare an IT major.

Hence, regardless of gender, students who experience early IT failure are less likely than students who do not to enter a major in IT. However, taking into account controls, the effect of early IT failure is weaker for women than it is for men (model 7). Table 1.4 shows the predicted probability that men and women will major in IT if they have experienced early IT failure. Men who fail are 36.6 percent less likely to major in IT than men who pass compared to an 18.6 percent decrease for women who fail compared to women who pass. While men are more likely to major in IT than women regardless of whether they experience early IT failure, the effect of early IT failure is

Table 1.3. Coefficients from Logit Models Predicting Probability of Entrance into an IT Major among Students Who Took at least Two IT Classes (N=8,500)

Variable	Model 1	Model 2	Model 3	Model 4	Model 5	Model 6	Model 7
Female	0.29***		0.28***	0.25***	0.26***	0.26***	0.26***
Early Failure in IT		0.53***	0.47***	0.43***	0.42***	0.41***	0.46***
Female * Early Failure in IT				1.79***	1.76***	1.75***	1.70***
Age					0.98***	0.97***	0.96***
Under-represented Minority					0.65***	0.67***	0.76***
Number of IT Courses							3.03***
Taken in First Two Semesters						3.10***	
First Semester IT GPA						0.89***	0.99
Institute (Community College)							2.60***
Constant	−0.193***	−0.00055	−0.357***	0.0223	0.451***	−1.64***	−1.76***
BIC	10,749	10,574	11,140	10,568	10,521	9,379	9,213
Log Likelihood	−5,366	−5,273	−5,561	−5,266	−5,233	−4,653	−4,566

* p<.10; ** p<.05; *** p<.01 (two-tailed)

Table 1.4.   Predicted Probabilities of Entering an IT Major from Logistic Regression Analysis, by Gender

	Men**	Women
Pass All Introductory-Level Classes	0.50	0.20
Failed at Least One Introductory Class	0.32	0.17
Percent Change	−36.6%	−18.6%

** predicted probabilities are significantly different at the p <.05 level

statistically significant for men but it is not for women. In other words, the impact of early IT failure was meaningful for men, the difference between failing and passing an introductory-level course had a real influence on their decision to persist and enter an IT major or switch course to another field. For women it did not, women's decision to enter the major was not influenced by their performance feedback, positive or negative.

To summarize the remaining effects, in general, older students, those with higher GPAs in their first semester classes, and underrepresented minority students are less likely than their counterparts to enter an IT major. First semester GPA is not significant after controlling for institute type, which represents the effect of community college compared to four-year universities;this suggests a relationship between institute type and early performance feedback rather than one between performance and persistence, defined here as subsequent entry into the major. Community college students were more likely to enter an IT major than their peers at four-year universities, and students were increasingly likely to enter an IT major as the number of IT classes they took in their first two semesters increased. The probability that students would enter an IT major approximately doubled for each additional IT class they took in their first two semesters.

The positive community college effect may reflect structural differences in the institutional contexts, though it is also possible that this effect is driven by the diversity of IT majors available at the community colleges. Computer science was virtually the only IT major available at four-year universities, while community colleges offered a broad selection of majors (e.g., computer game development, help desk and software support, etc.), some of which required considerably less technical sophistication than those offered at the four-year universities. Unlike the computer science majors at the four-year schools, which all required calculus for upper-level classes, very few community college computing classes required any math and none required calculus. Insomuch as math is a barrier to entering computing, this barrier did not exist at the community colleges in our study.

Discussion

We find that gender has a strong and stable effect on students' likelihood of entry into an IT major. Net the effect of early IT failure, age, underrepresented minority status, number of IT courses taken, first semester GPA, and institute type, women who took at least two IT classes are 75 percent less likely to enter an IT major than comparable men. While experiencing early IT failure is a strong negative predictor for men's entrance into an IT major, it is not a significant predictor for women. *Strikingly, women who pass all of their introductory-level IT classes are still less likely to enter an IT major than men who fail.* Failure is a significant obstacle for men but even failing an introductory-level class is not as much of a deterrent as being a woman.

We find this strong gender effect even in the subset of students who demonstrated more than just a passing interest in computing by taking at least two classes. The larger set of students who took at least one IT class contains 29,298 students, only 40 percent of whom are women, even though students can take introductory-level IT classes to meet general education requirements. When we restrict our analysis to only students who took at least two IT classes, women make up only 29 percent of students. Women are only 18 percent of students who entered an IT major, but they makeup 25 percent of students who subsequently left their IT major. At each step of the process toward graduating with an IT degree women opt out at higher rates than men. Stout et al. (2011) caution against interpreting this decision purely as "freedom of choice" and instead stress the importance of messages of belonging, or lack thereof, which shape women's decisions.

We speculated that a gendered response to early failure may be driving the underrepresentation of women in computing deterring women from entering the IT major. Our results do not bear this out. *Instead the decision to enter the major for the women in our analysis was not at all influenced by performance feedback.* Those women who experienced early IT failure were not significantly different from those who did not in their ultimate major decision. These findings do not support the hypotheses suggested by the literature on the biased self-assessment of women in math and science.

Specifically, we found no support for the hypothesis that women are more sensitive to negative performance feedback than men. Instead we found the opposite, *men were more sensitive to negative performance feedback than women.* Since this study focuses on women who are confident and interested enough in computing to take at least two IT classes our findings do not speak to women generally. While women, on average, appear to need more positive feedback to believe they are as competent as men (Correll 2001; Nelson and Cooper 1997), these women demonstrated more than a passing interest in computing and they are not like undergraduate women on average, the majority of whom will never take an IT class. Our findings are more in line with Cech et al. (2011) who find that self-assessment of math ability is not a significant predictor of persistence in engineering for men and women who are already engineering majors.

Among the population of undergraduate women who find their way to computing, despite the gendered obstacles and exclusionary messages prevalent at earlier stages, even the most negative performance feedback— failure—does not appear to be significant obstacle. By focusing on atypical women we discovered superior patterns of resilience to failure than men. *These findings point to the importance of agency among women amid gender-typed field constraint.*

Women who pursue a male-dominated STEM discipline must find ways to "do science," "do gender," or do both differently. They have already responded contrarily to the threat of poor performance, difficulty balancing work and family, and lost opportunities for romance than the literature on gendered deterrents from science suggested they would (Frome, Alfeld, Eccles, & Barber 2006; Park, Young, Troisi, and Pinkus 2011). Why then would failing a class be the factor that finally deters them? By studying these women, who are more resilient to negative performance feedback than women on average tend to be, we can better understand the conditions under which women will enter computing and other male-typed STEM fields and how to retain them.

The women in our analysis who pursue at least two computing classes seem to have a different relationship with grades and performance feedback than the literature on gender and biased self-assessment suggests. Future research needs to study how these women understand grades and how they developed their ulterior understanding in order to learn how to better inoculate other women against the typical effects of biased self-assessment.

These findings are particularly salient in light of Fox, Sonnert, and Nikiforova's (2011) finding that directors of programs for women in STEM tend to believe self-esteem is the biggest obstacle for women entering STEM fields. If self-esteem is the biggest obstacle for women, early IT failure is possibly the clearest, objective academic indication of low aptitude, and would likely confirm any self-doubt. Yet for the women in our analysis it did not. Perhaps their self-esteem was grounded in confidence in their ability to learn (a growth mindset). This growth mindset may have enabled them to see challenges and poor performance as an opportunity for growth and improvement rather than an indication of their lack of innate ability (Yeager and Dweck 2012).

Conclusion

Our findings point to the important intersection of identities between gender and major choice and have implications for how we understand women who enter male-dominated fields such as computing and engineering. Women must contend with professors and classmates who dismiss them and a larger culture of computing that excludes them (Margolis and Fisher 2003). They expect that potential employers and coworkers will attempt to measure their commitment and competence through their participation in stereotypically masculine activities, such as tinkering (Margolis and Fisher 2003; McIlwee and Robinson 1994). In order to navigate these fields they have to find ways to manage the assessments of their work and worth that may contrast with stereotypical performances of femininity.

As a result, women in these fields are not like women on average. There is an extensive literature that tells us how characteristics associated with normative femininity negatively impact women's entrance and persistence into STEM fields. However, *the women who do enter these fields, or test the waters via attempting classes before entering the major, are different.* We know far more about the women at the center of the distribution, the average women, than we know about those at the tails, the *atypical* women in STEM. By studying how women who choose to enter male-dominated STEM fields differ in their response to gendered obstacles, we can learn about resilience to stereotype threat and craft interventions better suited to helping all women. Resilience amid constraint is what the pipeline misses. Women who persist in computing, and in STEM fields more generally, demonstrate remarkable agency that the passivity of the pipeline ignores. Future research should focus on the tools resilient women possess, and how they obtained them, to broaden participation in computing.

Notes

1. An earlier version of this paper was presented at the annual conference of the Eastern Sociological Society (February 2013, New York, NY). Branch acknowledges support from NSF grant 0837739 and PI, W. Richards Adrion. However, all opinions and findings are those of the authors and do not necessarily represent those of the National Science Foundation. We thank Cecelia Cancellaro and Laura Hirshfield

for editing comments, and the undergraduate students who provided research assistance: Roma Chandhok, Jamilah Murrell, and Jonalis Carasquillo. Please send correspondence to: Enobong Hannah Branch (ebranch@soc.umass.edu); Department of Sociology, 736 Thompson Hall, 200 Hicks Way, University of Massachusetts, Amherst, MA 01003.

CHAPTER TWO

~

Is College Enough?

Gender Disparities in the Use of Science and Engineering Degrees in the Workforce
Margaret L. Usdansky and Rachel A. Gordon

Does graduating from college with a STEM degree equalize the field of STEM employment for women and men after college?[1] The short answer is no. Even when women major in natural sciences or engineering fields, they remain less likely than men to hold STEM-related jobs in the decades following graduation.

Are these employment differences large enough to matter? And, if so, what happens during and after college to explain these disparities? In this chapter, we explore the magnitude of differences in STEM employment among college graduates who majored in a STEM field and consider three factors related to the likelihood of subsequent STEM employment: the college graduate's gender and race/ethnicity; the STEM field she or he studied during college; and whether the graduate pursued additional education—inside or outside the natural sciences—after college. In addition, we consider other elements that could relate to gender disparities in STEM employment, including marital status and children (Fox 2005; Wolfinger, Mason, and Goulden 2008), although these family-related factors are less salient in our analysis than others because we consider graduates at mid-career—two to three decades after college—when the most time-consuming child care is likely behind them.

Gender disparities in STEM employment are important because women's underrepresentation costs them desirable, well-paying jobs in addition to depriving the United States of women's potential contributions to science and technology (National Academy of Sciences 2011). Jobs in STEM fields pay more, on average, than non-STEM jobs, and women employed in STEM fields earn one-third more than similar women employed outside STEM (Beede, Julian, Langdon, McKittrick, Khan, and Doms 2011). This earnings premium exceeds that of male STEM workers, resulting in a smaller gender wage gap among STEM workers compared to non-STEM workers (Beede et al.). Not only do STEM jobs represent important employment opportunities for women, scholars predict that the United States cannot meet growing demand for STEM workers without a demographic shift (increased representation of minorities and women) in STEM employment (National Science and Technology Council 2013).

Disparities in STEM employment among STEM college graduates also illustrate weaknesses in the often-used "pipeline model" of women's underrepresentation in the natural sciences. According to this model, women will achieve parity over time as more girls and women enter the pipeline by taking advanced math and science classes in primary and secondary school, selecting STEM majors in college and graduate school, and moving into STEM careers (Allen-Ramdial and Campbell 2014; Burke and Mattis 2007; Griffith 2010; Malcom and Malcom 2011). But growing research, including chapters in this volume, testifies to the limitations of the pipeline metaphor, which has been criticized for being too monolithic and overlooking variation in the pathways to STEM employment based on factors ranging from women's race/ethnicity to the climate of their chosen STEM field (Malcom and Malcom 2011; National Academy of Sciences 2011; Ong, Wright, Espinosa and Orfield 2011). The importance of further unpacking where and why the pipeline narrows or splits is demonstrated by the fact that even though increases in the number of girls and women entering the pipeline have reduced gender gaps in math and science achievement at the primary and secondary levels, they have not translated into equally large reductions in the gender gap in STEM employment.

The Present Study

This chapter addresses four research questions. First, what are the gender disparities in STEM employment among STEM college graduates at mid-career, and how have these disparities changed over time? Second, are the gender disparities larger for some racial/ethnic groups than others? Third, do differences in the STEM field studied during college play a significant role in maintaining the gender gap in STEM employment? Fourth, do differences in the educational pathways STEM graduates take after college, from seeking employment without pursuing an advanced degree to earning a PhD in a STEM field, contribute to the gender gap? As we examine these questions, we highlight college field of study and advanced degree attainment as the most salient contributors to employment differentials.

We measure gender within racial/ethnic groups because differences in STEM degree attainment and STEM employment vary by race/ethnicity (National Science Foundation 2015). Taking race/ethnicity as well as gender into account is also valuable because few datasets offer sufficiently large and diverse samples to allow consideration of race/ethnicity and gender (Riegle-Crumb and King 2010). This is a growing concern given the underrepresentation of blacks and Hispanics in the STEM labor force and the "double bind" faced by black, Hispanic, and Asian women STEM students and workers, who constitute minorities in their chosen fields on the basis of race as well as gender (Ong et al. 2011).

To fill this gap in the research, we utilize data from the National Science Foundation's Scientists and Engineers Statistical Data System known as "SESTAT," which provides a large and representative sample of the U.S. science and engineering labor force over time. SESTAT draws from ongoing surveys of recipients of science and engineering degrees at the baccalaureate level or higher, and recipients of non-science degrees employed in the sciences (Kannankutty and Wilkinson 1999). We define STEM degrees and the STEM labor force as comprising four broad fields: engineering; computing and math; the life sciences; and the physical sciences. This four-field aggregation is consistent with the practice of the National Science Foundation. Although it masks substantial variation among subfields, it enables us to create a comprehensible portrait of change in the STEM labor force over time.[2]

To answer our four research questions, we study seven cohorts of students who majored in a STEM field and earned a college degree between 1964 and 1988. We investigate the jobs these "STEM college graduates" ("STEM graduates" for short) held at mid-career, twenty to twenty-nine years later, when they participated in component surveys of SESTAT conducted between 1993 and 2008. This strategy allows us to examine trends over time in gender differences in STEM employment among workers who are well established in their careers, eliminating fluctuation in career pathways immediately after college. Because most STEM college graduates are employed at this mid-career stage, we compare the probability of employment in a STEM field to the probability of employment in a non-STEM field, excluding the small proportion of STEM graduates who were unemployed or out of the labor force. We further limit our analytic sample to respondents who attended college in the United States to avoid country-specific differences in science teaching and training during college.

Taking advantage of the large sample sizes in the nationally representative SESTAT data, we focus on the eight largest race-by-gender groups: non-Hispanic white men (N=51,903); non-Hispanic Asian men (N=3,405); non-Hispanic black men (N=2,435); Hispanic men (N=2,595); non-Hispanic white women (N=12,302); non-Hispanic Asian women (N=1,169); non-Hispanic black women (N=1,274); and Hispanic women (N=880). For simplicity, we use the terms "white," "black," and "Asian" in referring to non-Hispanics and refer to "race" as shorthand for racial/ethnic groups.

Sampling weights were applied so that the data reflect nationally representative trends. We present descriptive data to illustrate trends in the levels of STEM employment for each of our eight groups, and measure gender differences in the choice of a STEM field in college as well as advanced degree attainment after college. We use logistic regression to explore the extent to which the gender gaps in STEM employment related to six sets of factors: demographic characteristics, including gender, race, and nativity; college graduation cohort; parents' educational attainment; choice of STEM field; educational attainment after college; and living arrangements as measured by marital status and the presence of younger (less than six years old) and older (six-eighteen years old) children in the household.

We adjust our analyses using statistical procedures that take into account the participation of some SESTAT respondents in more than one of the seven SESTAT surveys (1993, 1995, 1997, 1999, 2003, 2006, and 2008) included in our study (Williams 2000). A comparison of respondents with and without multiple observations showed that both groups had similar profiles regarding our variables of interest. For example, 38 percent of respondents surveyed once and 37 percent of those surveyed more than once were employed in a STEM field. We created separate models for Asian, white, black, and Hispanic women and men to take into account the possibility that the relationships between college STEM field and STEM employment and between advanced degree attainment and STEM employment differ among the eight race-by-gender groups. Not surprisingly, given that the STEM graduates we studied had completed college twenty to twenty-nine years earlier, nativity, parental education, and living arrangements were not strongly associated with the likelihood of STEM employment at mid-career. In contrast, the educational pathways selected by STEM graduates during and after college strongly related to their likelihood of STEM versus non-STEM employment. Thus, we focus on these two factors in this chapter.

The Gender Gaps in STEM Employment

Figure 2.1 illustrates the levels of STEM employment among mid-career college graduates in 1993, the first year of our study, and shows disparities by gender within every race. The eight bars indicate the proportion of each group of STEM graduates employed in a STEM field at mid-career. For example, the solid black bar at the far left of figure 2.1 indicates that slightly more than one-third of employed Asian women STEM graduates (36 percent) held a job in one of the four STEM fields in 1993. This means that almost two-thirds of employed Asian women STEM graduates worked in non-STEM fields in 1993. How does this level of mid-career STEM employment compare to that of other groups? The three bars immediately to the right (distinguished by checkered, brick, and lined patterns) indicate that STEM employment levels were lower for other women STEM graduates. No

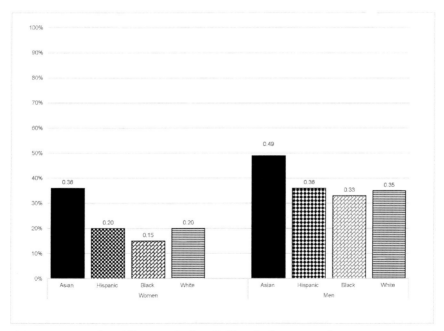

Figure 2.1.   Gender Differences in the Likelihood of STEM Employment among STEM College Graduates at Mid-Career, 1993.
Author's analysis

more than one-fifth of Hispanic, black, and white women STEM graduates held STEM jobs.

Within race, mid-career men STEM graduates (indicated by the bank of four bars at the far right of figure 2.1) were more likely to be employed in STEM than women graduates, differences of at least 13 percentage points in each case. Men experienced a similar pattern of variation by race, with approximately one-half of Asian men STEM graduates employed in STEM fields in 1993, compared to only about one-third of Hispanic, black, and white men STEM graduates. Interestingly, the sole case of gender overlap in levels of STEM employment occurred across rather than within race; Asian women were about equally likely to be STEM employed as non-Asian men.

Figure 2.2 traces STEM employment levels from 1993 to 2008, allowing us to examine change over time among our eight groups. Women are represented by solid lines and men by broken lines, with squares to distinguish Asians, triangles for whites, circles for Hispanics, and cross marks for blacks. Three broad trends emerge from figure 2.2. First, most of the lines rise, re-

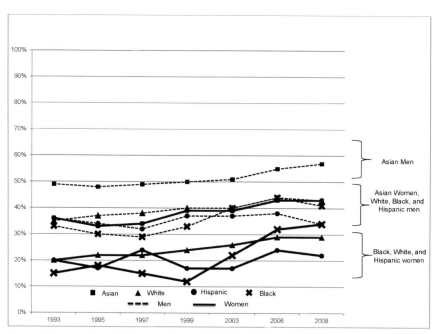

Figure 2.2. Gender Differences in the Likelihood of STEM Employment among STEM College Graduates at Mid-Career, 1993-2008.
Author's analysis

flecting modest increases in STEM employment between 1993 and 2008. Second, the lines cluster into high, middle, and low tiers of STEM employment, with Asian men occupying the top tier, white, black, and Hispanic men and Asian women occupying the middle tier, and white, black, and Hispanic women occupying the bottom tier. Third, these tiers remain stable over the time period with one notable exception: the rapid rise in STEM employment among black women STEM graduates after 1999, which brings them to parity with Hispanic men, the only group for whom STEM employment fell, albeit too slightly to represent a statistically significant decline.

Overall, STEM employment rose modestly between 1993 and 2008, with limited shifts in gender disparities. Asian and white STEM graduates experienced sizeable gender gaps in 1993 (13 and 15 percentage points, respectively) that remained virtually unchanged fifteen years later (14 percentage points for both groups). Hispanics and blacks experienced declines in gender disparities but to varying degrees and for different reasons. Hispanic STEM graduates experienced a modest decline in their gender gap in STEM employment—from 16 to 12 percentage points—that resulted from small declines in STEM employment among men coupled with small increases among women. Black STEM graduates were the only group to experience a large decline in the gender gap, which shrank from 18 to 7 percentage points (a gap too small to be statistically significant) as a result of large gains in STEM employment among black women and smaller gains among black men.

The Impact of STEM College Field on Subsequent STEM Employment

Our third research question asks, do differences in the STEM field studied during college affect STEM graduates' likelihood of STEM employment at mid-career? We begin by considering whether women and men STEM college graduates selected the same or different STEM fields to study during college. If women and men selected the four possible fields in equal proportions, choice of field would not contribute to gender disparities in mid-career STEM employment regardless of whether some fields were more or less likely to lead to subsequent STEM employment. Figure 2.3, however, illustrates significant variation by gender in the selection of STEM field during college. The eight shaded bars in figure 2.3 represent the proportion of STEM college graduates in each race-by-gender group majoring in each STEM field: engineering (black); computing and math (checkered); the physical sciences (brick); and the life sciences (lined).

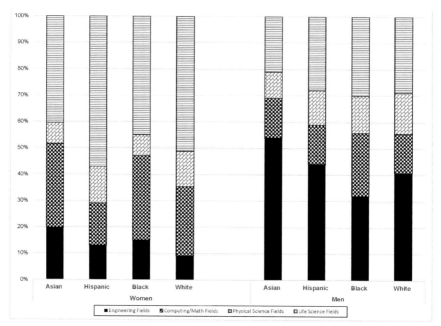

Figure 2.3.   Gender Differences in the STEM Field of Study of Mid-Career STEM College Graduates.
Author's analysis

Substantial gender differences are evident. Most striking is the case of engineering. Only a small minority of women STEM graduates studied engineering during college, from a low of less than one in ten white women to a high of one in five Asian women. In contrast, engineering was the field most often studied by male STEM graduates. More than half of Asian men STEM graduates and one-third or more of Hispanic, black, and white men STEM graduates studied engineering. The most common major among women STEM graduates, in contrast, was the life sciences, selected by more than half of Hispanic and white women and more than 40 percent of Asian and black women—but by fewer than a third of men STEM graduates. Smaller gender differences were evident in the selection of computing and math (more common among women STEM graduates) and the physical sciences (slightly more common among men and least common overall).

Did these differences in the field of study of STEM graduates affect their likelihood of subsequent STEM employment? To answer this question, we calculated the predicted probability of STEM employment for each of our eight groups based on the undergraduate field of study they had completed.

Figure 2.4 shows the first set of results of these logistic regression analyses, which compare outcomes for engineering (black bars) and life science (checkered bars). The levels of predicted STEM employment among those who studied engineering far exceeded those who studied life science for each of the eight race-gender groups. Among Asian women, for example, 65 percent of STEM graduates who majored in engineering fields were predicted to be employed in STEM at mid-career (black bar on the far left), compared to 22 percent of those who majored in life science fields (checkered bar on the far left)—a 43 percentage point difference. A similarly large 40 percentage point difference existed between Asian men in those two fields. Among the remaining race-by-gender groups, we generally see a 30 percentage point differential in STEM employment between the engineers and their life science counterparts. The exception is white women, for whom the differential is 22 percentage points. This reflects the fact that white women have the lowest likelihood of STEM employment given an engineering degree but among the higher likelihoods of STEM employment given a life sciences degree.

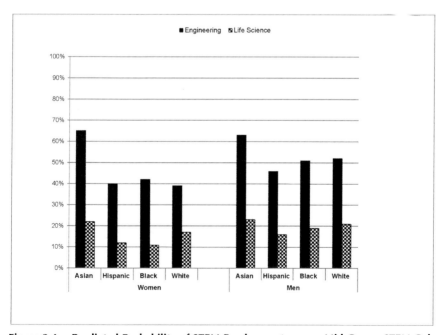

Figure 2.4. Predicted Probability of STEM Employment among Mid-Career STEM College Graduates by Undergraduate Field of Study: Engineering and Life Science.
Author's analysis

An additional question we can answer by examining figure 2.4 is whether a gender gap in the likelihood of STEM employment exists *within* fields of study by comparing the black or checkered bars for men and women of the same race. Particularly noteworthy in these comparisons is the absence of any gender gap for Asian engineering majors among whom 65 percent of women and 63 percent of men were predicted to be STEM employed. Although Hispanic, black, and white women who majored in engineering fields were less likely to be STEM employed at mid-career than men of the same race who majored in engineering fields, the respective gender gaps were often smaller than the overall gender gaps seen in figures 4.1 and 4.2. The gender gap for white women remained comparable to the overall gap, however, at 13 percentage points and was the only statistically significant gender difference among those majoring in engineering fields. Gender gaps among majors in life science fields were even smaller than those among engineers (and again only statistically significant among whites) but did not represent meaningful gains in job opportunities because all majors in life science fields experienced low odds of STEM employment.

In sum, for women STEM graduates as for men, the choice of an engineering field was associated with a relatively high likelihood of STEM employment at mid-career, especially compared to the odds for those in a life sciences field. In addition, majoring in an engineering field eliminated the gender gap in mid-career STEM employment for Asian women and reduced the gap for Hispanic and black women. For white women, however, a gender gap persisted even among those majoring in an engineering field. Although white women engineers had high levels of STEM employment, a substantial gender gap in STEM employment remained that was comparable to the gap of 14 percentage points experienced by all white women STEM graduates—regardless of field of study—over the 1993 to 2008 period (figures 2.1 and 2.2).

Figure 2.5 builds on these findings by illustrating the predicted likelihood of STEM employment for graduates of all four STEM fields. As before, solid black and checkered bars represent engineering and life science fields, respectively. Figure 2.5 adds computing and math fields (brick bars) and physical science fields (lined bars). Among women STEM graduates, majors in computing and math fields were more likely to hold a STEM job than majors in physical science fields (although these differences were statistically significant only among Hispanics and Asians), while men experienced similar odds of subsequent STEM employment across the fields. In computing and math fields, predicted levels of STEM employment were especially high for Asian women (almost half) and Hispanic women (42 percent). Moreover, gender

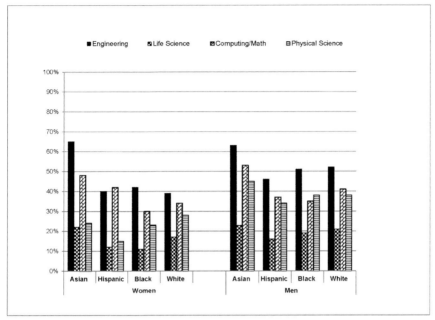

Figure 2.5.   Predicted Probability of STEM Employment among Mid-Career STEM College Graduates by Undergraduate Field of Study: Engineering, Life Science, Computing/ Math, and Physical Science.
Author's analysis

gaps in the likelihood of STEM employment among majors in computing and math fields were small and not statistically significant (Asians, blacks, whites) or non-existent (Hispanics). Among majors in physical science fields, who were less likely to be employed in STEM, gender gaps were larger.

Examining all four STEM fields reveals some consistent patterns. The probability of STEM employment at mid-career was greatest for graduates in engineering fields (with the exception of Hispanic women among whom majors in computing and math fields were slightly more likely to be STEM employed). Graduates in computing and math fields had the second highest likelihood of mid-career employment among women. Physical science fields came in third among women and tied with computing and math fields for second place among men. Graduates in life science fields were the least likely to hold STEM jobs at mid-career. Moreover, in most cases, gender gaps in the likelihood of mid-career STEM employment were small or non-existent among STEM graduates in the two fields most likely to lead to STEM employment: engineering and computing and math, with the exception of white women engineers. These findings indicate that differences in the fields women and men STEM graduates choose, and differences in these fields' subsequent likelihood of STEM employment, both contribute to the total gender gaps in STEM employment among Asian, white, black and Hispanic STEM graduates at mid-career. In this sense, the choice of a STEM field during college puts students not on a single path toward earning a STEM degree but on one of four distinct pathways, which vary considerably in their likelihood of leading to STEM employment.

The Impact of Advanced Degrees on Subsequent STEM Employment

Our fourth and final question concerns the impact of advanced degree attainment after college. Unlike college field of study, educational attainment after college did not vary greatly across our eight groups. Figure 2.6 indicates that, regardless of gender or race, approximately half of STEM college gradu-

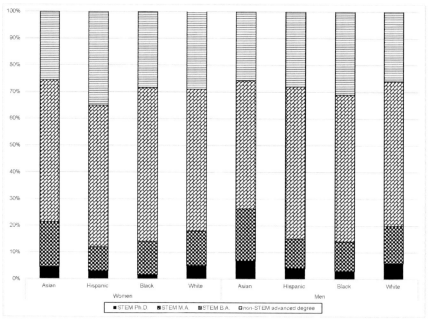

Figure 2.6.   Gender Differences in Advanced Degree Attainment among Mid-Career STEM College Graduates.
Author's analysis

ates reached the mid-career stage without having earned any degree beyond the STEM bachelor's degree (brick pattern), from a high of 57 percent of Hispanic men and black women to a low of 48 percent of Asian men. Differences in receipt of additional degrees varied modestly by race and little by gender. For example, Asian women and men were somewhat more likely to have earned a master's degree (checkered pattern) or a PhD (solid black) in a STEM field than non-Asian STEM graduates and somewhat less likely to have earned an advanced degree in a non-STEM field (lined pattern), such as law, medicine, or the social sciences. Across the eight race-gender groups, however, similarities in advanced degree attainment were more striking than differences.

However, STEM graduates who did and did not earn advanced degrees had quite different probabilities of mid-career STEM employment, as shown in figure 2.7. The majority of STEM graduates who earned a STEM PhD (black bars) were employed in a STEM field at mid-career, from a low of 60 percent among black men to a high of 76 percent among Hispanic men.

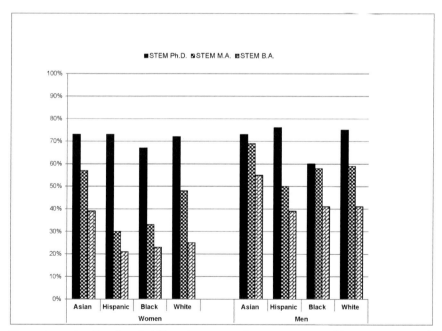

Figure 2.7.   Predicted Probability of STEM Employment among Mid-Career STEM College Graduates by Degree Attainment.
Author's analysis

STEM employment probabilities were somewhat lower among STEM graduates who earned a master's degree in a STEM field (checkered bars) and varied widely across the eight groups, from a low of 30 percent among Hispanic women STEM graduates to a high of 69 percent among Asian men STEM graduates. STEM graduates who did not earn any higher degree (brick bars) were less likely to be employed in a STEM field at mid-career than those who earned a master's or PhD in a STEM field. Graduates who obtained an advanced degree in a non-STEM field (not shown) had the lowest likelihood of STEM employment, ranging from 9 to 25 percent.

A marked relationship between higher degree receipt and the magnitude of the gender gaps in STEM employment is also notable in figure 2.7. Gender gaps in the likelihood of STEM employment at mid-career were small or non-existent among STEM graduates who went on to earn a PhD in a STEM field. Among white STEM graduates with a STEM PhD, for example, the predicted probability of employment in STEM at mid-career was 72 and 75 percent for women and men, respectively. Among black STEM graduates who earned a STEM PhD women had higher odds of STEM employment than men, 67 percent versus 60 percent. But gender gaps were substantial among STEM graduates who earned a master's degree (between 11 and 25 percentage points although only statistically significant for whites and blacks) or did not earn any advanced degree (between 16 and 18 percentage points and statistically significant for all races).

These results demonstrate that unlike gender differences in the choice of STEM field during college, gender differences in higher degree attainment after college were too small to have played a substantial role in gender differences in STEM employment for the cohorts studied. Likewise, gender differences in the likelihood of STEM employment among STEM graduates who earned a STEM PhD were too small (or, in the case of blacks, too favorable to women) to have contributed significantly to gender disparities in mid-career STEM employment. But large gender differences in the likelihood of STEM employment among STEM graduates who earned a STEM master's or did not earn any additional degree did contribute to the overall gender disparities in mid-career STEM employment evident among STEM graduates as a group. Thus, decisions regarding whether to pursue an advanced degree—and which degree to pursue—effectively sort students into distinct pathways with differing odds of subsequent STEM employment, with varying effects on overall gender disparities.

Discussion

Our research demonstrates that significant gender disparities in the likelihood of STEM employment persisted throughout the 1990s and 2000s, but these disparities varied by race. Between 1993 and 2008, the gender gap in STEM employment remained stable for Asians and whites at about 14 percentage points, declined from 16 to 12 points for Hispanics (largely reflecting slight declines in STEM employment for Hispanic men), and fell sharply for blacks—from 18 to 7 percentage points, reflecting black women's very low levels of STEM employment in 1993 as well as their unusually rapid gains in STEM employment between 1999 and 2008.

Our results indicate that the choice of STEM field during college, and advanced degree attainment after college, related to gender disparities in STEM employment but in different ways. STEM field of study in college was key. For example, we found women were less likely to study engineering in college, the field associated with the highest levels of mid-career STEM employment. In addition, women who studied engineering were less likely to hold a STEM job at mid-career than men engineering graduates (with the exception of Asians), although this gap was smaller than the overall gaps observed across fields. Gender gaps in the likelihood of STEM employment among STEM graduates who choose other majors, especially the physical sciences, also contributed to the overall gender gap in STEM employment. In contrast, degree attainment after college did not vary significantly by gender; men and women STEM graduates were equally likely to earn a STEM master's, STEM PhD, non-STEM advanced degree, or no additional degree. And women and men STEM graduates who earned a STEM PhD were equally likely—and highly likely—to hold a STEM job. But women graduates who did not earn any advanced degree and those who earned a STEM master's were markedly less likely to hold a STEM job at mid-career than comparable men of the same race.

In short, two of the most important patterns we find in these data involve differences in how women and men sort themselves into STEM majors, particularly engineering, and employment after receipt of a terminal STEM bachelor's or a STEM master's degree. Importantly, graduates with a bachelor's degree in engineering are uniformly and highly likely to be STEM employed at mid-career, but women pursue engineering degrees far less often than men. On the other hand, although women and men pursue STEM bachelor's and STEM master's degrees in similar proportions, once these degrees are in hand, women are less likely than men to be STEM employed.

The variation we document in gender disparities in STEM employment among Asians, whites, blacks, and Hispanics testifies to the importance of considering gender in combination with race in examining participation. Gender disparities in STEM reflect race-specific variation among men and women in attainment of STEM degrees and levels of STEM employment (Malcom and Malcom 2011; National Science Foundation 2015; Riegle-Crumb and King 2010). In some cases, gender disparities are smaller among black and Hispanic women because black and Hispanic men are disadvantaged relative to Asian and white men. For example, by 2008, overall gender disparities in STEM employment were smaller among Hispanics and blacks than among Asians and whites not only because of Hispanic and black women's gains since 1993, but also because of the comparatively low levels of STEM employment among Hispanic and black men STEM graduates relative to Asian and white men. In other cases, such as STEM master's degree recipients, black and Hispanic men experienced more favorable outcomes than black and Hispanic women did relative to Asians and whites of the same gender. These findings highlight the complexity of the relationships among gender, race, STEM field, and advanced degree attainment. In effect, each field constitutes a distinct pathway with a unique probability of leading to STEM employment at mid-career for women STEM graduates of a given race-ethnicity; advanced degree attainment after college also sorts women STEM graduates within each race into distinct pathways some of which are more likely than others to lead to STEM employment.

Conclusion

Our research holds a number of implications for policymakers seeking to promote greater gender equality in the STEM workforce. While a discussion of specific recommendations to modify or expand the many existing programs aimed at increasing women's representation in STEM fields is beyond the scope of this chapter, knowing where significant gender disparities in STEM employment exist and where they do not can assist policymakers in designing and evaluating programs. For example, our findings suggest that encouraging more women who enter college with an interest in STEM fields to consider engineering has the potential to increase STEM employment given the high levels of STEM employment among women STEM graduates who majored in engineering and the position of engineering as the second largest field within the STEM labor force (Beede et al. 2011). Our research also points to potential gains that might result from attracting more women to computing and math majors, not only because STEM jobs in this field are more numerous than in any other and are projected to grow rapidly (Beede et al. 2011), but also because women graduates who study computing are second only to engineering majors in their levels of predicted mid-career STEM employment, and gender gaps in STEM employment among computing and math graduates are small (Asians, whites, blacks) or non-existent (Hispanics). Despite these opportunities, computing and math is the only broad STEM field in which women's representation in the labor force declined between 2000 and 2009 (Beede et al. 2011).

In addition, our results highlight the importance of recognizing and addressing gender gaps in STEM employment where they remain. White engineering majors represent one such case in which women's mid-career STEM employment levels were relatively high but significantly lower than those of similar men. Marked gender disparities in predicted STEM employment also existed among graduates who earned a master's degree in STEM, and these disparities were particularly large among Hispanics (20 percentage points) and blacks (25 percentage points). An important future direction for programs and research would be to understand why such disparities in STEM employment exist within these majors and degrees.

STEM graduates who earned a PhD represent the most striking instance in which women appear to have reached parity or near parity with men, regardless of race. Since fewer than 10 percent of STEM graduates go on to earn a STEM PhD, the absence of a gender gap in STEM employment at this highest education level has limited impact on overall gender disparities in the STEM labor force. But it merits additional study both to elucidate factors that have promoted STEM employment among women STEM graduates who earn a PhD as well as the continuing underrepresentation of women in academia, especially among full professors at research universities (National Science Foundation 2015).

Our research is subject to some important limitations. Studying STEM graduates at mid-career allows us to examine graduates at a point when they are well established in their professions. But this also means studying older cohorts of graduates. Gender disparities in STEM employment may differ among more recent cohorts of STEM graduates in earlier phases of their careers. Further, we are not able to follow these STEM graduates longitudinally. The relationships we find between STEM field of study during college and mid-career STEM employment and between advanced degree attainment after college and mid-career employment are not necessarily causal. Our research offers a vitally needed nationally representative portrait of STEM employment among college graduates who studied a STEM field.

But we could not identify the mechanisms underlying the gender disparities we found.

Our results provide an important springboard for further research into how and why women college students who earn a STEM degree make decisions about which STEM field to study and whether or not to pursue an advanced STEM degree. Additional research could also shed light on other factors that influence the probability that a woman STEM college graduate will join the STEM labor force, including knowledge about employment opportunities in STEM and perceived barriers to STEM employment. Our findings suggest that taking race as well as STEM field into account could provide new insight into strategies to promote broader representation of women in the STEM labor force and respond to the growing demand for STEM workers in the United States (Beede et al. 2011; Vilorio 2014).

Notes

1. This research was supported by a grant from the American Educational Research Association which receives funds for its AERA Grants Program from the National Science Foundation under NSF Grant #DRL-0941014. Opinions reflect those of the authors and do not necessarily reflect those of the granting agencies. Yan Liu, of Syracuse University, assisted with data analysis. The authors also wish to thank Lisa Frehill and Katie Seely-Grant for their helpful comments.

2. The National Science Foundation also incorporates the social sciences into its definition of STEM fields. We excluded it here because our focus is on the use of science and engineering degrees in the workforce. Social science degrees are used across a variety of occupations thus we would expect the relationship between college major and mid-career employment to be less predictive for the field of social science than for the four fields we studied (engineering, computing and math, the life sciences, and the physical sciences).

PART II

DETOURS, OFF-RAMPS, AND GENDERED ROADBLOCKS IN SCIENTIFIC CAREERS

CHAPTER THREE

~

Women Faculty in Computing

A Key Case of Women in Science

Mary Frank Fox and Kathryn Kline

Women faculty in computing fields are a key case for the study of women in science.[1] Computing and the products of computing pervade modern life in communications, transportation, medicine, and numerous other areas (see Balka and Smith 2000). Computing—involving hardware (physical components of computers), software (machine-readable instructions for computers), and wide means of processing information—has been instrumental in the shift of the U.S. economy from manufacturing to services and technology and in economic growth (see Powell and Spellman 2004). Because of the centrality of computing in modern life, participation in these fields is consequential (Frehill and Cohoon 2015), and at the same time, challenging for women.

Women in Computing: Background, Context, and Aims

In the National Science Foundation's (NSF) classification of science/engineering, computer science is a field with uneven or little gain, and in some cases actual losses, in women's proportion of academic degrees over time (see table 3.1). Specifically, at the bachelor level, women's share of degrees in computer science increased slowly from the late 1960s to early 1970s (12 to 14.9 percent between 1968 and 1973), and grew notably in the late 1970s

41

Table 3.1. Degrees Awarded in Computer Science by Degree Level and Percentage Awarded to Women (in Parentheses), 1968–2013

	Doctorate	Master's	Bachelor's
1968	0	548	459
	(0.0)	(5.5)	(12.0)
1973	196	2,113	4,305
	(7.7)	(10.6)	(14.9)
1978	196	3,038	7,224
	(7.7)	(18.7)	(25.8)
1983	262	5,321	24,682
	(13.0)	(28.3)	(36.4)
1988	428	9,166	34,896
	(11.2)	(26.9)	(32.5)
1993	805	10,349	24,580
	(14.4)	(27.0)	(28.3)
1998	858	11,752	27,674
	(16.3)	(29.1)	(26.9)
2003	815	19,248	56,329
	(20.6)	(31.6)	(27.0)
2008	1337	16,497	34,559
	(22.7)	(26.6)	(17.5)
2013	1758	20,983	43,141
	(19.2)	(27.4)	(17.3)

Source: National Science Foundation, National Center for Education Statistics, The Higher Education General Information Survey, 1968–1883, and the Integrated Postsecondary Education Data System, 1988–2013 (Web CASPAR).

and early 1980s (25.8 to 36.43 percent between 1978 and 1983). Thereafter, the positive trend lost momentum, in the late 1980s through early 2000s, women's share declined and leveled (32.53 percent in 1988, 28.28 percent in 1993, 26.9 percent in 1998, and 27 percent in 2003). By 2008, women's share declined further to 17.5 percent and held steady at 17.3 percent in 2013.

Trends in women's attainment of master's degrees in computer science followed a similar trajectory as their bachelor's degree attainment, strong initial growth from the late 1960s to early 1980s followed by leveling or modest growth thereafter (see table 3.1). In doctoral degrees, women's share was less than 10 percent from the late 1960s, through the late 1970s, under 15 percent in the early 1980s to early 1990s, and only reached 20 percent in the 2000s (see table 3.1). These patterns observed in computer science degree attainment contrast with stronger, more linear growth in women's proportion of degrees awarded in life science, mathematics, statistics, and social sciences

(National Science Foundation, National Center for Education Statistics, 1963–1993, and the Integrated Education Data System [WebCASPAR], 1998–2013).

These statistics provide a context for putting forth a strategic case for women in computing, and for this chapter's focus on women faculty. As researchers, women faculty members are important to the size, creativity, and diversity of the scientific workforce and to human resources in fields regarded as consequential for national strength and innovation (Hanson 1996; National Academy of Sciences 2007; Pearson and Fechter 1994). Further, women faculty members contribute to the climate and culture of the university and the development of students. The percentages of women faculty in colleges and universities are positively associated with percentages of undergraduate women (Sharpe and Sonnert 1999), their choice of major (Canes and Rosen 1995), and their decision to major and complete a bachelor's degree in scientific fields (Sonnert, Fox, and Adkins 2007).

These findings provide further empirical evidence for the importance of women faculty as role models for undergraduate students (Astin and Sax 1996; Hackett et al. 1989; Stake and Noonan 1985; Xie and Shauman 1997). In graduate education as well, women faculty play an important role serving as primary advisors for a larger number of women doctoral students than do men, and having more women students on their research teams. Women also put significantly more emphasis on helping advisees across a range of areas, including more emphasis on the importance of interactional capacities, such as participating in laboratory meetings, making presentations, and interacting with other faculty (Fox 2003). For these reasons, it is critical to have women, as well as men, faculty in science.

It is not simply the presence of women faculty that is important but also the ranks that women hold. Women's share at rank of full professor is of particular interest because this senior rank is crucial to decision-making capacities in higher education and because the rank of full professor continues to constitute a challenge for women in academic science (National Academy of Sciences 2007; Stewart, Malley, and La Vaque-Manty 2007). Promotion to rank of full professor is an issue, in part, because compared with promotion from assistant to associate professor, the criteria for advancement to full professor are less clear, and in addition, no established timeline exists for this advancement (Britton 2010; Fox 2015; Misra, Lundquist, Holmes, and Agiomavritis 2011). Thus, women may linger as tenured associate professors without attaining full rank.

Given these issues, this chapter has three aims. First, it provides a nuanced profile of the proportions of women faculty, compared to men, by rank in computing fields (variously defined as computer science, information technology, and/or computer engineering), using published data from the National Science Foundation and from the Taulbee survey of the Computing Research Association. Second, it illustrates the potential opportunities and challenges for women's transition to higher ranks, using published evidence and arguments, including the case of "perceived chances for promotion among women associate professors in computing" (Fox and Xiao 2013). Finally, it depicts how institutional practices and policies to enhance women's rank and condition as faculty in computing would vary depending on the perspectives of "pipelines" compared to "pathways" that appear in existing research literature.

Comparing pipelines to pathways constitutes a unifying theme of this volume. This chapter points to the importance of pathways for women faculty in computing. In doing so, it emphasizes that transitions to, and within, academic computing are dynamic processes reflecting the features and forces of institutional settings in which women are employed (and earlier, educated)—with complex outcomes that are not necessarily orderly, expected progressions from one stage or rank to another. This contrasts with the pipeline view of uni-directional links between education and careers with the fundamental issue being "keeping women in the pipeline" so that they emerge, in turn, into careers that also have an expected sequence of progression. Institutional practices and policies often correspond to the pipeline as opposed to a pathways perspective. Our aim is to emphasize the practical implications of such perspectives ("points of view") for "solutions" to improve the condition of women in science (see Fox, Sonnert, and Nikiforova 2009, 2011).

To illustrate, a study of U.S. programs targeted to improve the participation and performance of undergraduate women, as majors in science and engineering fields, found that activities organized to support positive outcomes for women in science embody conceptions of what is thought to be problematic about women in science and engineering. In both the survey (Fox, Sonnert, and Nikiforova 2011) and interviews (Fox, Sonnert, and Nikiforova 2009) conducted in this study, the directors of these initiatives reveal that the programs' definitions of barriers facing women are primarily individually based (e.g., attitudes, aptitudes, background of women) or structurally based (e.g., teaching environments that portray science and engineering as masculine, that isolate women from social concerns, or take a "weed-out" orientation for students). Definitions have a strong bearing on solutions and the most successful programs (in terms of improving the proportions of undergraduate degrees awarded to women) have a more structural, compared to individual, perspective and orientation (Fox et al. 2009). However, programs' perspectives do not necessarily align, in turn, with typical activities that they implement, particularly when these involve actions that interfere in ongoing laboratories or classrooms that frequently operate as independent and unfettered domains in academic science (Fox et al. 2011).

A Profile of Women Computing Faculty, by Rank

Providing a nuanced profile of women faculty in computing requires giving attention to: 1) variable definitions of computing, 2) types of institutions represented, and 3) completeness of information on gender and rank over time. This involves a judicious approach to the sources and their utility as well as their limits. A widely used source of data (and therefore important for consideration) is that based on the Survey of Doctoral Recipients, and reported publically–without need for a restricted license–in the NSF Reports on Women, Minorities, and Persons with Disabilities in Science and Engineering. The Survey of Doctoral Recipients uses a sample of persons under age seventy-six who earned a doctoral degree from a U.S. university in a science, engineering, or health field.

The data available (1994–2015) on women faculty in computing, specifically, are both useful and in other ways limited. First, the data represent full-time and part-time faculty in both four-year colleges and universities. However, for faculty, the fields of computer and information sciences are combined (the separate category of computer science is not publicly available[2]). In addition, for the years 1994–1999, data on faculty do not appear by gender and rank; rather, they appear only with classifications of tenured, tenure track, or not and women and men. The data on faculty, by rank and gender, are available for 2001–2013, and are assembled here in table 3.2 (for reasons not explained in the NSF Reports, no data were available on faculty rank by gender and field in 2000).

We observe the following trends (see table 3.2). First, across this period, the representation of women among assistant professors was close to 20 percent, varying from a low of 16.67 percent in 2001 to a high of 25 percent in 2010. Second, the representation of women among associate professors increased in a slow and mostly steady fashion from 15.99 percent in 2001 to 19.23 percent in the 2013. Third, in 2001, the representation of women among full professors was less than 6 percent; fluctuated between 8.57 percent and 9.09 percent in 2003–2008; and reached but did not exceed 12.5 percent in 2013.

Table 3.2. Computing Faculty in Universities and Four-Year Colleges by Academic Rank and Percentage Women (in Parentheses), 2001–2013

Year	Full	Associate	Assistant
2001	2,240	2,690	1,270
	(5.80)	(15.99)	(18.11)
2003	3,500	3,400	3,600
	(8.57)	(14.71)	(16.67)
2006	2,800	2,300	2,400
	(10.71)	(17.39)	(20.83)
2008	3,300	2,500	2,200
	(9.09)	(16.00)	(22.73)
2010	3,300	2,400	1,600
	(12.12)	(16.67)	(25.00)
2013	3,200	2,600	1,900
	(12.50)	(19.23)	(21.05)

Source: National Science Foundation, *Women, Minorities, and Persons with Disabilities in Science and Engineering Report* (2004–2015), Tables: H-21 (2001), H-22 (2003 and 2006), 9-23 (2008, 2010, 2013).

The Taulbee survey, conducted annually by the Computer Research Association (CRA), produces high quality and comprehensive workforce data on computing faculty. The survey-responses are collected from doctoral-granting departments of computer science and computer engineering in the United States and Canada, from 1993 to the present, and include a selected group of information science departments, starting in 2007–2008. The CRA has taken steps to filter out electrical from computer engineering responses for faculty data. Response rates of the solicited departments are consistently high: 67 to 91 percent. For each year, data[3] on faculty appear by gender and academic rank and are available online (with an archive of the full set of years).

The Taulbee data (see table 3.3) show patterns of gender and rank among the computing faculty in doctoral-granting departments over nearly two decades (1994–1995 to 2013–2014). In these data, the percentage of women among assistant professors ranged over time, from 13.6 to 24.6 percent in an upward trend that was not continuously linear. Specifically, in 1994–1995, women represented 20 percent of the assistant professors, with a decline to 13.6 percent in the early 2000s, and an increase to 26.2 percent in the later period of 2000s. Women's representation among associate professors, on the other hand, doubled from 10.1 percent in 1994–1995 to 20.5 percent in the most recent period (2013–2014), exhibiting strong growth. Women

Table 3.3. Computing Faculty in Doctoral-Granting
Departments by Academic Rank and Percentage Women (in
Parentheses), 1994–2014

	Full	Associate	Assistant
1994–1995	1,144	968	624
	(5.1)	(10.1)	(20.0)
1999–2000	1,595	1,157	904
	(7.8)	(12.8)	(13.6)
2004–2005	1,911	1,276	1,363
	(9.8)	(12.5)	(17.3)
2009–2010	2,204	1,675	890
	(12.6)	(15.9)	(25.8)
2013–2014	2,228	1,530	833
	(13.3)	(20.5)	(24.6)

Source: Computing Research Association, Taulbee Survey Report (1995–2014),
Tables: 13 (1994–1995), T-21 (1999–2000, 2004–2005, 2009–2010), F-6
(2013-2014).

represented only 5.1 percent of the full professors at the earliest time point
(1994–1995) and their representation grew steadily but slowly, reaching
13.3 percent in 2013–2014. Thus, we can summarize women's gains within
doctoral-granting departments in computing as follows: 1) their representation among assistant professors grew in a moderate, but not necessarily linear,
trend; 2) representation among the associate professors grew notably; and 3)
representation of full professors grew steadily but slowly.

Challenges to Women's Advancement in Rank

In 2008, the NSF released a report entitled "Thirty-Three Years of Women
in S&E Faculty Positions," finding that women's share of tenured and
tenure-track positions in 2006 was the same (28 percent) as their share of
doctoral degrees in science/engineering in the 1958–2004 period, but that
women's share of full professor positions (19 percent) was not. In an analysis
of cross-sectional data for college faculty members in science, matched with
aggregate field level and institutional data, Kulis, Sciotte, and Collins (2002)
conclude, more broadly, that the link between women's representation as
doctoral recipients and representation as faculty members is neither simple
nor direct, and that the size of the doctoral supply is "not [a] uniformly consistent predictor of their level of faculty representation" (687).

At the same time, the argument of "demographic inertia" holds that the
representation of women at given academic ranks are subject to the existing
gender and age distributions that affect the proportional representation of

new PhDs, including women. This would mean that potential lags exist between the timing of the hiring of women, and their proportional representation among academic ranks within institutions (Hargens and Long 2002). In an analysis of outcomes of women and men in scientific fields with data from the Survey of Doctoral Recipients, Shaw and Stanton (2012) use a design that separates out such effects of demographic inertia. They report that computing, along with mathematics, is one of the two scientific fields in which gender differences in transition from graduate school to an academic career are most pronounced and that "although much progress has been made, gender differences [in these fields] remain comparable with those in many other disciplines 30 years ago" (3739).

Earlier longitudinal studies that followed sets of individuals over time were more resolute. A classic study of biochemists (Long, Allison, and McGinnis 1993) found that, after controlling for publication productivity, women's advancement is lower and slower than men's. In their analysis of women and men who are past recipients of prestigious postdoctoral fellowships, Sonnert and Holton (1995) report also that in the non-biological scientific fields, women's advancement in academic rank was lower than men's. These research designs are expensive to implement, and more recent longitudinal findings have not been available.

Women Associate Professors and Their Reported Chances for Promotion

A study using unique data collected in surveys (2006–2007) of women associate professors in computing fields addresses women's own perceptions of their chances for promotion to full professor (Fox and Xiao 2013). The faculty members surveyed represent the universe of women associate professors, ascertained in a complete canvas of the websites of 233 institutions (217 U.S., 16 Canadian) that were members of the Computing Research Association. From the canvas, Fox and Xiao identified a total of 286 women associate professors, who were then surveyed. Removing ineligibles (e.g., retired, moved to another employment sector), the overall response rate to the surveys was 66 percent.

Perceptions about advancement to full professorial rank are not, of course, the same as actual promotion. However, women's perceptions of their chances for promotion have implications for whether they will put themselves forward for advancement. This is because, unlike the promotion from assistant to associate professor, advancement to full professor does not have a given schedule or timeline, is at the discretion of faculty members, and likely links to faculty members' own perceptions of their prospects.

In the Fox and Xiao study, characteristics of the associate professors' home departments, as well as the professors' individual characteristics, were used to predict perceived chances of promotion to full professor, which respondents reported as excellent/good (compared to fair/poor). Among a range of work practices, productivity, and interests considered as predictors of chances, the variable—collaborating with faculty in the home unit on research proposals or publications within a prior three-year period—is a strong, positive predictor of excellent/good chances for promotion. Further, among a range of characteristics of departments and universities considered in the study, the strongest predictor of chances is being in a department perceived to be "stimulating/collegial."[4]

Collaboration with faculty in a home unit may be an indicator of faculty members' social integration into their departments. Associate professors, who collaborate with other faculty in their home unit, may be incorporated socially and intellectually into the department for potential reasons, including research topics and/or approaches and styles of doing research compatible with other faculty members. The perception that the climate of the home unit is stimulating/collegial may be a cause, effect, or both of reported chances. Whatever the relationship, it is noteworthy that simply being in an environment perceived as "stimulating/collegial" positively predicts perceived chances for promotion as excellent/good (compared to fair/poor).

Collaboration and departmental climate are not "fixed" matters. Rather, they are social and organizational features, subject potentially to approaches that bring faculty together in ways that enhance possibilities for collaboration and/or actively shape positive environmental climates—and thus, the pathways for faculty. An interesting case study of an academic science department (Jordan and Bilimoria 2007) that achieved "cooperation, inclusion, and research productivity" indicates that such features may be created through "constructive interactions." These interactions involve collegial exchange in formal and informal settings; opportunities for knowledge sharing that allow faculty to learn about work and convey norms and behaviors; relational interactions that build trust and concern for others; and problem-solving interactions involving the sharing of materials and expertise, funding for equipment, and support for writing proposals (230–232).

This method of department intervention leads us to a broader assessment of institutional practices and policies to enhance women's rank and condition as faculty in computing.

Institutional Practices and Policies
Reflecting Pipeline and Pathways Perspectives

The existing literature on women in science reflects both pipeline and pathways perspectives. The perspective adopted has practical consequences for the steps that institutions and departments could take to improve the status of women faculty in computing. Pipeline versus pathways perspectives offer different emphases and possibilities for intervention and change. We see this in key features of the literature reflecting these two perspectives. Purposefully comparing them to one another enhances our understanding of each perspective and highlights the differences in their implications for solutions to improve the condition of women faculty in computing, particularly.

In 1983, the Rockefeller Foundation issued a report (Berryman 1983) describing the representation of women and racial minorities among doctoral holders in scientific fields with the "pipeline" metaphor. The metaphor depicted straight links between educational stages and between education and occupational outcomes, such that the issue was women "leaking" from the scientific pipeline. In the two decades following, the pipeline metaphor was probably the most common perspective on women's underrepresentation in science. The literature on pipelines emphasizes factors including: 1) uni-directional progressions assumed to operate for women in science; 2) preferences and choices of individual women; 3) deficits of women that result in "leakage" in the pipeline; and 4) effects of family formation, with implications for potential solutions.

Most fundamentally, literature from this perspective emphasizes a point in the original Berryman paper (1983:4), persistence in the pipeline. This appears, for example, in a final report to NSF on "Investigating the Incredible Shrinking Pipeline for Women in Computer Science" (Gruer and Camp 1998), underscoring accurately that women make up decreasing proportions of degrees awarded at increasingly higher levels (bachelor's, master's, doctorate). It also accurately highlighted women's declining share of bachelor's degrees awarded between 1983 and 1998. The emphasis is on the "supply" of women and increasing the supply early in the educational sequence so that more women enter the pipeline at younger ages and continue in scientific careers. The proposed solution is: increase the supply, the sooner the better.

Literature in the pipeline tradition also points to women's educational and career preferences and choices, as major factors governing their underrepresentation in science (Ceci and Williams 2011). In their meta-analysis of forty-seven interest inventories (503,188 respondents), Su, Rounds, and Armstrong (2009) find a large sex difference in the dimension of "Things/

People," with men preferring work with things, and women with people. Sex differences, favoring men, also appear for specific measures of engineering, science, and mathematics interests. As a result, researchers have extended women's limited interest in things to presume girls' preference for careers focusing on people (rather than things), with implications for women's absence from math-intensive fields of computer science, as well as chemistry, engineering, and physics (Ceci and Williams 2011).

In her summary of "the woman problem in computer science," Lagesen (2006) points to other characteristics of individuals that have been cited as contributing to women's lower experience with and interest in computing, specifically, lower confidence with computer skills and lower self-efficacy (sense of control) in relation to computing and computers. From the pipeline perspective, the solution to these issues is to "correct the deficits," that is, enhance women's interest in things compared to people, vocational interests in science/engineering, and confidence and self-efficacy with computing. The focus overall is on individual women and their shortcomings that, if corrected, are believed to help stop the leaking of women from the scientific pipeline (Blickenstaff 2005:369).

Studies from the pipeline perspective also focus on women's "fertility/lifestyle choices" as hindering their progression (Ceci and Williams 2011), especially in academic science (Goulden, Mason, and Frash 2011). The argument is that women are more likely than men to leak out of the scientific pipeline prior to receiving tenure in a college or university and that this owes to "family formation"—marriage and childbirth. In this case, proposed solutions tend to concentrate on potential family benefits such as paid parental leaves, tenure-clock extensions, child care supports, as well as no-cost extensions on research grants for caregiving responsibilities (Goulden et al.2011).

The literature on pathways, in contrast, emphasizes progression that is neither direct nor simple, owing to factors that include: 1) organizational culture and climate that influence women's careers in computing; 2) evaluative practices in academic science; and 3) institutionalized procedures, including those involved in hiring senior faculty members. Solutions to improve the condition of women faculty in computing would address the settings in which they work, in ways that go beyond assumptions about the preferences and choices of individual women, and their supply in the pipeline.

Attention to organizational culture involves consideration of the shared values, beliefs, and behaviors within organizations that can become constructed as "masculine," reflecting men and their interests (Caroll and Mills 2006). Such a culture creates boundaries, by gender, for those who are more, compared to less, valued in the organization with implications for the interaction, communication, and exchange that are important to performance in science (see, for example, McIlwee and Robinson 1992). Technical fields, such as computing, may be prone to masculine organizational cultures because the machine-like terminology, sense of control emphasized in problem-solving, and images and stereotypes of the "ideal computer scientist" are more associated with men than women (Carroll and Mills 2006; Edwards 1990; Lagesen 2007). Such organizational cultures of computing can be reshaped, however, in ways that include expanding approaches to problem solving, featuring women as well as men on departmental websites and promotional materials, and transforming the physical environment of the workplace in videos and posters on site so that they reflect both women and men faculty in computing (Hayes 2010; Cheryan, Davies, Plaut, and Steele 2009; Varma 2007).

Processes of evaluation are the means of assessment and the levers for promotion in academic science. These are fundamental organizational processes (Branskamp and Ory 1994; Seldin 1984; Whitman and Weis 1982) that embody the priorities of units (Wilson and Beaton 1993). Clarity of evaluation, the issue of "how much of what kind of work is enough" (Huber 2002:78), is salient for women scientists who are more likely than men to report that they do not understand the criteria for evaluation in their science unit (Roth and Sonnert 2011), and are less likely to report that criteria for tenure and promotion are "very clear" to them (Fox 2015). Clarity of evaluation draws attention in various reports and initiatives to support positive participation and performance in academic science (and other fields of higher education), including a report of the American Association of Higher Education (Rice, Sorcinelli, and Austin 2000), an analysis of U.S. medical colleges (Bunton and Corrice 2011), the report of the Collaborative on Higher Education (COACHE 2006), and the NSF-ADVANCE Institutional Transformation program to support the advancement of women in academic science and engineering (Bilimoria and Liang 2012; Fox 2008).

Additionally, data from a survey of women and men faculty in nine U.S. research universities in computer science, engineering, and sciences point to unexpected patterns in clarity of evaluation, by gender (Fox 2015). Among men, both formal and informal organizational indicators, as well as field, predict their reported clarity. Among women, only informal indicators, namely speaking daily with faculty in home units and being in units perceived as having a collegial climate, predict their clarity of evaluation; the formal indicator of time (seniority) in the unit does not predict women's clarity. Implications are that time in the institution and presumably exposure to evaluative processes and outcomes do not significantly increase the probability of very clear criteria of evaluation among women (although they do for men). Rather, factors that increase women's clarity are linked to their social integration within units: speaking daily with faculty about research and being in units that they perceive to be collegial. These are issues of social pathways in science.

A third set of factors are institutionalized procedures of organizations that produce gender inequalities in positions, promotions, and salaries in not necessarily conscious ways (Reskin 2003). In a case study of a large public university, Roos and Gatta (2009) focus on such organizational mechanisms of inequality in the organization's own practices of rewarding and promoting faculty. One mechanism is the practice of boosting faculty members' salaries, based on the outside offers received. Those less able to take advantage of the strategy are women who are more likely than men to have spouses with careers that affect whether they are moveable. Another mechanism is the active recruiting of faculty from outside the university for special (enhanced) appointments. This can result in biases favoring men who are less encumbered by careers of spouses and more moveable for these special positions, with the organization taking risks in efforts to recruit men at high and special ranks, and with women more likely to be hired as assistant professors who need to rise through the ranks. The implications are that inequalities in gender, rank, and rewards do not necessarily result from a conscious motive to discriminate but rather as "ways of doing business" in the organization.

Solutions then involve institutional changes that identify and change the mechanisms that produce gender inequities by clearly deliberating and addressing existing organizational procedures including hiring, salary rewards, and advancements in rank (Fox 2008). These entail, in turn, potentially long-term, purposeful, and explicit transformations in management and leadership, reward structures, and ways of thinking about an organization's goals and means of achieving them (Levy and Merry 1986; Nutt and Backoff 1997; Wischnevsky and Damanpour 2006).

Conclusion

Computing is a strategic field for innovation and influence, but the field has been challenging for women. Computer science shows uneven or limited gains, and in some cases actual losses, in women's share of degrees attained over the past four decades. Women faculty members are critical because they contribute to basic and applied research and to the development of both undergraduate and graduate students. The academic ranks—not merely the presence—of women faculty are important because higher rank confers status, and capacity for increased decision-making and impact within colleges and universities. For these reasons, this chapter accomplished three aims: 1) it provided a nuanced profile of the percentage of women faculty by rank in computing fields, defined variously as computer science, information technology, and/or computer engineering; 2) illustrated the challenges and opportunity of women's transitions to higher academic ranks; and 3) depicted how solutions to enhance the condition of women computing faculty vary from the perspectives of pipelines compared to pathways.

In doing this, we found that the profile of women faculty in computing fields depends, in part, on data sources used, and thus we took a judicious approach to sources. At the same time, both the NSF data (that are publically available) and the Taulbee data (compiled by the Computer Research Association) point to trends that may be characterized as: 1) an increase in women's share of positions as assistant professors that, while not continuously linear, is upward so that women constitute about 20 to 26 percent of faculty at this rank in the current period; 2) growth in women's share of positions as associate professors reaching 20 percent; and 3) an increase in women's share of positions as full professors that has slowly and steadily increased, but not exceeded 12 to 13 percent. Women's advancement in rank warrants attention. More needs to be understood about the relationship between the proportions of doctoral degrees awarded to women in computing fields and their transitions to academic careers and ranks over time. However, existing evidence points to the importance of social pathways—including women's social integration into departments of academic science.

Actual steps to improve the status of women computing faculty vary depending on the perspective taken (pipelines or pathways). A comparison of the solutions that would result from one perspective compared to the other points to the importance of structural remedies that address features of the settings in which women faculty work, and issues that go beyond assumptions about preferences and choices of individual women that contribute to their persistence within a scientific pipeline. In keeping with this, promising solutions include 1) attention to the organizational culture in ways that support the positive participation of both women and men; 2) clarity of processes of evaluation, openly conveyed and communicated in settings that integrate women into the social fabric of departments; and 3) identification and proactive changes in ongoing institutional mechanisms that produce gender inequities in positions, promotions, and rewards. These, in turn, have the potential to reduce the challenges, and improve the opportunities, of women faculty in computing fields.

Notes

1. The Alfred P. Sloan Foundation's support of this project is gratefully acknowledged.

2. The SESTAT public variable is "computer and mathematics," and the Report on *Women, Minorities, and Persons with Disabilities in Science and Engineering* categorizes the variable as "computer and information scientists" (and cites SESTAT).

3. Data are unweighted, reflecting the scope and range of the departments surveyed.

4. A factor analysis identifies this construct based on responses to five scaled items about perceptions of the departmental environment/climate as fair, exciting, helpful, creative, or inclusive.

~

CHAPTER FOUR

Does the Road Improve in the Land of the Tenured?

Exploring Perceptions of Culture and Satisfaction by Rank and Gender

Julia McQuillan, Mary Anne Holmes,
Patricia Wonch Hill, and Mindy Anderson-Knott

My job satisfaction increased significantly becoming a full professor . . . that's the top academic title that you can get.

> —Full Professor, Woman, STEM department, 2012,
> Midwestern University, R1

I must have been really naïve because I thought when I became a full professor I would be able to do what I wanted to do, and that really hasn't happened . . . This, you have to have so many grants and you have to have so many publications a year does not lend itself to the kind of research I am doing . . . The evaluation process does not make me feel comfortable. I enjoy my job, my research, I enjoy my students a lot . . . but the evaluation process does not match what I thought it would be as a full professor.

> —Full Professor, Woman, STEM department, 2012,
> Midwestern University, R1

The quotes above indicate that for some faculty the road of scientific careers in the land of the tenured and fully promoted can be, but is not necessarily, as smooth as pre-tenured faculty hope it will be and many administrators assume that it is. As Bozeman and Gaughan (2011:158) describe so well, "Given that tenure is essentially a condition of continued employment as an academic faculty member, it seems straightforward that *tenure is a determinant of job satisfaction*. Tenure implies senior status and by definition means job security." Yet the second quote above suggests that for some faculty, tenure, and specifically being a full professor, may not be the "promised land."

We confronted the question of gender and rank specific faculty needs when we designed a pilot survey for our National Science Foundation (NSF) ADVANCE application. Our goals were straightforward; we wanted to recruit, retain, and promote more women in science, technology, engineering, and math (STEM) departments. We also wanted to focus on broader inclusion goals (e.g., race/ethnicity, sexuality, and disability status), but had to work within the expectations of our funding. We debated if we needed to go beyond assistant professors for our research. At the time (2007) we planned to use the popular Harvard Collaborative on Academic Careers in Higher Education (COACHE) survey, but it only included pre-tenure faculty and we were committed to a community-based participatory research approach (McIntyre 2008). We therefore held group and individual meetings with women STEM faculty and department chairs as we wrote the proposal. Several associate and full professor women expressed frustrations and challenges. We also heard stories of highly successful women who had left the institution even with tenure and at the rank of full professor. In addition, we recognized that faculty have to go up for tenure or leave the institution, but that they never have to go up for promotion to full professor, and therefore the issues relevant for tenure could be different than the issues relevant for promotion to full. We therefore decided to survey faculty of all ranks.

These pilot data supported the extra efforts involved in converting the survey items to be relevant not only to assistant professors, but also to associate and full professors. For several items designed to measure department culture and individual satisfaction, full professor women had lower scores than associate professors, and assistant professors had the highest scores. For men the patterns were reversed; therefore men, but not women, found well-paved roads in science careers post tenure and promotion.

Our ADVANCE-Nebraska team research director, Dr. Christina Falci, led efforts to create a new survey for our project that included faculty across rank, and expanded the measures of department culture and faculty satisfaction (the Faculty Network and Workload Study [FNWS] is described in our ADVANCE-Nebraska Annual Report 2011–2012[1]). To further understand the survey data patterns, we hired the University of Nebraska Bureau of Sociological Research to conduct focus groups with associate and full women STEM faculty. We analyzed the transcripts from the focus groups for themes and to more fully explain the patterns that we identified from our survey data. In this chapter we summarize the mean scores of several measures of department culture and faculty satisfaction by gender and rank including: 1) general perception of positive culture, 2) clarity of the tenure process, 3) workload fairness, 4) how much colleagues value one's research, 5) family supportiveness, and 6) intention to stay at the university. We also briefly summarize key insights from the focus groups to add depth to the descriptive statistics.

We recognize that family demands can also differentially influence work satisfaction by gender (e.g., Mason and Goulden 2004), yet prior research with the same data suggests that family-related demands are not a factor in faculty satisfaction (Watanabe and Falci 2014). We therefore provide information on several measures of faculty work satisfaction, identifying gender and rank specific information helpful for change efforts. Just as maps and information about local conditions improve journeys, our goal is to inform efforts in the lands of assistant, associate, and full professors.

If we had not listened to women faculty, we would have focused on faculty who already have the most positive perceptions of their department cultures and highest satisfaction: pre-tenured faculty. If we had not surveyed all STEM faculty, we would not have recognized that men at the associate level have lower perceptions of department culture and lower satisfaction than men at the assistant and full level. In the following pages, we discuss the literature on workplace culture and job satisfaction, we share our survey results on perceived workplace culture by rank and gender and we use our subsequent focus groups to explore what might be driving our findings. We then look at the sociological literature to assess why there are differences by rank and gender in some findings, but not others. Finally, we discuss implications for other institutions that want to retain women STEM faculty of all ranks.

Why Focus on Faculty Perceptions of Department Culture and Satisfaction?

Satisfaction among faculty matters to institutions because higher job satisfaction leads to higher productivity (Fox and Mohapatra 2007), and lower job satisfaction leads to higher turnover (Callister 2008; Watanabe and Falci 2014). Recruiting faculty takes considerable time and money, and large start-up packages often take years to pay off. Therefore it makes sense to take steps to ensure high job satisfaction. Job satisfaction for faculty often reflects perceptions of department practices and policies such as equity (equitable pay, equitable access to resources), collegial relationships among colleagues and with administrators, a feeling that one can grow professionally, job security, recognition for work and contributions (Gappa, Austin, and Trice 2007), as well as autonomy, academic freedom, and having excellent students (Winkler 1982).

Prior, and somewhat dated, research found that both within and outside academia, the higher the rank of a person in an organization, the greater his or her job satisfaction, in part because of greater responsibility, higher salary, prestige, and more intrinsically rewarding work (Herzberg et al. 1959; Oshagbemi 1997a). It follows that job satisfaction should be higher among faculty at higher ranks. Studies from the late twentieth century confirmed this assumption: tenured faculty had higher mean satisfaction scores than non-tenured or pre-tenured (tenure track) faculty and full professors reported higher levels of job satisfaction than faculty at assistant or associate rank (Tack and Patitu 1992; Oshagbemi 1997a). Pre-tenured faculty may be concerned with job security, a major factor in faculty job satisfaction (Gappa et al. 2007). More recently, Trower and Bleak (2004) revealed that considerable demands on time and struggles to achieve work-life balance have become important contributors to lower satisfaction among pre-tenured faculty, particularly women. Before we surveyed the associate and full professor women, we expected to confirm the finding that higher rank is associated with higher satisfaction and lower rank is associated with lower satisfaction

For centuries faculty were men, therefore the job was designed around the "ideal worker" norm of a person with few family demands (e.g., Gappa et al. 2007; Williams 2000; Xu 2008). Women do not fit the ideal worker norm, and each increase in rank could be associated with an even bigger "mismatch." The extensive research on "chilly climates," initiated by Hall and Sandler (1982), focuses on gender specific actions that do not welcome women. Our measures of department climate and faculty satisfaction are more general and can apply to men or women. We were unsure if women who persist despite potholes and barriers, and reach the peak of academic STEM careers (i.e., tenured associate and full professors), would have higher satisfaction than women assistant professors.

Below, we describe the ways in which we gathered information to answer our questions about rank, gender, and perceptions of culture/satisfaction. We then provide descriptions of the measures, graphs showing the means by rank and gender, and interpretations. We complete the empirical information with a brief summary of the focus group data. Finally, we discuss the meaning of the findings relative to prior research, and summarize suggestions for improving department cultures to support satisfaction among all faculty of all ranks.

Getting to Know the Local Terrains

We conducted our project survey in March of 2011. The goal of the survey was to measure faculty networks, climate/culture perceptions, and faculty productivity. The study design for the FNWS consisted of a mixed mode survey: faculty had the option of filling out the survey on the web or via mail questionnaire. Overall, there was a 73.1 percent individual response rate. Our results may underestimate dissatisfaction as those who suffered the most probably left the institution before reaching the rank of associate or full professor. FNWS is a census drawn from the population of STEM and Social and Behavioral Science Departments at the University of Nebraska, Lincoln. We limited this analysis to the subsample of 414 tenured or tenure-track faculty members in twenty-four STEM departments.[2] We focus on comparisons between men and women within each measure rather than comparing across measures because the scale ranges differ between some items.

Our project focus groups with associate and full professor women followed the survey in the fall of 2012. The facilitators that we hired conducted three focus groups, each consisting of six-eight women, with a total of twenty-one participating. The protocol included a broad range of questions on subjects including the tenure and promotion process, job satisfaction, retention, and the impact of spousal employment. Faculty were also asked to discuss policies they thought would be useful in recruiting and retaining tenure-track STEM women faculty. The focus group conversations were transcribed and coded for major themes. The themes, with accompanying quotes, then led to a set of recommendations for the senior administrative team at the university (see chapter 12).

Survey Patterns: Perceptions of Department Culture Indicating Level of Satisfaction General Positive Department Culture

Figure 4.1 shows the mean scores for positive department culture for STEM faculty by gender and rank. Positive department culture is a scale composed of five variables. Faculty were asked how strongly they agreed or disagreed, ranging from 1 to 5 (5=strong agreement), with the following statements: a) "Faculty in my department are supportive," b) "Faculty in my department enjoy working together," c) "Faculty in my department spend time getting to know one another," d) "Faculty in my department are sometimes rude to one another," e) "Tension among faculty in my department make it uncomfortable working here' (the latter two variables were reverse coded).[3]

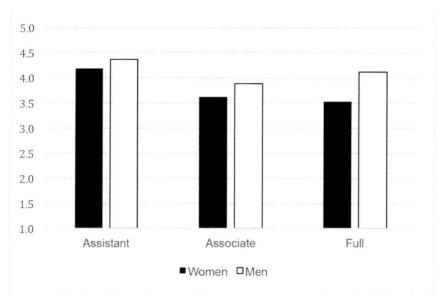

Figure 4.1.   Perceptions of Positive Department Climate by Gender and Rank. Note: Number of participants by gender and rank in the figures: Assistant Women (N=31), Assistant Men (N=71), Associate Women (N=26), Associate Men (N=69), Full Women (N=15), Full Men (N=202).
Author's analysis.

For all groups the means are above the mid-point of the scale (between 3 and 4), indicating fairly positive perceptions of department culture. In general, satisfaction with department varies by both gender and rank. Women at the assistant level have higher positive culture perceptions than women at higher ranks. Associate professor men have lower positive culture percep-tions than assistant and full professor men. At every rank, men have higher average positive culture perceptions than women.

Clarity of the Tenure Process

Figure 4.2 shows the mean scores for clarity of the tenure process for STEM faculty by rank and gender. Clarity of the tenure process is a scale composed of three variables. Faculty were asked on a scale of 1 to 6 (1=Very Unclear, 6=Very Clear) to what extent are each of the following aspects of tenure and promotion in your tenure home department clear or unclear: a) "The body of academic work considered," b) "Academic work performance expectations (i.e., quantity and quality of the work), "The steps involved in the process."[4]

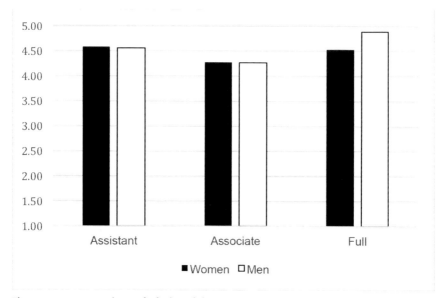

Figure 4.2.　Perceptions of Clarity of the Tenure Process by Gender and Rank.
Author's analysis.

Associate professors (both men and women) perceive the tenure process the least clear compared to assistant and full professors. Only among the full professors is there a notable gender difference, with women perceiving the tenure process as less clear than men. Both men and women who recently went through the tenure process (associates) find the process the least clear. It is important to note that for the tenured associate and full professors, these are a sample of people who successfully navigated the process of tenure and promotion, while those who likely found it most unclear consequently left the university after not receiving tenure. These findings are similar to the patterns identified by Fox (2015) in a study of the clarity of tenure in nine universities. Fox found that time at an institution is associated with clarity of tenure evaluation for men but not women, and that within departments, informal interactions have stronger associations with the clarity of the tenure process, particularly for women.

Workload Fairness Culture

Figure 4.3 shows the mean scores for perception of workload fairness for STEM faculty by rank and gender. Workload fairness distribution is com-

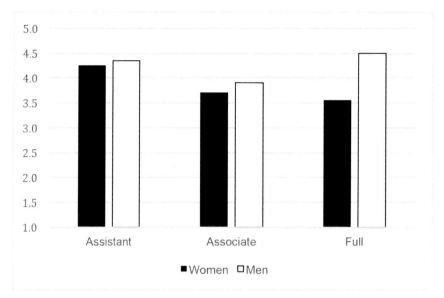

Figure 4.3. Perceptions of Workload Fairness by Gender and Rank.
Author's analysis.

posed of four variables that ask faculty to rank fairness from 1 to 5 (1=Very Unfair, 5=Very fair). Within their tenure home department how fair is the following: a) "Rotation of service committee assignments," b) "Evaluation of faculty performance," c) "Distribution of faculty salaries," d) "Distribution of department resources."[5]

Among women the trend is a linear decline in perceived workload fairness as rank increases. Women assistant professors perceive workload as the most fair, and women full professors as the least fair. In contrast the trend for men is curvilinear; assistant and full professor men have higher perceived workload fairness scores than men who are associate professors. At each rank, women have lower perceived workload fairness than men, but the gap is largest among full professors.

Culture around Valuing Research

Figure 4.4 shows the mean scores for the perceived value of research for STEM faculty by rank and gender. The value of research perception is based on how strongly faculty agree with the following statements: a) "I have received positive feedback about my research from department colleagues," b)

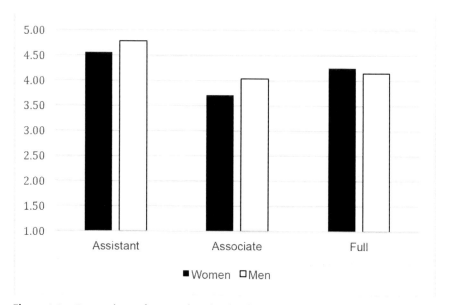

Figure 4.4. Perceptions of Research Valuation by Colleagues by Gender and Rank.
Author's analysis.

"Faculty in my department recognize the contributions I make to my field,"
c) "Faculty in my department value my research."[6]

Among both men and women, the pattern is curvilinear, with assistant
and full professor perceptions higher than associate professor perceptions.
Among full professors, women have slightly higher scores then men.

Family Supportiveness Culture

Figure 4.5 shows the mean scores for family supportiveness perception for
STEM faculty by rank and gender. Department family supportiveness is a
scale composed of four variables that measures faculty's perception of their
department's policies and general acceptance of work/family balance issues.
On a scale of 1 to 5 faculty were asked how strongly they agreed or disagreed
with the following statements: a) "My colleagues are respectful of my effort to
balance work and home responsibilities," b) "In my department, faculty may
comfortably raise personal or family responsibilities when scheduling work
activities," c) "My colleagues do what they can to make family obligations
and an academic career compatible," d) "I am hesitant to talk about my family life with other faculty in my department" (reverse coded).[7]

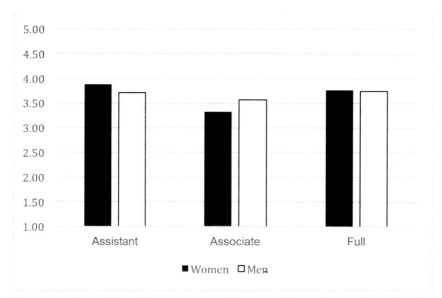

Figure 4.5.   Perceptions of Department Family Supportiveness by Gender and Rank.
Author's analysis.

For men and women there is a curvilinear pattern for the family support-iveness scale. Assistant and full professors have higher scores than associate professors. At the assistant and full ranks, women have slightly higher scores than men, but at the associate level men have higher scores than women.

Desire to Stay

Faculty ratings regarding their desire to stay are given in figure 4.6. The de-sire to stay on the UNL scale is composed of four variables that ask faculty to rank on a scale of 1 to 5 (5 = strong agreement) how much they agree or disagree with the following statements: a) "I would be happy to spend the rest of my career in this department," b) "It would take a lot to get me to leave this department," c) "I have seriously considered leaving this department," d) "If I could leave this department right now, I would" (the latter two variables were recoded).[8]

Among women the trend is linear and negative: assistant professors have higher scores than associate professors, and full professors have the lowest scores. In contrast, the trend is curvilinear for men professors. Among the men, assistant professors have the highest desire to stay, followed by the full professors, with the score for associate professors much lower. At all ranks

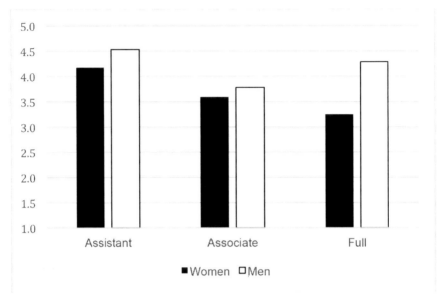

Figure 4.6. Faculty Rating of Desire to Stay by Gender and Rank.
Author's analysis.

women have lower desire to stay than men, but the difference is most extreme among full professors.

In Their Own Voices

The pattern of results showing that associate professor women had worse
perceptions of their department culture than assistant professor women, and
that in some cases perceptions were even lower for full professor women,
suggested the need for further investigation. We therefore added the focus
group data to the survey data, a mixed-method strategy that informed our
actions (Creswell 2012). Because some of the associate level men were also
less satisfied than assistant professor and full professor men, we presumed that
ideas for improving the experiences of associate professor women would help
all associate professors.

As the quotes at the beginning of this chapter indicate, some faculty did
find that the land of the full professor was better than the terrain of pre-
tenure life. In some departments women had considerable help, for example:

> I spoke with my colleagues in my department and they were supportive so I
> went up [for promotion]. So, they gave me pointers because I was going up

early . . . so for me it was not a problem. Expectations were well laid out . . . my department was supportive.

Another full professor woman in a STEM department did not perceive any difference between the experiences of men and women:

> I actually think that in my department, the expectations are very much the same for everybody . . . this big pressure to get tenure because that's a big deal, because of course if you don't get tenure you don't have a job. . . . I don't feel like the pressures have changed and I also feel like the expectations were exceptionally clear. And have always been exceptionally clear . . . it's the quality of the work that's being evaluated.

Both associate and full professors were asked to describe how their job satisfaction has changed since becoming an associate or full professor, particularly what factors have increased or decreased satisfaction. Consistent with the standard image of tenure making it possible to take risks and go in new directions with research, some associate professors reported being able to do what they want research-wise:

> I feel like after being tenured, there was a lot of pressure taken off because I can do the research that I want and not really care about having, you know, having that many publications a year.

Not all women, however, found that the reality of achieving tenure matched their hopes. Some of the women did not get to take advantage of the promise of more research freedom from tenure because they were expected to do more service, such as university award committees, faculty senate, or the college Promotion and Tenure committee. For instance, one professor described her experience:

> For me before I was [tenured], I couldn't wait because I felt like that would allow me to pursue some of these research avenues that I hadn't been pursuing yet because they might be a little bit more risky, or . . . but I haven't had any time. Which makes it even more frustrating, so probably my job satisfaction has decreased because I felt like I should now be able to do these things but yet there's just no time because of service.

For some women, and presumably some men, given the patterns in the survey data, large service roles appear to be major potholes that get in the way of tenured professors who want to explore exciting new research routes.

Also consistent with the idea of being more vested in the department, some women were pleased to have a stronger voice as associate professors:

> One way in which job satisfaction increased is I felt like I had a stronger voice in the department, was taken more seriously by members of the department. It makes a big difference.

Yet not all women experienced the rise in status associated with promotion to associate or full professor. Instead, at least one woman experienced inconsistency between her status as a full professor because she was treated as a lower status "woman":

> . . . after I got full professor . . . there was "ok, she's there and now, you know, we can ignore her pretty much." And I feel even more isolated I would say, so the male faculty I . . . when you are younger they can big brother you and . . . kind of treat you like a little sister but then when you get older they don't really, they can't really treat you like a little sister anymore, and so you are even more excluded I guess than when you were younger. . . . I feel more separated from the faculty than I ever did . . . I feel that people still respond to me like a woman rather than a full professor.

Rather than feeling more embedded and connected with the department after tenure and promotion, there was a sense of now being on one's own, but still needing a support system. As one associate professor described:

> And when you are associate professor too, what I have noticed is that you kind of had a support system when you were assistant professor. When you get to be associate professor I don't know what happened to that support system, I mean, all of a sudden. . . . It just seems like you are almost on your own, which is ok, but, but it doesn't help in terms of trying to figure out what the expectations are when you go up for promotion or tenure.

This faculty member raises an important point. Depending on personal relationships—social networks—to disseminate vital information for promotion will disadvantage those who are more socially isolated. The experience this professor describes resonates with the insights from Fox and Xiao (2013) who found that the key predictors of women's perceived chances for promotion reflect social integration (e.g., collaboration with faculty with home unit) and department culture (e.g., being in a unit that they report as having a "stimulating/collegial" climate).

In response to questions about policies and practices that could help faculty make their careers more successful, several faculty members described frustration with low valuation of service, a need for service, and no consequences for faculty who do not do service. One faculty member explained:

> There is an active undervaluation of service, and that's what I thrive on . . . I do a lot of the advising. . . . It's just not valued at all. And that's not a gender thing, that's across the university. . . . It's a drain on time and it's a lot of effort.

These quotes provide insights regarding why many women associate professors, and even some women full professors, are less satisfied after earning tenure. The challenges that faculty identified with promotion processes (e.g., consistency, clarity, transparency, rigid expectations, and inclusion of personal information in the process) could lead some faculty to be so discouraged that they do not even want to seek full professor. Some women did see and experience the benefits that can come with tenure and promotion, however, including a sense of job security, a stronger voice in the department, enjoyment of work, and the perception that their work was valued.

One of the largest stressors was high service demands and low valuing or respect for service, particularly when service was perceived as undervalued and an unfair burden on women. Some women experienced lower job satisfaction at the associate or full professor level if they had less guidance and support, and if they felt more isolated in their department. The discrepancy between expecting to be treated with more respect but instead experiencing less respect and recognition as a woman first, and a faculty member second, created even more dissatisfaction. There was a mix of positive and negative experiences among the associate and full professor women in STEM departments, suggesting that some departments have created cultures that can help faculty to remain connected, supported, valued, and productive at all career stages. We next link our findings to prior research and describe strategies to improve department cultures and faculty satisfaction at all ranks.

Job Satisfaction for Assistant Professors

In general, our results indicate that, unlike some previous studies (Trower 2012; Xu 2008; Hagedorn 2000; Oshagbemi 1997a; Tack and Patitu 1992) but similar to others (Sabharwal and Corley 2009; Mathews 2014), faculty at the assistant professor rank have the most positive faculty experiences. In contrast, faculty at the associate professor rank and women at the full professor rank have more negative experiences. The inconsistent results from prior research and in the focus group data suggest that local culture plays an important role in faculty experiences. From our work on ADVANCE, we knew a few full professor women faculty who had low job satisfaction; yet we were surprised by the contrasting patterns between men and women by rank for some measures (e.g., general department culture, workload fairness, and intention to stay) and the similar curvilinear patterns for men and women for other measures (e.g., clarity of the tenure process, one's research being valued, and department family supportiveness).

Why might job satisfaction be highest for assistant professors? We suggest that one factor is that they have just been hired into, one hopes, their "dream job." Presumably they are satisfied with their salary and start-up packages and perceive a collegial, supportive environment. Our institution does provide considerable support for new STEM faculty by providing grant proposal-writing workshops and administrative support for obtaining funding for research. In many departments, first- and sometimes second-year faculty are provided some teaching relief and/or summer salary to aid in launching their research careers. In addition, women at this rank probably experience less gender discrimination or implicit bias, since they were hired despite any bias of the selection process.

In addition, as one of the focus group members suggested, at the assistant professor level the older faculty may treat the younger women professors as "little sisters." Therefore the women's gender and professor status are more consistent in that they are "less than." But when women increase in status through promotion and tenure, their male colleagues do not know how to reconcile the higher status (associate or full professor) with the lower status (woman). Rather than confront the confusion or discomfort, the male faculty likely avoid the women faculty, resulting in some of the greater isolation some of the associate and full professor women described. In the absence of clear formal guidelines for successfully navigating mid-career challenges, women professors will have less support to navigate their new territory. If associate and full professor women are seen as "women" more than as "professors," then they are likely to be asked to do more of the department "housekeeping" service work such as advising undergraduate students (Misra, Lundquist, Holmes, Agiomavritis 2011; Pyke 2011). Indeed many women STEM faculty did not want to be associated with the ADVANCE grant because they expected that it would increase the salience of their identity as a woman and decrease their salience as a professor, plus add to their already high service loads. We agreed, and worked to include more full professor men in the time-consuming labor of transforming the institution to recruit, retain, and promote more women in STEM.

The Climate for Tenured and Promoted Professors

There are several possible reasons why perceptions of general positive culture in the department is lower for associate compared to assistant professors. We expect that the reasons for lowered satisfaction depend on how long the individual has been at the associate professor rank (Geisler, Kaminski, and Berkley 2007). Britton (2012), based on interviews with associate professors, reports that those who are at this rank for seven years or more perceive themselves as highly burdened with "academic reproduction": teaching and advising service. For newly minted associate professors there can be a sort of post-tenure "depression" or "mid-career crisis" wherein they begin to re-assess and re-adjust as they seek to find renewed interest and perhaps even a new path for the next phase of their careers. Similar to the women in our focus groups, some faculty report spending less time on research and more time on service work and teaching, and less satisfaction with having the time to keep current in the field and with workload (Baldwin, Lunceford, and Vanderlinden 2005).

We also found evidence that for many faculty, all of their attention has been focused on getting tenure; once they have achieved it, many wonder what the next career stage will bring. Additionally, we found evidence that faculty perceive the loss of the support and mentoring they had when they were pre-tenure faculty (Mathews 2014; Baldwin, Lunceford, and Vanderlinden 2005). At our institution, men at associate professor rank have the lowest climate scores for each factor that we measured. It may be that men feel the fall from "golden boy" (assistant professor) rank to a secondary or tertiary status more than women, who are generally conditioned to accept second-class status.

Why do departments expect faculty to know how to handle the new responsibilities that come with tenure and promotion? There seems to be an assumption that tenured faculty have "made it" and therefore can figure out the next steps with ease. Baldwin et al. (2008) used in-depth interviews to map the terrain of mid-career faculty, and found unique needs for professional development support. Several other studies highlight the importance of addressing the mentoring and professional development needs of mid-career faculty (Alstete 2000; Awando, Wood, Camargo, and Layne 2014; Baldwin, Lunceford, and Vanderlinden 2005; Britton 2011, 2012; Canale, Herdklotz and Wild 2013, Geisler et al. 2007; Mathews 2014; Strage and Merdinger 2015; Terosky, O'Meara, and Campbell 2014).

Transparent guidelines and explicit support and mentoring for faculty are exceptional and usually focused on pre-tenure faculty (Trower 2012). Even less transparency and guidance is provided for associate and full professors, exemplified by this quote from a study on mid-career faculty: "To sum it all up, you're pretty much left to your own devices" (Baldwin et al 2008:46). In general there are fewer resources for faculty at associate rank than at assistant rank. For example, NSF CAREER grants and other early stage grants and professional society awards focus on pre-tenure faculty. The next stage of grants and awards tends to be for fully mature STEM faculty. At the same time that they lose support and guidance, mid-career faculty also perceive an increased teaching load and greater expectations for service and advising (Pyke 2011; Britton 2012; Mathews 2014).

Much of the information and guidance necessary to succeed at each level of the faculty career comes from informal relationships (Bird 2011); few institutions have specific mid-career roadmaps (Britton 2011, 2012). There are exceptional institutions that provide explicit support for mid-career faculty; these institutions highlight extensive possible actions for faculty, chairs, departments, and institutions to improve satisfaction and success for faculty at all ranks (Baldwin et al. 2008).

In the absence of explicit support for navigating the new demands and expectations faced by associate and full professors, faculty need to gain necessary information and guidance through informal relationships (Terosky et al. 2014). Yet as departments become less homogeneous and faculty are asked to do more in the same amount of time, trusting informal personal relationships to spread essential information for faculty success becomes more precarious. Examples of how to clarify this process include communicating: How many years is typical at the associate rank before promotion is possible? Is an international reputation expected, and in what ways can such a reputation be demonstrated?

To make explicit what is often presumed through implicit informal interactions, department members could work together to create rubrics with clear expectations for what is expected to reach full professor, and what the expectations are for those at the full professor level. It is less important to specify the number of articles, books, conference presentations, or grants, and more important to have conversations and attempt to capture general guidelines that provide more than "we'll know it when we see it" (Canale et al. 2013; Strage and Merdinger 2015; Awando et al. 2014). It is likely that having department-wide conversations about what faculty are expected to contribute to the department at different career stages will help everyone better recognize the contributions and needs of faculty at different ranks.

We found at UNL that department chairs and heads were not always aware that the criteria for promotion were not clear. Once alerted, however, most administrators began an annual review for each associate professor and provided feedback on how well the associate professors were tracking for promotion. The service load of these faculty should be considered seriously, as service disproportionately falls to women, who are generally told "Just Say No," a tactic widely demonstrated to be ineffectual and particularly damaging for women faculty (Pyke 2011).

For associate professors, clarity of expectations for the next career move is essential but may not be enough. Baldwin et al. (2005) provide extensive lists of promising practices to help mid-career faculty, including: an orientation to the mid-career experience for newly tenured faculty, leadership development opportunities, workshops for chairs/directors to provide skills for career guidance, motivating faculty, and faculty evaluations, providing funds to help faculty "retool," providing second "start-up" packages for faculty who change research areas, engaging in more assessment and planning with faculty, including meaningful career plans and clear expectations regarding requirements for full professor, feedback on progress toward full professor, conversations about how faculty can best contribute to the department, college, or profession, performance data relative to department and rank, nominating mid-career faculty for awards, providing incentives for service contributions, and providing praise and thanks. Many of these same ideas could work for full professors.

Conclusions

Our self-study revealed missing road signs, rough roads, and the realization that only some people get the maps. Our university may be unique, but we suspect that it is not. Indeed several of the patterns that we identify are consistent with patterns from other institutions (e.g., see Fox and Xiao 2013; Fox 2015). Overall we find that for associate compared to assistant and full professors, indicators of clarity of evaluation, valuing of research, and support for families are lower. Our hope is that institutions of higher education that want to retain, support, and help faculty thrive throughout their careers will include faculty at all ranks in their efforts. Providing maps to help navigate the roads for associate and full professors will minimize wasted time and energy on failed tenure and promotion cases (see chapter 12 for more information on creating roadmaps). The skills, knowledge, and abilities that helped faculty to gain tenure are not necessarily effective in the world of associate and of full professors. We recognize that there has been more emphasis on mid-career faculty in recent research, but we know of no other studies that show the gaps between women and men full professors in some areas of culture and satisfaction. For most universities the number of full professor women in STEM fields is relatively small, therefore finding out if there are changes that could improve their situation is likely to incur minimal time and effort, but could result in substantial benefits to the institution.

We focused on identifying areas that can benefit from changes in policies, practices, mentorship, and professional development by gender and rank. Our data show the value of questioning assumptions about the ubiquitous benefits of tenure and promotion and "one size fits all" faculty development and support practices. In addition, institutions could use self-study to explore whether faculty take advantage of tenure by taking more risks and going into new research directions. If they do not, could this explain lower satisfaction for associate professors? And what are the barriers to enjoying the benefits of tenure? Our experience shows that the processes of self-study, of flexible routes to faculty success in response to findings, and evaluation of intervention efforts can have a major impact for all higher education institutions.

Notes

1. http://advance.unl.edu/projectdocs/advanceannualreport20112012.pdf.

2. Because this is not a random sample, tests of statistical significance are not appropriate.

3. The scale on positive department culture has a good reliability as indicated by a chronbach's alpha of 0.86, with all variables loading onto one latent construct at above 0.7, explaining 64 percent of the variance in a single latent construct.

4. The scale on clarity of the tenure process has a very good reliability with a chronbach's alpha of 0.90, and all of the factor loadings above 0.7, explaining 84 percent of the variance in a single latent construct.

5. The workload fairness scale has good reliability with chronbach's alpha of 0.85, with factor loadings at 0.7 or above, with 69 percent of the variance explained by a single latent construct.

6. The valuing research scale has good reliability with chronbach's alpha of 0.92, and all of the factor loadings above 0.9; these variables explain 86 percent of the variance in a single latent construct.

7. The scale on family supportiveness culture has a good reliability with a chronbach's alpha of 0.77, all of the variables had factor loadings above 0.6; these variables explain 62 percent of the variance in the latent construct.

8. The stay at UNL scale has a very good reliability with chronbach's alpha of 0.9, with factor loadings at 0.8 or above, and 78 percent of the variance is explained with a single latent construct.

~

CHAPTER FIVE

Potholes and Detours on the Road to Full Professor

A Tale of STEM Faculty at Two Liberal Arts Colleges

Catherine White Berheide

Women are underrepresented at the rank of full professor in the United States (National Science Foundation [NSF] 2013) as well as other countries (e.g., Wroblewski 2014).[1] Even though they comprise a higher proportion of full-time faculty at four-year colleges than at research universities in the United States (West and Curtis 2006), Perna (2001) found there was no difference between the two types of institutions in the probability of women reaching the full professor level. Furthermore, when only the natural sciences, technology, engineering, and mathematics (STEM) disciplines were considered, the number of women at the rank of full professor at undergraduate colleges also mirrored their underrepresentation at research universities, especially in the physical sciences (Ellemers, Van den Heuvel, de Gilder, Maas, and Bonvini 2004).

The greater presence of women on the STEM faculty at colleges implies that they encounter fewer roadblocks in their careers at these institutions than at universities and yet they still have not achieved parity at the highest rank. Even though the research expectations tend to be lower at colleges than at universities, the teaching and service demands are higher and more ambiguous (Wolf-Wendel, Ellen, and Ward 2006). The barriers to reaching full professor may, therefore, be different for women faculty in STEM departments in colleges than in universities. Most studies of the underrepresentation of STEM women at the full professor level have been conducted at research universities (e.g., Geisler, Kaminsky, and Berkley 2007). This chapter uses mixed methods to explore whether STEM women at two elite liberal arts colleges encounter the same problems on the road to full professor that STEM women encounter at research universities.

The Nonlinear Career

Instead of the leaky pipeline metaphor that many researchers (e.g., Riger et al. 1997) have used to explain the large numbers of women, and the even larger numbers of women of color, who drop out of STEM fields at each stage of an academic career, Hill, Secker, and Davidson (2014) used the concept of a nonlinear career. According to Hill et al. (2014), different types of events, such as a late start, caring responsibilities, and health problems, may have produced nonlinearity. They classified these nonlinear events as either pauses where time was taken out of the labor force, diversions that forced faculty to reduce their workload or deliberately slowed their career progress, or hijacks that halted advancement.

Ten of the thirteen women faculty they interviewed at an Australian university experienced caring for children, the most frequently mentioned nonlinear event, as a diversion that slowed their career progress. The second cause of nonlinearity was taking on a service role, eight of the thirteeen women faculty reported that doing so had hijacked their advancement. In contrast, only two of the fourteen men faculty reported that caring for children had diverted their careers and another two that assuming a service role had hijacked their careers. Furthermore, women faculty experienced more instances of nonlinearity (4.5 on average) than men did (1.9 on average). The cumulative effect of these interruptions on advancement was greater for women than for men.

I argue that STEM women who pursue faculty careers encounter barriers in the workplace that hinder their progress toward promotion to full professor. Some of these barriers slow their progress; others halt it. In this chapter, I focus specifically on potholes, such as chilly department climates, that can leave women stuck as associate professors as well as on detours, such as administrative and service responsibilities, that delay, or even hijack, women's promotion to full professor at two highly selective liberal arts colleges.

The Chilly Department Climate Pothole

Previous research (e.g., Roos and Gatta 2009) has demonstrated that chilly department climates have hurt the advancement of STEM women. Fox and Xiao (2012) found women associate professors in computer science who reported that their department had a competitive and stressful climate assessed their chances of promotion negatively. At a major technological university, women faculty rated supportive relationships with colleagues as more important than men did (Bilimoria, Perry, Liang, Stoller, Higgins, and Taylor 2006), and yet more women than men engineering faculty at research universities reported lack of support from colleagues (Jackson 2004).

Carr, Schmidt, Ford, and DeShon (2003) described workplace climate as shared perceptions of formal and informal organizational policies, practices, and procedures. They identified three components of organizational climate: affective, instrumental, and cognitive. The affective dimension referred to involvement with people and interpersonal relations; the instrumental to work processes, structure, and extrinsic rewards, such as pay and promotion; and the cognitive to intrinsic rewards, such as autonomy and meaning. Callister (2006) concluded that the affective dimension, that is interpersonal relationships, was key to a supportive department climate.

One of the few studies of a predominantly undergraduate institution (Borland and Bates 2014) found that STEM women full professors also experienced a chillier and less collegial climate. They reported "less support for professional advancement than men, as well as collegial exclusion, isolation, and gender hostility" (Borland and Bates 2014:118). In contrast, less senior women had not experienced these climate problems, perhaps because of the increasing number of women among the STEM faculty. Chilly department climates clearly had an effect on women's promotion opportunities in the past, but climates may be warming up today in those STEM departments that have increasing proportions of women faculty.

The Rocky Road to Full Professor

Gender schemas are a set of implicit ideas about sex differences that affect expectations of men and women as well as evaluations of their work (Valian 1998). For example, Moss-Racusin, Dovidio, Brescoll, Graham, and Handelsman's (2012) experiment found that 127 STEM faculty from research-intensive universities in the United States rated a laboratory manager application that was randomly assigned a man's name as significantly better qualified for the position than the identical application with a woman's name; being a woman *caused* the application to be evaluated more negatively. Another study that examined 500 letters of reference for medical school faculty positions also revealed implicit gender bias. Letters for male applicants were longer, raised fewer doubts, and were more likely to mention research, whereas those for women more often mentioned teaching (Trix and Psenka 2003).

In the Netherlands, women in the natural sciences who sought promotion to full professor were measured against a masculine standard of the ideal scientist. As a consequence of applying gender schemas to evaluations of faculty competence and performance, men were consistently overrated, while women were underrated (Van den Brink and Benschop 2012). Both Van den Brink and Benschop (2012) and Borland and Bates (2014) found instances where assessments of women's competence were negatively affected when men regarded their appearance as too young or too feminine. In short, empirical evidence indicates that gender bias still affects personnel decisions.

This problem of gender bias in personnel decisions is exacerbated by a lack of clarity concerning criteria for promotion to full professor. In Austria, women encountered gender bias in three phases of the process of applying to become a full professor: "missing or unspecific procedural guidelines, peer reviews and gendered assessment criteria" (Wroblewski 2014:294). At Massachusetts Institute of Technology, Bailyn (2003) found that evaluation criteria, timing expectations, and authorship conventions had a differential impact on the careers of women faculty. Women in STEM departments at a different major technological university in the United States reported that gender affected their likelihood of being promoted to full professor because the standards were applied inconsistently (Fox and Colatrella 2006). Not surprisingly, then, women and men experience the promotion process differently (Gunter and Stambach 2003) with women typically reporting less positive experience.

The Administrative/Service Detour

A third explanation for why so few women have been promoted to full professor is that women perform more service work than men, detouring them off the road to full professor (Misra, Lundquist, Holmes, and Agiomavritis 2011). Small numbers of women faculty in STEM departments has often left them bearing heavier workloads than men in areas such as advising students, mentoring other women, and providing gender diversity on committees (Rosser 2014). According to Awando, Wood, Camargo, and Layne (2014:216), women reported being pushed into more service than men, including committee work and administrative responsibilities, "sometimes by choice, but often in response to demands of departments," leaving them with less time to devote to research. Consequently, women spent more time on activities that were not strongly valued in promotion decisions while men were free to concentrate on their research, which was the most important criterion for promotion to full professor.

Data Sources

The research presented here examined the full professor promotion experiences of faculty at two highly selective private liberal arts colleges in the same metropolitan area in the northeast. Both have approximately 2,300 students and 180 tenure-line faculty. Although both have been co-educational for forty years, their histories as single-sex institutions have left legacies including different gender ratios in the student body and different curricular emphases. The former women's college still had more women students (60 percent) than the former men's college (50 percent). The former men's college had larger programs in STEM, while the former women's college had larger programs in the arts and humanities and did not even offer an engineering major. About 40 percent of students at the former men's college graduated with a STEM major while less than one-quarter of the students at the former women's college did. These differences in curricular emphases may have explained why women comprised only 38 percent of the entire tenure-line faculty at the former men's college compared to 48 percent at the former women's college.

This chapter analyzes data collected from focus groups, personnel records, and a survey. The departments faculty worked in have been categorized as STEM and non-STEM. For most of the analyses presented in this chapter, I limited STEM to the natural sciences (i.e., biology, chemistry, environmental studies, health and exercise science, geology, and physics), computer science, mathematics, and engineering. For the focus groups at both colleges (and the analysis at the former women's college of time spent at the rank of associate professor before promotion to full professor), I included the social and behavioral sciences (i.e., anthropology, economics, government, psychology, and sociology) along with the STEM disciplines because the number of STEM women faculty, especially at the full professor rank, was too small to analyze them separately.

In the fall of 2008, I conducted four focus groups with STEM and social science women associate and full professors at each college to discuss their experiences with both the tenure and promotion to full professor processes. The two associate professor groups contained the eight women who had been in that rank longest on each campus. The full professor group at the former women's college included all eight women at that rank in the STEM and social science departments. At the former men's college, it included a sample of the women full professors from STEM and social science departments. Each focus group lasted between sixty and ninety minutes. The focus group data helped frame the research questions, develop the questionnaire, and interpret the results of the survey and personnel data analyses.

We administered a web-based questionnaire to all tenured and tenure-track faculty at both colleges in the spring of 2009 (see Berheide and Anderson-Hanley 2012). The survey instrument largely consisted of questions developed for measuring the climate for women at research universities (see Callister 2006; Khare and Owens 2006; Settles et al. 2007). A response rate of 70 percent with 237 completed surveys was achieved. Women had a higher response rate, especially those in the STEM disciplines, than men, which means the response rate was slightly higher at the former women's college than at the former men's college. As a result, women constituted almost half the respondents. I rely on the two types of quantitative data (survey and personnel records) to uncover gender differences in promotion experiences.

Gender Differences at the Rank of Full Professor

In 2009, 48 percent of STEM and social science men but only 35 percent of STEM and social science women had achieved the rank of full professor at the former men's college. Similarly 44 percent of STEM and social science men and 38 percent of STEM and social science women at the former women's college held the rank of full professor. At the former women's college, six of the seventeen STEM and social science men at the associate professor rank could be characterized as stuck whereas only two of the eleven STEM and social science women had been associate professors for more than seven years. There was no gender difference in the number of years these stuck associate professors had been in rank (fifteen on the average). Thus, there was a gender difference in rank at both colleges, and it was twice as big at the former men's college as at the former women's college.

Satisfaction with Opportunity for Advancement in Rank

Given that fewer STEM women than men were full professors at both colleges, I expected women to be less satisfied than men with their opportunity for advancement in rank. The survey asked faculty, "How satisfied are you with the following dimensions of your job?" The last of the seventeen dimensions was "my opportunity for advancement in rank." The faculty were given a six-point Likert satisfaction scale (1=very dissatisfied to 6=very satisfied) for their response choices. While STEM women at the former women's college did indeed express lower levels of satisfaction than men, contrary to my expectations, there was no gender difference in satisfaction with opportunity to advance in rank at the former men's college.

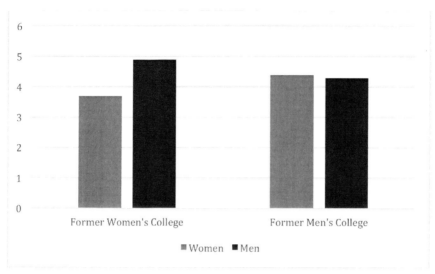

Figure 5.1. Mean Satisfaction with Opportunity for Advancement in Rank for STEM Faculty by Gender and by College.
Author's analysis.

The mean satisfaction for STEM men at the former women's college was 4.9 compared to 3.7 for STEM women, which was over a one-point difference on this six-point scale (see figure 5.1).[2] In contrast, there was no appreciable difference in mean satisfaction for STEM men and STEM women, 4.3 compared to 4.4, respectively, at the former men's college. On the average, men at the former women's college were basically satisfied whereas both men and women at the former men's college were just somewhat satisfied and women at the former women's college did not even reach somewhat satisfied. It is somewhat surprising that on the average the STEM women at the former men's college were not more dissatisfied with their opportunity for advancement than the STEM men given that there was a greater gap in the proportion of women who had reached the rank of full professor than at the former women's college.

What Explains the Gender Difference in Satisfaction with Opportunity for Advancement? The Chilly Climate Pothole

One explanation for the gender difference in satisfaction with advancement at the former women's college may be that women experienced chillier department climates than men did, ones that reduced their chances of success and affected the seemingly objective measures of performance involved in promotion decisions (Berheide and Anderson-Hanley 2012). Differences in the quality of department relationships fully explained gender differences in satisfaction with opportunity for advancement among the entire faculty, not just the STEM faculty, at the former women's college (see Berheide and Walzer 2014). Limiting the analysis to STEM faculty revealed that there was a gender difference in the quality of department relationships at the former women's college, but not at the former men's college.

The survey included five of six items Callister (2006) used to measure the quality of relationships at a research university. These items were: communication is good among the people in my department; the people in this department trust each other; there is a strong sense of "family" in my department; I feel really close to most of my co-workers; and the best thing about this job is the people I work with. Faculty rated each statement on a six-point Likert agreeability scale (1=strongly disagree to 6=strongly disagree). Individual responses to the five items were summed and then divided by five so that scores on the index ranged from a low of 1 to a high of 6. Higher scores indicated better relationships within the department.[3]

As figure 5.2 indicates, there was a notable difference in mean scores on the good department relationships index for STEM men and women, 4.5 and 3.7, respectively, at the former women's college but not at the former men's college (STEM men=4.6; STEM women=4.7). STEM men at both colleges and STEM women at the former men's college rated the quality of their department relationships about a full point higher than STEM women at the former women's college. The mean for women at the former men's college as well as both sets of men fell between agree and somewhat agree whereas the women's mean at the former women's college did not even reach somewhat agree. The quality of department relationships was strongly correlated with satisfaction with opportunity for advancement in rank at both the former women's college (r=0.46) and the former men's college (r=0.50).[4] Better department relationships were associated with STEM faculty's assessment of their opportunity for advancement in rank at both colleges, with the lower ratings of the quality of department relationships by STEM women at the former women's college being associated with their lower level of satisfaction with their opportunity for advancement in rank.

The Rocky Road

Next, I used assessments of the promotion process as a measure of instrumental climate, which is the second component of department climate (Callister

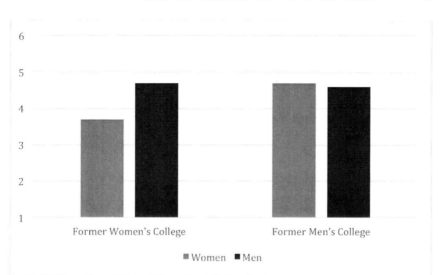

Figure 5.2.   Mean Scores on Good Department Relationships Index for STEM Faculty by Gender and by College.
Author's analysis.

2006). The full professor promotion process index drew on the same six items that research universities have used to assess faculty perceptions of the tenure and promotion processes (Khare and Owens 2006). We revised the wording of the items to create ones that referred specifically to promotion to full professor. The items as revised were: I am/was satisfied overall with the process of being promoted to full professor; I understand/understood the criteria for achieving promotion to full professor; I receive/d feedback on my progress toward promotion to full professor; I feel/felt supported in my advancement to full professor; senior colleagues are/were helpful to me in working toward promotion to full professor; and I feel there is/was a strong fit between the way I do/did research, teaching, and service and the way it is/was evaluated for promotion to full professor. Faculty rated each statement on the six-point agreeability scale. The scores on the six items were added and then divided by six, resulting in an index ranging from a low of 1 to a high of 6. Higher scores represented a positive experience with the process of being promoted to full professor.[5]

We only administered these promotion questions to faculty for whom promotion to full professor was the next step in rank (i.e., associate professors) and those who had successfully navigated this promotion process at their current college (i.e., full professors), thereby eliminating from the analysis assistant professors and anyone who was hired at the rank of full professor. Consistent with Borland and Bates's (2014) results using these same questions at a public college, there were no appreciable differences between STEM men and women at either of these private colleges in their assessment of the process of promotion to full professor.

The perceived competence index operationalizes the third cognitive component of department climate and consisted of two of the three items Callister (2006) used: I am confident about my ability to do my job; and I am self-assured about my capabilities to perform work activities. Faculty rated these two statements on the six-point agreeability scale. The two items were summed and then divided by two, resulting in an index ranging from a low of 1 to a high of 6. Higher scores indicated a higher level of self-reported competence.[6]

Unlike the pattern of gender differences for satisfaction with opportunity for advancement and good department relationships, which were found only at the former women's college, the differences in the mean scores of STEM men and women on the perceived competence index were notable at both the former women's college (5.6 and 4.8, respectively) as well as at the former men's college (5.5 and 5.0, respectively), although the gender difference was greater at the former women's college (see figure 5.3). Men in STEM

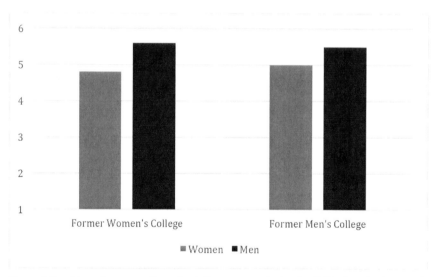

Figure 5.3. Mean Scores on Perceived Competence Index for STEM Faculty by Gender and by College.
Author's analysis.

departments at both colleges were more likely to strongly agree that they were confident about their abilities and self-assured about their capabilities to do their jobs while women were more likely to merely agree with these statements.

This dimension of department climate was only weakly correlated with satisfaction with opportunity for advancement in rank at the former women's college ($r=0.22$), and it was not correlated at all with satisfaction at the former men's college ($r=0.07$). Consistent with previous results for the entire faculty (Berheide and Walzer 2014), the component of climate that made departments chilly enough for STEM women to be associated with a reduction in their satisfaction with their opportunity for advancement in rank was the affective one, specifically the quality of department relationships.

While it may not have explained the gender difference in satisfaction with opportunity for advancement, the gender difference in scores on the competence index may exacerbate a structural problem that surfaced in the focus groups, *uncertainty over when to stand for promotion*. A former STEM department chair's remark that promotion to full professor did not have a fixed timeline sparked the following exchange in a focus group for women associate professors:

> First Social Scientist: I actually am not convinced that there's any benefit to me in pursuing to full. I figure now I have tenure, so I'm just going to do things I like—my research, my classes.
> STEM Faculty: See I'm very similar.
> First Social Scientist: You know . . . I'm not convinced that I should be pursuing this the way I was pursuing tenure itself.
> Second Social Scientist: Why? Because it's no pressure to do what you want to do? But it's pressure to try to be promoted? Is that it?
> First Social Scientist: Well, not that it's necessarily pressure, like, but what am I going to get? If I'm not going to get anything out of it, I'm not going to purposely try to accomplish it. I'm just going to do already what I'm doing.
> Current STEM Program Director: I'm the same way because titles don't motivate me in any way, shape, or form. And so there's really, I'm doing what I like to do, and so there's no motivation to go through because the process itself, I think, is probably pretty emotionally draining just as tenure was because you're being judged by a group of people.

Later in this discussion, a former social science chair, who was still an associate professor, asked, "What if all the women decided not to go for full? I started thinking about that as I was listening to the three of you say I may not do it." These women may have needed a signal that they were ready to be promoted, especially if implicit gender bias within their department led to them feeling as if they were merely competent in contrast to men who were given strong positive signals about their competence.

Thus, women STEM faculty, perhaps because of the slightly lower levels of confidence and self-assurance that they reported compared to men, may be less likely to put themselves up for promotion to full professor. A STEM department head that Awando et al. (2014:213) interviewed observed that women faculty might wait longer because "they want everything to be perfect." A STEM faculty member described this pothole differently later in the same focus group discussion of timing, "A lot of people won't run/ask to be promoted because they don't want to be turned down." Women's greater uncertainty about when they were ready to stand for promotion may be another part of the explanation for why STEM women were underrepresented at the rank of full professors at colleges as well as universities. If they encountered a department climate that actively discouraged them, as was the experience of one-third of the women but only two of the men interviewed at a public college (Borland and Bates 2014), they would be less likely to put themselves up for promotion.

In sum, there were gender differences on two of the three dimensions of department climate, affective and cognitive. A gender difference in the quality of department relationships was found only at the former women's college while a gender difference in a sense of competence was found at both colleges. There was no apparent gender difference in the assessment of the promotion process. Neither were there any gender differences among STEM faculty in feeling isolated, department climate for women, or departmental support for family obligations (see Berheide and Linden 2015).

Other factors in addition to affective and cognitive department climate may also help explain STEM women's dissatisfaction with their opportunity for advancement in rank at the former women's college. In particular, the former men's college has two roads to promotion to full professor while the former women's college only has one. The second road takes longer but it allows faculty whose teaching and service loads may have adversely affected their scholarly productivity to be promoted to full professor (for more information, see Berheide and Walzer 2014).

The Administrative/Service Detour

To explore the effect of service on time to promotion at the former women's college, which had only one road to full professor, we analyzed the records of the twenty-nine STEM and social science faculty who had been promoted to full professor at that college to examine whether it took women longer to achieve that rank than it took men. As of fall 2009, eight women and twenty-one men in STEM and social science departments had reached the rank of full professor at the former women's college. Personnel records for STEM and social science tenure-line faculty at the former women's college provided the sex, date of hire, rank at hire, date of promotion for each successive rank, and dates of service as a program director or department chair when applicable.

As reported in Berheide, Christenson, Linden, and Bray (2013), on the average, STEM and social science women had held the position of associate professor for a mean of ten years, and men nine years, before being promoted to full professor.[7] Because the women's college had changed its norms to reduce the time to promotion to full professor, we disaggregated the data by date of hire. This further analysis showed that it took women hired in 1987 or earlier an average of eleven years to be promoted from associate to full professor, while it took men ten years. Both women and men hired after 1987 earned promotion to full professor more quickly but the one-year gender difference remained. Women hired after 1987 held the rank of associate professor for an average of nine years before being promoted to full professor, while men were promoted after eight years. On the average, women spent two years longer than the seven years Britton (2012) set as the standard for a timely promotion to full professor while men only spent one year more as an associate professor. Thus, while both men and women experienced a delay in their promotion to full professor, the delay for the more recent cohort of STEM women still averaged one year longer than for men.

What was the effect of service as a department chair or program director while an associate professor on time to promotion to full professor? Specifically, did STEM and social science faculty who took on these leadership positions at the former women's college spend more time as associate professors before they were promoted to full professor than faculty who did not assume these positions? Among full professors, there was no gender difference in time to promotion for those who had not administered a program or department for more than a year before their promotion to full professor (fifteen men and four women); the average was nine years for both men and women. In contrast, there was a gender difference between the time spent in the rank of associate professor for those who chaired a department or directed a program, for longer than a year, while they were still associate professors. Women spent an average of eleven years in rank, while men only spent ten years. Thus serving as a department chair or program director, on the average, delayed promotion to full professor by one year for men and two years for women compared to faculty who had not assumed these roles mid-career. In sum, women paid a steeper price for their administrative service to the former women's college than men did.

The promotion delay associated with administrative service also fell on a higher proportion of the women than the men. Half of the STEM and social science women (four out of eight) but only twenty-nine percent of the men (six out of twenty-one) who had achieved full professor had served a full term, typically four years, as a department chair or program director while at the associate rank. This pattern of more women taking on administrative duties that delayed their promotion to full professor has been found at research universities as well. For example, all six STEM women faculty Awando et al. (2014:214) interviewed reported that they were engaged in administrative and service work that was not valued while men "concentrated their efforts in conducting research and seeking grant funding, activities that are more valued in promotion than teaching and service."

While there was one case at the former women's college of a woman associate professor chairing a STEM department because she had already turned her attention away from her research, in the other cases, women associate professors were pressured to become chairs or program directors before their promotion to full professor with their research agendas suffering as a result. A few STEM men, and even fewer STEM women, have successfully resisted becoming department chair until after their promotion to full professor. For some of those who were unable to resist, service delayed their promotion, for others, it hijacked their careers, leaving them stuck at the associate professor rank and unable to get their research back on track to become promotable.

The focus groups conducted with women associate professors in STEM and social science disciplines on each campus provided further evidence supporting this explanation for the delay in promotion to full professor. Specifically, taking on administrative leadership positions came up as a detour that diverted their attention from the activities that would lead to promotion to full professor. Administering departments and programs as well as mentoring counted as service, but promotion to full professor in a timely manner at these two colleges required faculty to reach a standard of excellence in research in addition to teaching and service.

Conclusion

This study of STEM faculty at two highly selective private liberal arts colleges revealed, first, that similar to research universities, women were less likely than men to hold the rank of full professor. Second, at the former men's college, there was no gender difference in satisfaction with the opportunity to advance in rank, while at the former women's college, similar to what Khare and Owens (2006) found at a public research university, STEM women were less satisfied than STEM men. There was also a gender difference in the quality of department relationships at the former women's college, but not the former men's college. The quality of department relationships was strongly correlated with satisfaction with opportunity for advancement in rank at both colleges suggesting that supportive department climates can keep women faculty from getting stuck in potholes they encountered on the road to full professor.

Third, this study demonstrated that serving as a department chair or program director before being promoted to full professor delayed the promotion for both men and women, but it delayed the promotion for twice as long for women. Furthermore the proportion of STEM women who assumed these administrative roles while at the rank of associate professor was almost double that of men. For some STEM women and men associate professors, the detour they took when they chaired their departments or directed an interdisciplinary programs hijacked their advancement to full professor. A few became stuck as associate professors because their administrative responsibilities hurt their ability to produce the scholarship necessary for promotion, particularly at the former women's college where there was only one road to full professor. In the meantime, their peers who had not been detoured by administrative responsibilities passed them by as they moved unimpeded along the road to full professor.

What do colleges and universities need to do to improve the process for promotion to full professor, especially for STEM women? As Van den Brink and Benschop (2012:87) argued in their analysis of the opportunity for women to achieve the rank of full professor at Dutch universities,

> To bring about change, the system itself must change. . . . Gender inequality practices need to be undone. Academics ought therefore to reflect on why these gender imbalances persist in higher positions, how they come about and who benefits from keeping them in place. More structural action should include interventions that change "the way we do things here."

What structural changes need to be made? Associate professors need clear and transparent guidelines that indicate what is necessary for promotion (Britton 2010). Retaining and promoting STEM women faculty also requires warming the chilly climate by improving the quality of department relationships. According to Fox's (2015) study of nine major research universities, more collegial department climates, and speaking with colleagues daily, were the strongest predictors of the degree of clarity STEM faculty, especially women, reported that they had regarding the criteria for promotion.

Another way to provide clarity and transparency would be to hold a workshop (Awando et al. 2014) or a faculty forum (Buch, Huet, Rorrer, and Roberson 2011) for associate professors on how to develop a successful application for promotion. Awando et al.'s (2104:207) evaluation of just such a workshop found that it was,

> important both in terms of the interaction participants have with recently promoted professors and the information provided about requirements for promotion to professor at the university level. Both men and women participants described the workshops as a resource to help them know what qualifications are required for promotion to professor.

One purpose of this meeting would be to clarify the criteria by providing a vehicle for operationalizing the general language in written personnel policies as it applies to the cases provided by individual faculty in specific disciplines.

Furthermore, colleges and universities need to ensure that their process results in women as well as men standing for promotion to full professor in a timely manner. Since the timeline for promotion to full professor is not predetermined, some faculty, particularly women faculty as the focus groups revealed, were unsure about when to stand for promotion. Approximately half the faculty, including STEM faculty, at these two colleges indicated that they were not getting feedback on their progress toward promotion to full professor and that their senior colleagues were not providing help (see Fox, Berheide, Frederick, and Johnson 2010). The focus groups also revealed that this lack of feedback and lack of mentoring decreased the likelihood that they would apply for promotion to full professor. Thus problems with the promotion process, especially lack of feedback and help from senior colleagues, created more potholes, while regular support and guidance, especially from chairs, smoothed the road.

Therefore, associate professors need to receive regular evaluations of their progress toward meeting the criteria for promotion to full professor. At some universities, associate professors received annual letters of evaluation from their department chairs (e.g., Awando et al. 2014). Those letters need to include feedback on the associate professor's progress toward promotion. The associate professors, often women, who chaired many of the departments at these two colleges were less able to provide that feedback, since they had not yet successfully gone through the promotion process themselves. In such cases, the colleges need to create an alternative mechanism for providing annual developmental feedback on an associate professor's progress, including the chair's progress, toward advancement in rank.

Colleges and universities need to stop asking associate professors to assume administrative responsibilities that take them away from the research that leads to promotion. Given the service pressures at most colleges and universities, especially in small departments, if taxing associate professors with this work is unavoidable, additional steps should be taken to minimize the deleterious effects of heavy service loads on the prospect for promotion. Awando et al. (2014:216) recommended that department chairs and administrators be aware of "the disproportionate demands of service often placed on women compared to men." Chairs and deans have a responsibility to make sure that women faculty are not detoured off the road to promotion to full professor by service and administrative responsibilities. Institutions can facilitate continued research productivity while engaging in academic leadership, by providing additional support, such as greater release time, longer fully paid leaves, more internal research funds, or paid research assistants. Alternatively, colleges and universities could, as the former men's college has done, create more than one road to promotion to full professor, one that rewards faculty for taking on administrative duties and other service responsibilities that are essential for the institution to function (Berheide and Walzer 2014).

In sum, STEM women will be more successful in environments in which they have positive relationships with their colleagues, in which their competence is affirmed, in which they do not carry a disproportionate share of the service and administrative responsibilities, and in which their service, especially administrative service, is valued positively in personnel decisions in proportion to its time demands. In addition, colleges and universities need to develop personnel procedures for providing feedback to associate professors about their progress toward meeting the standards for promotion. If they do so, more women in all disciplines would be promoted in a timely manner. Revising the process of promotion to full professor in these ways would remove the potholes and detours that STEM women encounter on the road to becoming a full professor.

Notes

1. This research is based upon work supported by the National Science Foundation under Grant Numbers 0820080 and 0820032. Any opinions, findings, and

conclusions or recommendations expressed in this material are those of the author and do not necessarily reflect the view of the National Science Foundation or Skidmore College. Direct correspondence to Catherine White Berheide, Department of Sociology, Skidmore College, Saratoga Springs, NY 12866, cberheid@skidmore.edu, 518-580-5415. An earlier version of this paper was presented at the Eastern Sociology Society meetings, March 2013. I want to acknowledge the contributions to this chapter of Lisa Christenson, Senior Personnel; Ana Lordkipanidze, Rena Linden, Jessica Kong, and Rachelle Soriano, the undergraduate research assistants for this phase of the project; and Anita Miczek and Linda Santagato, the administrative assistants. In addition, Co-Principal Investigator Cay Anderson-Hanley, and the other undergraduate research assistants Tara Kelley, Emily Cooper, Joelle Sklaar, and Kayleigh Kahn, did invaluable work on the larger research project. I would also like to thank Mary Campa, Alice Dean, Amy Frappier, Kimberley Frederick, Holley Hodgins, Muriel Poston, Monica Raveret Richter, Barbara Danowski, Kristin Fox, Suthathip Yaisawarng, and especially Brenda Johnson for their contributions to the larger National Science Foundation funded project.

2. This difference and all the other differences in means that I report in this chapter are statistically significant at the $p<0.05$ level. I do not report the tests of statistical significance because I am analyzing population data rather than a sample.

3. A Cronbach's alpha of 0.89 indicates that the internal consistency of the relationship quality index is high.

4. Both these correlations and all other correlations reported in this chapter are significant at the $p<0.05$ level.

5. The Cronbach's alpha is 0.90, indicating that the internal consistency of this index is excellent.

6. The Cronbach's alpha is 0.84, indicating good internal consistency.

7. Years in rank as an associate professor was calculated by subtracting the year promoted to associate professor from the year promoted to full professor. For those who served as a program director or department chair when they were not yet a full professor, years of service in that administrative role was calculated by subtracting the date they assumed the role from the date they completed their term of service. Those who had not become a director or a chair before being promoted to full professor were coded as having zero years of service.

PART III

WHAT THE PIPELINE MISSES: GENDER PERFORMANCE AT WORK

~

CHAPTER SIX

Crisis of Confidence

Young Women Doing Gender and Science

Laurel Smith-Doerr, Timothy Sacco,
and Angela Stoutenburgh

In our larger study of the social organization of collaboration in chemical science laboratories, a curious pattern emerged when coding the data.[1] Young women scientists were routinely experiencing a crisis of confidence. While a large body of literature in psychology investigates the gender differences in confidence from an individual perspective (e.g., Kling, Hyde, Showers, and Buswell 1999; Mahaffy 2004), we are interested in the contexts in which scientists work and display their expertise. This chapter examines gendered contexts and the different displays of confidence they produce. The methodological approach for our larger project is inductive: rather than beginning with hypotheses and testing them, we begin with qualitative data from interviews and field observations in laboratories and use those data to build theory about the organizational contexts that may be producing barriers to collaboration between men and women chemical scientists.

In this chapter, rather than expecting all scientists to experience the pressures of laboratory life in the same way, or even all women scientists to face the same barriers, we consider the ways that the simultaneous identities of being a woman and being young matter and intersect in a way that is different for young women and young men, and for older women and older men scientists. By "young" we mean scientists in graduate school, a postdoc position, or a bench science industry job supervised by others.

Our approach derives from insights developed in intersectionality theory. The theory of intersectionality has been extremely useful in understanding the different ways that women experience inequality (e.g., Collins 1990). For example, women of color face different barriers in science than white women, as Mia Ong's (2005) path-breaking study of physicists demonstrated. More policy-oriented reports, like the *Double Bind* report from the National Academies of Science (Malcolm, Hall, and Brown 1976), have long noted the dearth of women of color in science and the particular barriers they face in science careers, but from a less theory-driven perspective.

We did not find any existing literature examining the intersection of age and gender in science. The effect of age in science careers has been studied by economists, but without focusing on the simultaneous effects of gender. In what may be the most comprehensive analysis of age and science to date, economists Stephan and Levin (1992) examine how age and success are linked in scientific careers, but look only at male scientists. Some studies have indicated that in recent years young scientists have a harder time attaining research grants than older scientists (Matthews, Calhoun, Lo, and Ho 2010), though others have attributed this trend more broadly to the rising age of scientists in the United States over time (Arbesman and Wray 2012).

Science Careers, Age, and Confidence

Ong's research on the intersection of race and gender in science has been an important contribution to the study of scientific careers. Although age was not a focus of Ong's research, one woman physicist in the study (Ong 2005:605–6) hints at the importance of the age dimension in confidence:

> What I learned from my male classmates is, don't even say, "This is what I thought." Say, "This is the way it is." (Interviewer: Did you learn to speak like that?) Fortunately or unfortunately, I learned to speak some of it. Because for me, it was a survival mechanism. I see the older women in the field, and I see they've appropriated [the language] as their own. And I'm against that because I think that goes against my very nature as a female. I don't feel that. . . . The words that indicate you're not confident— I think, I am not sure, but —That's such a part of scientific thought, to have some space, but that's not part of the male ego. But it's very much a part of how I think.

Ong uses this quote as an example of how women of color view the existing culture in science and in some ways resist it; but her paper does not consider the intersection of age and gender.

Another study that inspired us to examine the gender and age intersection in science careers is that of Cech, Rubineau, Sibley, and Seron (2012). Based on survey research with undergraduate engineering majors, the authors develop the concept of professional role confidence: "individuals' confidence in their ability to successfully fulfill the roles, competencies, and identity features of a profession" (Cech et al. 2012:641). This important research finds that college men have greater professional role confidence than women and that this gap contributes to the attrition of women from engineering majors.

Their paper hints at the intersection of age and gender; the discussion speculates, "as professionals gain more experience in their field, their understanding of the professional role likely becomes more complex and nuanced" (646). The authors cannot investigate this suspicion about developmental change, however, because like many studies, their data are collected on only one science career age level—in this case, students. It is also limited by the survey method. The social interactions where expertise confidence (a form of professional role confidence) is developed cannot be seen in this type of study, which asks about individual perceptions at one point in time. In order to examine the intersection of age and gender in the performance of confidence in scientific settings, one must draw on qualitative data and field observation methods, which is what we do in the following pages.

Data and Methods

Our data come from both interviews and ethnographic observations in labs. The 106 interviews with chemical scientists were conducted in four settings, including three academic and one industry lab. These sites represent a spectrum from basic academic to industrial: one was a traditional chemistry lab; another was an academic lab run by a principal investigator (PI) returning from a career in industry; a third was a large research center with applications for industry; and the fourth was a lab group in an industrial firm. Taken as a whole, the diversity between our research sites encapsulates a broad spectrum of contemporary chemical science research. The private and public university settings and industrial firm represent many of the organizations and organizational hybrids that populate the landscape of contemporary science (Frickel and Moore 2006).

Observations were conducted at weekly lab meetings across our research sites. From the observations among the regular lab members, we have field notes on seventy-two different presentations. Of these presentations, thirty-six of the presenters were men and thirty-six were women. In this chapter all names used are pseudonyms, to protect the confidentiality of respondents.

At the academic sites, interviews were conducted with faculty principal investigators (PIs), postdoctoral researchers, graduate students, and other individuals affiliated with the lab groups including technicians and staff. At our industry site, we interviewed bench scientists, lab technicians, and managers. We requested interviews of all scientists involved in the labs we observed, either in person or via email. Interviews lasted between forty-five minutes and one hour.

Thematically, interviews focused on interviewees' experiences with research collaboration, the focal area of the broader NSF-funded project. We asked about respondents' histories of collaboration, people with whom they have collaborated, characteristics of good and bad collaborations, and about the desired outcomes of collaborative research. In addition, we asked respondents what led them to become scientists and how they ended up in the position they held at the time of the interviews. Members of our research team transcribed the interviews; transcripts were then coded using Atlas.ti, a qualitative data analysis software. We used an inductive approach to coding: rather than beginning with preconceived categories, we let the themes central to this analysis emerge through line-by-line coding. The central finding in this chapter—the crisis of confidence for young women—emerged from inductively coding the observational data; it was not a topic that we had originally planned to study in the larger project.

Presentations were central to the lab meetings we observed at our academic sites, providing an opportunity for the lab group to learn about the work of peers and offer advice about how research could be strengthened. Even for newer members to the lab who may not have had ongoing research, presentations were still central. In these cases, newer members read and reviewed a journal article or a general literature review, then presented a summary of the published work to the group. These journal articles were often related to broad research themes of the lab, although on occasion presenters disclosed choosing articles out of personal interest in the topic despite a lack of relevance to the knowledge produced by the lab group. The symmetrical nature of our recorded observations provided an opportunity for comparisons between women and men.

The common routine of presentations across our sites speaks to institutionalization within science. In our interviews, we asked our interlocutors what happened to knowledge produced via collaboration. Publishing was typically the first answer interview respondents discussed. Describing the presentation of results in some public forum—whether meetings, conferences, or colloquia—was the second most frequent answer. Presenting work orally in front of a group, lecture style, is a common practice for communicating scientific knowledge. Not only does the lab presentation situation allow for the communication of information with peers in the group, but it is also meant to serve as a professionalization tool that permits preparation for more public forums. Graduate students are expected to begin presenting at lab meetings on a regular basis very early in their careers. The weekly "check-in" meetings that we visited regularly at the industry site did not have presentations built in as routinely as the meetings observed at the three academic sites. The presentations at the industry site were more often held with multiple lab groups and at times we were not allowed to visit because of proprietary intellectual property concerns. As a result, the primary focus of our analysis for this chapter is on our three academic sites, with a small number of examples brought in from our industry site data where relevant.

Findings

In this section, we first examine narratives of expertise that emerged from our interviews. We then discuss the findings that emerged from our observational data in relation to lab presentations. We conclude this section with a discussion of the structures that govern science careers, and how (using an intersectional lens to understand gender and age) these structures shape the interactions in the lab and impinge on young women scientists in unique and detrimental ways.

Narratives of Expertise from Interview Data

The interviews revealed that talk about expertise is quite standard and normative. Collins and Evans (2002) offer a clear definition of expertise, according to traditional scientific norms: "Only those who 'know what they are talking about' should contribute to the technical part of technical debates" (113). Our interview data fit with this normative narrative. Not much variation exists by gender and age groups in talk about expertise, which seems rather clear, and even cut and dried in the interviews. One interview with a graduate student from the research center, whom we call Deanna, provides an illustration of the expertise narrative, including how those who have knowledge are those who should apply it: "[T]he field of what I do, which is surface science and analytical chemistry, can be applied to any number of things." In this instance, analytical chemistry is an approach that can be applied to "any number of things," however, it cannot be done by anyone. It requires expertise.

Expertise is something that all of our respondents discussed with ease in interviews. When asked to talk about collaboration, most respondents brought up a standard narrative about expertise driving collaboration in science. Consider the following pair of quotes from interviews with two graduate students from different universities in different states that sound very similar. Gabriel, from Dr. Paul's lab, said:

> I think that the strongest motivator is expertise. Look, the advancements in research and the scope of knowledge out there are just amazing. It's not something that you can consume and handle by yourself. You need others to complement your knowledge and your expertise.

Fiona, from Dr. Brian's lab, said:

> I think it always starts out with an idea. They have some idea; they have some end idea in mind. "This is what it could do. In the end, wouldn't that be great?" And then they find that there are whole things that they don't know or they don't know how to approach it or they don't have the resources. And then they go find somebody who can. And I think that's always the beginning of a collaboration for most scientists.

The narratives we heard supported existing scholarly writing about expertise as: capacity to accomplish tasks better and faster (Eyal 2013), devices to answer specific disciplinary questions (Fuchs 2001), and learned skills that can be assessed by standard performance criteria (Lynch 2014).

Expertise discourse is a way for scientists to construct boundaries around their expertise (e.g., Gieryn 1999), including scientists' argument that uncertainty in problems like climate change requires scientific experts (Zehr 2000). Previous literature on inequality in expertise often focuses on how scientists work to maintain this boundary, as when advocacy groups face an "expertise barrier" erected by scientists (Parthasarathy 2010). This chapter, rather than considering the boundaries of science, looks within science to see how expertise is learned and how it is contested, particularly for young women scientists.

In the expertise narratives we heard in interviews, status differences sometimes did emerge. For example, Cassandra, a graduate student in the academic chemistry lab notes: "Before I take anything to Dr. Michelle [the PI], I think about it. She's my boss, and do I want to go to my boss with a problem, or rather a problem and a solution? So I always talk to my lab mates first and we talk about it. Then I can say, 'I ran into this problem, but we have a solution.'" Cassandra's comment about working on presenting an

"expert" solution to the PI of her lab reveals how status hierarchies sometimes appear in discussions of expertise. At the same time, her discussion is
still fairly standard rhetoric of producing solutions and solving problems in a
rather linear fashion.

Although we heard a few narratives like Cassandra's about the status differences in the establishment of expertise during graduate student training,
we find that in both the literature on expertise (e.g., Eyal 2013; Lynch 2014;
Collins and Evans 2002) and in the routine narratives on expertise by our
respondents, there is little acknowledgment that not everyone's expertise is
counted in the same way. As we cover below, the gender inequalities that
arise among young experts in training do not appear in the ways expertise is
talked about, but rather in the ways expertise is performed and in the reactions to those performances.

Presenting and the Crisis of
Confidence from Observational Data

In our observations of presentations, where students were required to demonstrate their expertise, the picture was less straightforward than the interviews
suggests. We noted fifty-two instances where a lack of confidence was clearly
displayed, and forty-five of those displays were by young women. Lack of confidence was displayed in verbal apologies, crediting colleagues rather than
taking credit, explicitly declaring that one was nervous, or having an unsure
tone of voice that questioned rather than asserted; in addition, physical
signs of nervousness appeared in body language and positioning within the
presentation space. Table 6.1 shows a clear gendered and aged trend—young
women are displaying a crisis of confidence often, young men much less so.

Table 6.1. The Gendered Crisis of Confidence in Lab Presentations

	Young Women	Young Men
Instances where lack of confidence displayed	45	7
Types of instances		
Apologetic	12	2
Giving credit to colleagues, unsure of own expertise	3	0
Physical signs of nervousness	20	3
Declares nervousness	4	2
Unsure tone	6	0

Source: N=72 presentation observations, 36 women presenters, 36 men presenters.

Notes: Multiple instances of lack of confidence in some presentations. No displays of lack of confidence by
    older men or older women scientists.

There were no instances we observed of older women or men scientists displaying a lack of confidence in the lab presentations.

The younger, or less experienced, scientists are distinguished from "older" scientists who occupy faculty positions or supervisory positions in industry. We did not encounter any examples of non-traditional, physically older graduate students in their late thirties or forties, and we did not encounter any PIs who were younger than late thirties. This physical and career age perfect correlation reinforced the aged hierarchy in academia. Dr. Michelle, a PI, described it as a medieval guild structure:

> I had two undergraduate faculty supervisors and then I had a PhD advisor, and a postdoc [advisor], and you learn both good and bad all along. I think science—especially experimental science—has sort of a medieval cultural training, with a sort of apprenticeship with a journeyman and a master—and that sort of thing.

In Dr. Michelle's apt metaphor, students are apprentices, postdocs are journeymen, and faculty are masters. Postdocs are a more borderline position in this age/authority structure as they gain more expertise. We noticed that gender was often a determining factor in how much expertise a postdoc was believed to have in the lab—women postdocs were questioned more often, as some of the data presented below will show. A key feature to note in the description of lab hierarchy in "journeyman" and "master" terms is the clearly gendered language that describes these positions tied to both age and expertise. Dr. Michelle was not the only scientist to describe the academic system in these apprenticeship terms.

We turn next to a few specific examples of how the gendered crisis of confidence (summarized in table 6.1) appeared in context from the observational data. A recurring theme that emerged from our field notes was the apologetic tone employed by young women during presentations. Psychological research has found gender gaps in apologies, in that women apologize more than their male counterparts (Schumann and Ross 2010). What our ethnographic research demonstrates is the interactional context of those apologies, and how they can accumulate. Coding the presentation situations revealed that small apologies, such as for mispronouncing a word, sometimes cumulated in larger admissions of lack of expertise, as in the following excerpt from field notes taken at the lab led by a PI who returned to academia from industry. Denise, a graduate student, is presenting the findings of a recently published journal article to the lab members:

> Denise presents a journal article she has chosen. She goes to the board and begins describing the paper. Members of the group follow along as she explains

the paper's different elements. Several times while explaining, she stumbles on certain words and names, which she then apologizes for. At a later moment she says, "I was a little confused [by the paper], I don't understand how they got to this result."

Performing expertise is not as clear cut as it is in the normative narratives about expertise, particularly for young women. Young women apologized during twelve of thirty-six different presentations in our observation, while young men only apologized during two of thirty-six presentations.

In another example, Sheila, a female graduate student, begins her presentation with an apology:

> Dr. Paul invites Sheila to present her article. When she gets to the front of the room, she begins by telling the group "I apologize in advance for this paper." She goes on to say that she recognizes how "complicated this article turned out to be," and with a deep sigh continues, "if I knew, I wouldn't have chosen it." [A few minutes later] Sheila goes to the board and draws two schematics to illustrate a point. Dr. Paul asks a question about one of her explanations; she corrects her earlier version saying, "Sorry, I misspoke."

In this case, Sheila appears to anticipate that her presentation will go poorly and is concerned that she will not have the technical expertise to present the article adequately to her peers. When the PI questions her about a diagram she was drawing on the board, her response is not to talk through the point, which was the typical response for the young men we observed. Rather, she apologizes and says she "misspoke." Sheila's response indicates that she views this presentation as less of a learning experience and more of a situation that reveals her subpar level of expertise.

The most common observation of a crisis of confidence in young women scientists' presentations were of physical signs of nervousness. Commonly observed signs include fidgeting, getting caught on words, and a lack of eye contact or other forms of reluctance to engage with the group in a presentation. During a presentation in the traditional academic chemistry lab, Cassandra exhibited a few of these physical signs of nervousness:

> Cassandra, the newest student on the project, begins her presentation. She stands off to the side of the room, away from her laptop with PowerPoint slides located in the center of the room. While presenting, she fidgets back and forth between her legs. Her voice is shaky, and she stumbles on her words. Sentences are filled with "um"s and she licks her lips. She tries clearing her throat several times as she talks. Approximately 5 minutes into the presentation, she pauses momentarily to collect herself.

At our public university site, young women presenting tended to sit directly next to Dr. Brian, the PI. In contrast, the young men chose to sit wherever was convenient, giving the appearance of being more comfortable in that context. Young women's body language and positioning spoke of a crisis of confidence in twenty out of thirty-six presentations, while young men exhibited physical signs of nervousness in only three of thirty-six presentations.

Another physical sign of nervousness was losing one's breath while speaking. The following example is from the traditional academic lab where Nayla, a postdoc, is presenting:

> Dr. Michelle [the PI] interrupts Nayla's presentation. She tells Nayla, "There is a link with one of your graphs. What is it?"
> Nayla: "Are you asking me or the class?"
> Dr. Michelle: "I think you are missing a pedagogical link . . ."
> Nayla: "Oh, what I showed last week?"
> Dr. Michelle: "Yeah, you've got to remind people and show them the link. They won't do that on their own."
> Nayla returns to her presentation, but seems shaken up. Her voice sounds breathy, and she seems more nervous. It takes her a couple slides before she gets back into the groove of presenting.

Again, rather than the presentation being a chance to learn or take mild suggestions, these situations for young women seem to be highly charged and fraught with meaning about one's expertise that lead to being physically shaken. Yet also note that it is not uncommon for young women scientists to be interrupted during their presentations, and that is discussed further below.

An alternative presentation situation, to review the effect of interruptions, is the laboratory safety walkthrough. Sasha, who was the Lab Safety Monitor in Dr. Brian's lab, walked fellow students through the lab to search for violations. Placed in a position of authority with punitive powers for students that violate lab protocol, Sasha should speak with expertise on lab safety. However, periodically throughout the walk Dr. Brian would stop and direct interrogating questions to Sasha:

> When Dr. Brian first pointed out the labeling on a bottle to Sasha he asks pointedly, "What the hell is that?" He continues, "Sure, Kellen and *I* know what this is . . ." but Sasha, does she know?
> Sasha is quiet, head tilted down, and takes notes on her notepad. Later on in the walk-through Kellen asks Dr. Brian a question. Turning around suddenly, Dr. Brian asks Sasha, "Did you understand what he just said?" Again, Sasha is put on the spot in front of the entire group.

In each of these moments Sasha is the sole target of Dr. Brian's questions. And while the PI intends them to be teaching moments—confidence boosters, such as giving permission to "Use your mean voice!"—Sasha is barely able to respond verbally, let alone physically.

As in the example of Nayla, young women scientists sometimes lose their voice, literally. Or in the case of Sasha, young women scientists are not able to use their voice before the "conversation" moves on.

Context of the Crisis

As discussed above, however, our approach focuses less on individual action in isolation and more on understanding the social interaction and organizational contexts that shape the crisis of confidence for young women. In our observations, we note that hierarchical status orders may be underlined and highlighted in the presentation situation by interruptions and corrections, and deference behavior that acknowledges the expertise of higher-status scientists. This deference can quite often be gendered and shrouds a detrimental paternalism as a form of mentorship. For example, during one young woman's presentation (Alice), the primary investigator (Dr. Brian) interrupts to speak on her behalf. Dr. Brian's interruption is motivated by his *enthusiasm* for Alice's work and its implication. But rather than asking Alice to speak to her project's significance—perhaps even working with her beforehand to prepare that component of her presentation—he speaks about her project *for her*, effectively removing her from her own presentation.

Higher-status scientists repeatedly interrupt students' presentations to capitalize on teaching moments. Consider the excerpts from field notes in table 6.2, which displays two different presentations with interruptions in the traditional academic lab, one with Eva and one with Malcolm. In each, the PI is teaching the student by interjecting comments during the presentation.

In both cases, Dr. Michelle interrupted in a way that disrupted the flow of their presentations. In Eva's case, Dr. Michelle points out a mistake that ends up not being a mistake. Rather than calmly addressing this, Eva's demeanor changes, she becomes nervous, and continues to be nervous even after it comes to light that the mistake was, in fact, not her fault. Malcolm, on the other hand, is interrupted with a joke, the room erupts into laughter and he pauses without letting it affect his demeanor.

Similarly, when Dr. Brian interrupts his graduate student's presentation with a clarifying question, Clark rebuffs with, "Great! I didn't even make it through the title slide!" What follows is a long one-on-one conversation between the PI and the graduate student, where Clark stands up and goes to

Table 6.2. Two Examples of Correcting Mistakes in a Traditional Academic Chemistry Lab

Eva	Malcolm
Eva, a graduate student, begins her presentation confidently, but after a few moments Dr. Michelle, the PI, points out a mistake.	Malcolm, a first year graduate student presenting a published literature review says: "first I want to give a little info on cancer drugs."
Eva stops talking as she tries to offer a correction; it is obvious she doesn't quite know what to say. Her voice trails off, until all of a sudden she realizes that it's not really a mistake, but rather a strange notation pulled from an article.	Dr. Michelle [wry tone]: "*anti*-cancer maybe . . ."
	Everyone in the room laughs.
Dr. Michelle interjects a few more times as Eva continues through her slides. Eva becomes more and more nervous, and has lost her seemingly calm demeanor from the beginning of her presentation.	Malcolm seems very calm. He laughed off the "anti-cancer comment." There is also no shakiness audible in his voice and very few "ums." Like the other lab members, he writes out all of the molecule diagrams on the board as well as all the equations. However, he does make some effort to turn around and make eye contact with the group. His breathing is normal.

Source: Fieldnotes, on two separate occasions

the dry erase board to illustrate his answer. Like Malcolm, Clark uses humor to temper what could have been a disruptive moment and uses the interruption as an opportunity to engage in a direct and collaborative conversation with his PI.

An interesting question to ask of these data is how the students experience the interruptions. As a young woman, Eva seems to experience the interruptions as a pointing out of flaws in a less than perfect performance of expertise. On the other hand, Malcolm seems to experience the interruptions as light hearted joking from which he can learn. The response to mistakes may be shaped by different expectations of young women and young men, and the seriousness with which they are expected to stick to a normative, static definition of expertise. This normative definition of expertise was widely shared in the narratives about scientific work, but the performance expectations seem to differ in the intersection of gender and age as we can see in the interactions.

Interruptions at times were interjections about how to do presentations. Corrections are thus sometimes about style, as well as about substance. For example, in an interview in the industry setting, Michael, who is the most senior manager for the lab group, describes this kind of situation when he is instructing a younger scientist:

> We have to teach them how to be an effective presenter. Like Lucy was talking about [her presentation], "Do I have to stand up?"
> "Yes, you have to stand up. Yes." [Michael says this in an insistent voice, and laughs. He then looks aside as if addressing Lucy in a space next to him]. "Yes, I have to teach you how to be an effective presenter and standing up is the first thing. Don't keep asking. Because you're not progressing."

In our data, this kind of "helping" where the style of the presentation was corrected in front of the group happens more often between older men and younger women. An unintended consequence of these types of interruptions was the underlining of status differences, which often fall along age and gender lines.

Another kind of "help," that seemed to us somewhat less than helpful, was when older men scientists interrupt younger women scientists while they were presenting to offer up their own expertise in place of the presenter's:

> Rosa began her presentation, which was focusing on her work-in-progress. After a few slides she began to speculate about some of the results that she had been getting. After this, Sheila interjects and poses a question to Rosa. After a moment, Dr. Paul—he PI—speaks up, answering and clarifying Sheila's question.

Rather than giving Rosa the opportunity to respond to a question she received from one of her peers, the lab PI interrupts and answers the question for her. This can be interpreted as the PI having doubts about Rosa's ability to adequately answer the question asked of her. This type of interruption was very rare in the interaction between PIs and young men, while more common between PIs and young women. These instances point to structural mechanisms that perpetuate the conceptions young women have of their professional capabilities—that create conditions ripe for a crisis of confidence.

Consider another example from the same lab group where an older male scientist steps in and provides answers or clarifications for the young woman scientist presenting. In this case, the older male scientist is a very advanced graduate student (Martin), who supervises the younger graduate student Denise:

> Denise is presenting her work-in-progress. Soon Dr. Paul interjects with a clarifying question; Denise answers—but Martin adds more points to her

answer in an authoritative voice. Denise is new to the lab, and it has quickly become clear she is working under the auspices of Martin. After Martin finishes, Matilda makes a suggestion about the experiments. Again, Martin responds saying "Yes, that's interesting" despite this being Denise's presentation. Gabriel then asks a question, which Denise answers. But Martin then turns to Denise and says: "yes, but do you know why we chose [that] base?" To which she answers: "no."

This kind of "help" was not a phenomenon we observed between older men and younger men in similar situations. Denise is apprenticing under Martin, an advanced graduate student preparing to leave the lab; this type of apprenticeship is common.

In our interviews, we asked our respondents about how people new to the lab learn about professional responsibilities. Typically, students report that they "learned through doing," but also that they were more likely to turn to an older graduate student or postdoc than to their PI for mentorship. Part of socialization into a lab was to be included on a project, in which a more experienced graduate student supervised the younger student's work. Through this relationship, newer students were educated about the lab's data, and techniques used to analyze the data and draw scientific conclusions. In this case, however, rather than let Denise work through the questions herself—and to learn—Martin interrupts her following Gabriel's question and addresses her in a way that brings to the fore her lack of expertise, undermining the authoritative and expert role she would typically have during a presentation. This degree of undermining a lab group member's expertise was rare, but taken in conjunction with more subtle instances of senior (usually men) members of the lab asserting their expertise during the presentations of young women, this points to structural conditions in which young women's expertise and authority over their area of study is held under a more extreme degree of scrutiny than their young male counterparts' experience.

Another acknowledgment of status differences, revealing how they align with gender and age differences, came from explicit statements about the greater expertise of older men by younger women. Here is an example in the academic lab with the PI (Dr. Paul) who formerly worked in industry:

Dr. Paul asks Dr. Melvin (another faculty member) a question, and the two of them engage in a lengthy exchange. After some time, Matilda—the postdoc—interjects to ask a clarification question. She begins her question with a shy smile and the following qualification, "My question is less complex [compared to Dr. Paul's]," and pauses before stating her question.

Matilda is lowering expectations of the group, signaling that the exchange between Paul and Melvin is expert territory, not to be entered easily. Matilda is not new to the chemical sciences; rather, she is the lab postdoctoral researcher. She has already obtained her PhD, and holds a position of authority within the lab. Yet she still questions herself and devalues her skill in a public way when entering into conversation with the male faculty at the meeting. In general, graduate students and postdocs (more often young women) defer to faculty (more often older men) by giving credit or otherwise explicitly acknowledging their status and expertise.

Conclusion

Young women talk about expertise in the same normative way as everyone else; yet a crisis of confidence is displayed in presentation situations by young women and not by other age/gender groups in the labs. There appears to be amplification of a lack of confidence in hierarchical settings where age and gender are confounded with status—particularly through interruptions and deference to expertise. Candace West and Don Zimmerman define "doing gender" as the interactive processes that go into performing gender and "managing situated conduct" (1987:127). Our findings suggest that the institutions of science and the notion of expertise are gendered, and operate to the detriment to young women training to be scientists. Young women in the chemical sciences were less confident in performing their expertise than their young men scientist colleagues. They were more apologetic and more physically nervous when addressing their research group.

There are a number of psychological arguments that could be made to explain these findings, such as men's egos lead them to apologize less (Engel 2001). Here we point instead to the social structures and social institutions that govern daily life and shape social interaction. In this study, not only did young women devalue their expertise and undermine their expert authority over their area of specialty with their apologies for example, but older, predominantly male researchers in positions of power also undermined the expertise of young women—sometimes under the premise of instructing or mentoring them. The interplay between these two statuses seems to create a feedback loop that reinforces structures that value the expertise of men and devalue the expertise of women.

While our focus in this chapter is the lab presentation situation, and young women seem to experience a crisis of confidence that is not shared by experienced women scientists in that context, there may be other locations in science where older women faculty experience barriers and challenges to their expertise. For example, other research finds that the classroom presents a significant student gender bias toward women faculty; and in chemistry specifically, women faculty are judged and evaluated more harshly by their students than men faculty (Hirshfield 2014).

A strength and contribution of our study is to examine gender performances during the presentation situation in labs, which is common and routine practice across all four of our sites ranging from traditional academic to industry labs. The early years of graduate school are a career period when many young women consider leaving academia (Ferreira 2003; Cech et al. 2012), and they coincide with the crisis of confidence in presentation situations, which seem to produce difficult interaction contexts. In this study, the PIs may think they are helping by harshly critiquing, speaking over, or answering for young women students in the lab but these interactions on a daily basis add up to differential treatment that may have unintended consequences of decreasing women's retention in academic science. The postdocs Matilda and Nayla, whom we describe above, had a similar experience to graduate student women. The postdocs' experience indicates that it is not simply a matter of progressing through graduate school to alleviate the crisis of confidence.

If a gendered crisis of confidence is happening in these common laboratory situations, what can be done? We do not have specific policy prescriptions, but would raise some questions for consideration. Could there be more formal training for presentations, not just for the presenters but also for the mentors and the audience? Would experiments with different forms of presenting that shake up the traditional hierarchy shed light on possible ways of de-emphasizing the ever-present status differences and the individual spotlight? For example, the individual presentation might be designed as more of a team panel presentation; or the PI could present on an article from an area that is new to the PI and work through the vulnerability in acquiring expertise with the students. Whether or not policy interventions or new ways of doing lab presentations can be developed, more research is needed on the largely unexamined yet routine social organization of lab presentations. Lab presentations should be a place where young and new scientists learn to be experts, but it is important to understand how following the "way it has always been done" tends to reinforce traditional gender inequality by playing into career age based expertise.

Note

1. Earlier versions of this paper were presented to annual conferences of the American Association for the Advancement of Science (February 2015, San Jose,

CA), and the Eastern Sociological Society (February 2013, New York, NY). Smith-Doerr acknowledges support from NSF grant 1064121/1413898, however, all opinions and findings are those of the authors and do not necessarily represent those of the National Science Foundation. We thank Anna Branch for extensive editing comments, and our colleagues on the larger project that investigates collaboration in the chemical sciences who collected some of the data: Jen Croissant, Claire Duggan, and Itai Vardi. Please send correspondence to: Laurel Smith-Doerr (Lsmithdoerr@soc.umass.edu); Institute for Social Science Research, Bartlett Hall, Hicks Way, University of Massachusetts, Amherst, MA 01003.

CHAPTER SEVEN

~

Who's the Expert?

Gendered Conceptions and Expressions of Expertise by Chemists-in-Training

Laura E.Hirshfield

Women face numerous challenges in academic science. While there have been measurable improvements, women still fall short in several key areas of scientific career success compared to men. Their salaries are lower (Toutk-oushian and Conley 2005); they are promoted at a slower pace (Valian 1998); and they drop out of science, technology, engineering, and math (STEM) majors, graduate programs, and careers at higher rates (Xie and Shauman 2003). Discussions of women's difficulties along the STEM pipeline often focus on the points at which they "leak out." Rather than focus on "leakage," this study explores the challenges that women scientists who persist experience. Specifically, I investigate the professionalization of academics during graduate school and in postdoctoral fellowships, to examine how gender impacts conceptions and expressions of expertise.

Women graduate students and faculty members in traditionally male disciplines (including most STEM fields) are at a greater risk of experiencing gender discrimination and harassment (Ecklund, Lincoln, and Tansey 2012); are burdened with extra formal and informal service responsibilities (such as sitting on diversity committees or mentoring women students, sometimes called "identity taxation") (Hirshfield and Joseph 2012); and receive less mentoring than their men colleagues (Johnsrud 2002; Moss-Racusin, Dovidio, Brescoll, Graham, and Handelsman 2012). Gendered stereotypes also lead to lower expectations of women's ability and harsher evaluation of women's research accomplishments, particularly in the sciences, where knowledge production is paramount (Steinpreis, Anders, and Ritzke 1999; Wenneras and Wold 1997). However, since expertise and knowledge are differently valued and expressed depending on particular social and gendered contexts, it is important to examine more fully how expertise and status are linked, as well as how these links might impact women's success in academia and science (Evans 2008; Keller 1985; Harding 1991).

In this chapter, I explore expectations about and expressions of expertise in men and women chemists-in-training to investigate an important avenue through which women scientists may face barriers to success. I focus in particular on how expertise is established, portrayed, and interpreted in daily interactions, and whether gender plays a role in these processes. Given the importance of knowledge and expertise within the field of science, divergent methods of expressing and demonstrating knowledge may diminish women scientists' ability to compete with their men peers. I argue that men chemists are more likely to be seen as experts, both by other men and by their women peers, because they are more likely to be viewed as highly knowledgeable, more likely to gain specialized knowledge, and more likely to volunteer their knowledge or to accept others' definitions of their expertise in group settings. Some women are also more likely to be seen as experts regarding knowledge that is related to successfully navigating the academic program, the research group, or the laboratory itself, rather than science more broadly.

Science, Expertise, and Gender

Academic disciplines train students to specialize not only in their relevant knowledge bases, but also in the different norms, work patterns, and interpersonal interactions that take place within these disciplines (Anderson, Louis, and Earle 1994; Becher 1987; Evans 2008). Further, graduate school socializes students to become members of the graduate student community, of the academic community as a whole, and of their discipline or field (Austin and McDaniels 2006). Although graduate school is intended to prepare students for the academic job market and for life as a faculty member, most graduate students find their preparation to be lacking.

Within groups, knowledge and expertise are often linked with status. Indeed, a professional's power and authority are rooted in both her specialized knowledge and her control over interpersonal situations (Larson 1979). Thus, interactions with other group members and members' judgments of an individual's knowledge and expertise can become key factors in determining who will have status and power within a group. However, experts do not always need a record of excellent performance to convince others of their abilities or knowledge, but can use impression management to project self-confidence to imply to others that they are highly skilled (Goffman 1959; Shanteau 1988). There are several key ways that individuals' expertise are judged: 1) credentials, which might include certification, course work, or graduate degrees; 2) an individual's track record, or demonstrations of previous success in a given field; or 3) long-term participation or experience in the field (Collins and Evans 2007).

Expertise is also directly linked with knowledge, of which there are several relevant forms. Explicit knowledge is easily classified, recorded, and communicated through formal (often written) language (Polanyi 1966; Nonaka, Toyama, and Nagata 2000). Tacit knowledge, on the other hand, involves unspoken rules that are not easily transmitted, tend to be abstract and obscure, and can be communicated much more easily through active interaction with others (Collins 1974). An important example of tacit knowledge, in the context of this analysis, is knowledge about how to use scientific equipment. Finally, another key type of knowledge in the natural sciences is local knowledge, or information that is specific to the limited context within which individuals work (Knorr-Cetina 1981; Cambrosio and Keating 1988). For scientists, this is the laboratory or university. This kind of knowledge might include information about where to find certain kinds of glassware, how a particular piece of troublesome machinery works, or how best to approach specific peers and advisors for help.

Unsurprisingly, gender is related to men and women's access to knowledge and ability to be perceived as experts. Gendered expectations about what kinds of educational, career, and behavioral choices are appropriate influence how men and women are understood and evaluated by their students, peers, and superiors (Valian 1998). In the natural sciences, long-held cultural associations between masculinity, male bodies, rationality, and science, grant men access to expert status much more quickly and easily than their women peers (Keller 1985). When assumptions of men's "natural" superior technological skill are questioned, the social construction of these assumptions becomes more obvious (Abiss 2007). On the other hand, gendered patterns of interaction affect how men and women communicate their expertise to others (Crosby & Nyquist 1977; Hirshfield forthcoming). Indeed, there is good evidence that women are more likely to use speech patterns that moderate the strength of their statements or make their comments sound tentative. These behaviors include hedging (such as beginning a comment with "I'm not sure, but") or disclaiming their expertise entirely (Leaper and Robnett 2011).

While previous research has explored definitions of expertise and gendered experiences in sciences, few studies have brought these areas of research together. Thus, in this chapter I ask: "How do men and women in chemistry training programs (i.e., graduate students and postdoctoral fellows) conceptualize and express their expertise and knowledge? How do principal investigators and fellow graduate students and postdocs identify experts? And, in what ways are these conceptualizations, expressions, and identifications different for men and women chemists-in-training?" Given previous research demonstrating that women feel that they are less likely to be seen as experts and that they receive less respect from faculty than their men peers (Fox 2001; Johnsrud 1995), qualitative research exploring knowledge and expertise in these settings is important for understanding these processes more completely. Further, insight into the development of gender differences in expressions of expertise has significant implications for women's success in academic science.

Method

This study draws on data collected during nine months of ethnographic observation in the research laboratories of five groups in the chemistry department of a large research university, from 2009 to 2010, as well as forty in-depth semi-structured interviews, and select content analysis of lab manuals and websites.[1] I concentrated my analysis on chemistry because, at the time of my study, the majority of practitioners in industry, academia, and doctoral programs were men (Hill, Corbett, and St. Rose 2010). On the other hand, women were making significant headway in the field. Specifically, 33.1 percent of the workforce and 34.3 percent of graduate students were women at the time of this study, and these proportions have been increasing steadily.

The proportion of women faculty in chemistry at this university was fairly low (approximately 25 percent), but within the past eight years, the proportion of women has doubled. Women graduate students represented nearly half of the total graduate student population (49.2 percent), which was above the national average. By contrast, the department was not very racially diverse: roughly 84 percent of graduate students were white, 5 percent were Asian, 4 percent were Latino/Hispanic, 4 percent were black or African-American, 1 percent were American Indian/Native American, and 1 percent were unknown/unreported (NSF 2009). In choosing groups to observe, I identified those that had more than six students, as well as a principal investigator (PI) who was early in their career. Of the thirteen professors I contacted, five agreed to be involved in my study.[2] Of these groups, two were led by men (Professors Mitchell and Moore) and three by women (Professors West, Williams, and Worth).[3] The smallest group I observed had nine members in it (not including the PI), and the largest had twenty-one.

The first phase of my data collection involved ethnographic observations that occurred over the course of nine months, comprising over 120 hours. Using an inductive approach, I noted interactions between the group members, how speakers and group members presented themselves in meetings and in the lab, and variations in teaching or mentoring modeled in each group. In total, I observed fifty-six graduate students and nine postdocs, as well as their five principal investigators. The groups I observed varied in their percentage of women members (23 percent to 60 percent), in terms of race and ethnicity, and in proportion of various scientists-in-training (undergraduate, graduate, and postdoc).

I was able to interview over half of the population I observed: in total, 40 semi-structured interviews of graduate students and postdocs, 19 of whom were men and 21 were women. My primary focus was on graduate student training and experiences, so the majority (n = 37) of my interviews were with graduate (PhD) students, though I interviewed three postdocs about their experiences as well. While race and other social factors such as age, class, and sexual identity likely also impact the negotiation of knowledge and expertise, I was unable to limit the possible pool of respondents based on these factors due to issues of access. I recorded relevant demographic information using a short demographic survey and these factors were considered during analysis. Ten of my interviewees were international students, which is comparable to representation of international students in the chemistry department; whereas all but one of the domestic students I interviewed were white.

Interviews lasted roughly one to 1.5 hours, most were conducted in private office spaces. A sampling of topics discussed include: lab dynamics and relationships within their research group; experiences with teaching and authority in the classroom; and their overall images of scientists. The quotes from field notes and interviews I include in the following sections are examples of representative patterns in my data; they have been lightly edited for clarity.

My analytic strategy involved open and focused coding (Emerson, Fretz, and Shaw 1995). This analysis focuses mainly on themes that emerged from these data; specifically, the use of authority and expertise in graduate experiences, group norms, and student mentorship. Given my interest in social inequality and identity, I paid particular attention to any patterns that emerged regarding gender, race, or nationality. Lastly, within the themes and trends I explored, I was careful to look for disconfirming evidence and occasions when the patterns I expected did not emerge.

Results

In examining expertise in a scientific lab, I paid particular attention to who graduate students and postdocs turned to for help or advice in solving problems in their work. In the absence of direct ascriptions of expertise, I assumed that those individuals to whom students turned for advice were viewed as experts by those seeking help because individuals are likely to seek advice only from those they deem likely to have sufficient knowledge (Haythornthwaite 2006). Past research demonstrates the importance of clear communication about "who knows what," as well as how individuals' standing as an expert can become crystallized within a group, both of which are addressed in this study (Wegner 1986; Haythornthwaite 2006). Indeed, the graduate students and postdocs I observed described a variety of factors that they used to determine whom they should go to for advice about their chemistry.

The simplest factor chemists-in-training used to determine who they should ask for support was basic proximity: participants often looked to those around them for input. However, although factors such as proximity often influenced who participants *talked to* about their work, ascriptions of expertise were the primary factors through which chemists-in-training determined who to go to for *advice*. Students and postdocs assessed the following: overall skill, talent, or intelligence; specialized knowledge regarding instruments or chemistry subtopics; and expertise about individual research groups, departments, or career paths (i.e., local knowledge). These assumptions of knowledge and expertise were also greatly affected by gendered patterns of presentation and interaction in group settings.

Overall Skill, Talent, or Intelligence

Unsurprisingly, many of my participants told me that when they needed help they sought out the most senior students or postdocs in their labs. For example, Sarah explained that in terms of science-related questions, "I do think there's definitely a seniority thing there where, Anthony is a senior member. . . . Steven, Chad, I'm forgetting one of them, Kyle, are kinda the senior members right now, and so you tend to gravitate to those people, I think" (Williams lab, white woman). Indeed, there was a clear link in participants' minds between the seniority of graduate students and their overall skill in the lab: the most advanced graduate students in each lab were expected to be the most knowledgeable and to be the "best" chemists in the groups.

Students also articulated that other factors, such as being a "really excellent scientist," shaped their choices for experts and helpers. Kira explained this concept well when discussing Sean's skill and proficiency, describing him as one of the students who others tended to listen to and go to for advice. When I asked her to tell me more about why students went to him for help, Kira said, "He's so good . . . he's phenomenal. I'm just like gosh, how does he know all this stuff? He [asks] such good questions" (Kira, Mitchell lab, white woman). Kira implied in this comment that she was extremely impressed by Sean's knowledge and ability. Andrea's comments about two of the students in her lab were very similar in sentiment:

> There's [one] student who is actually a third- or fourth-year, and I'm a fifth-year. . . . And he's brilliant. He gives me advice all the time. . . . [And another student] is very, very knowledgeable. He's also brilliant. It kinda makes me see these people who are just so damn smart, and I'm like man, I feel like I'm a moron, you know. (Andrea, West lab, white woman)

Both Kira and Andrea idolized the intellect of the men, using words such as "brilliant" and "phenomenal," while diminishing their capabilities by extension saying, "gosh, how does he know all this stuff" or "I feel like I'm a moron." Both of these sentiments suggested that they were intimidated by their (men) peers at times, a sentiment that was not echoed by the men in these groups.

Kira's earlier comment that Sean asks "such good questions" also highlighted one of the ways that students and postdocs use group meetings: to elicit information about how "smart they are" or "how good at chemistry they are." Quan explained this phenomenon, judging students or postdocs' intelligence or skill during group meetings more fully:

> We have new postdocs coming in all the time. After a week people start to realize whether or not he's good, what field he's really good at, and also people will look at the old papers he published, the old work he had been working on . . . people will realize whether or not [you're] good or which area you are good at really quick. We have group meetings, so people ask questions, people get feedback, and you can always have a good idea about how good a person [is]. (Quan, Williams lab, Asian man)

Since postdocs enter research groups with higher external credentials than the graduate students in the group, but often have less direct knowledge about the specific instruments or reactions that each group works with on a regular basis, they face a unique set of challenges to their expertise. Thus, group meetings, especially postdocs' first presentation to their new research group, are an important opportunity for them to demonstrate their expertise and for the rest of the members of the group to determine whether they are worthy of being considered experts.

Notably, in the course of my observations in group meetings, in the lab, and in my interviews, I frequently overheard comments or was told directly about approximately eight "stellar" scientists. Of those who were either described to me or who I overheard being called "so good," all were men, with the exception of one third-year woman graduate student in the Williams lab. Indeed, within most of the groups, at least one graduate student was clearly seen as superior to the others by other group members, as well as by his or her PI, and in most cases, that student was a man. In the case of the Williams lab, the woman graduate student shared her role as "superior" or "star" of the lab with at least one other man student.

Specialized Knowledge and Expertise

When graduate students and postdocs required help with their chemistry they generally employed one of several methods. The simplest method for a group member to determine who they should ask for help was to simply ask around the lab to find someone who had previously worked with the particular compounds, reactions, or syntheses for which they needed help. Usually this occurred in small one-on-one conversations, but sometimes it also involved more public conversations such as the one Joseph described:

> . . . something will come up, and I'll just mention out loud, like Ahmed, Jun, whoever else is around, do you guys know anything about whatever. Somebody'll say "oh, I know that Maria from the Moore group did that, you should go ask her." (Joseph, Mitchell lab, white man)

In the process of asking around the lab, students may gather information about who had done a specific reaction, as well as discuss who is particularly adept, expert, or knowledgeable at working with specific compounds, running columns, or using instruments. Importantly, lab members' knowledge about others' expertise and skill is contingent upon students' and postdocs' willingness to advertise or flaunt their knowledge to others, which may be gendered (see Hirshfield forthcoming).

Group meetings are designed to provide students and postdocs an opportunity to practice presenting their research, as well as to receive feedback from their principal investigator and peers. They also provide a chance for group members to learn what their peers are working on. Recalling who gave presentations on related topics in group meetings is another method group members used to determine expertise. As Michelle explained, "Yeah . . . from group meetings we get a good feel of what other people's projects are, so if you can sort of keep track of that in your head . . . you can just get a feeling of who [a topic is] most relevant to" (Williams Lab, white woman). The most common model for research meetings was one in which the members of the group presented their research on a rotating basis.[4] Given the size of the groups (and periodic interspersed practice talks and literature meetings), each student or postdoc usually presented their work at most once a semester. In this model, it was difficult at times for students and postdocs, especially those who were new to the group, to learn what all of the group members were working on. In fact, the only way that people could share their knowledge or establish their expertise was through their questions and comments. Thus, one key way to establish expertise was to ask questions that began, "when I ran a similar reaction using this other method, I found . . . ;" this style was more frequently used by male students and postdocs.

Additionally, several of the graduate students in these labs were asked to become experts about specialized topics or, more commonly, machines or instruments needed in the lab. While it was common for both men and women students and postdocs to be assigned roles and responsibilities in the labs, which often included responsibility for machines used in group chemistry, when members of the group or the principal investigator decided that a new machine or instrument should be purchased, men students more often took the lead in becoming knowledgeable about safety and best practices for them. There are two possible reasons that these students were more likely to be men. First, there is evidence that boys are more likely than girls to be exposed to computers and technology during childhood and adolescence (Abbiss 2008). Second, there is a strong cultural association between men and technology (Wacjman 1991; Clegg, Trayhurn, and Johnson 2000). This link is related to stereotypes about gendered differences in technological skill and ability. Accordingly, men graduate students seemed more likely to be aware of new technologies (and to recommend to their PIs that they purchase them). Men were also more likely to be viewed as experts about current instruments in their research groups. When graduate students were asked to learn more about a particular machine, their role as expert in the lab was usually made clear to the entire group during group meetings. In most of these cases, the student taking on the role of expert had expressed a particular interest in a process or instrument, received training on that process or machine (either at the university or at a seminar elsewhere), and returned to the group to answer questions and teach them more about it.

The third way that graduate students and postdocs learned about others' knowledge was that the PI directed them to a group member whose expertise was most related to the topic of concern. This happened most frequently in the Williams lab, especially during group meetings. This also particularly solidified the sense that specific people in the lab were (and should be) considered the experts in specific topics or fields. While Professor Williams sometimes privately told her students to seek help from their peers in her individual meetings with them, she also asked particular students to give their help in group meetings. In the process, she announced their expert status to the entire group. In some cases, she simply advised students who had previously done similar work to help their more junior colleagues so as not to "reinvent the wheel." For example, during one group meeting (Williams Group Meeting 7.31.09), Professor Williams turned to Ethan (the most senior member of the group) to ask him why he thought something was happening in the presenter's results, making it clear that the presenter's work was related to Ethan's, and Professor Williams felt Ethan could provide insight into the strange results. Similarly, in a group meeting several months later, the entire group had a long discussion about how to use a particular method for synthesis that Joanna, the presenter, was struggling with:

> Professor Williams asked Steven how he did something so that he could pass along this information to Joanna. He hadn't done it. She then asked Quan how he did it. He hadn't done it either. Then Steven said that Adriana had done it and so Professor Williams turned to her and Adriana explained how she did it to Joanna. (Field notes, Williams Group Meeting 10.8.09)

Professor Williams's goal here was to elicit information for Joanna to help her successfully complete a synthesis. Yet, in calling upon particular students, she marked them as people she expected to have had experience with the process they were discussing (though they had not), and also as people whose knowledge and advice was worth listening to. Notably, throughout the conversation, Adriana, who was the only person in the group who actually *did* have experience with the method the group was discussing, did not speak up and describe her experience until she was specifically called upon by Professor Williams.[5]

In other cases, groups of lab members, rather than individuals, were asked to help out presenters when they were struggling or when a question arose during a presentation. In these instances, members were identified as experts in a particular area and were asked to speak up. For example, during one meeting in the Williams Group I noted the following exchange:

Professor Williams: Do any of the organic folks know?
    Adam starts to talk, but Professor Williams interrupts and asks, "Where's Sachi? Didn't you do your seminar on . . . ?"
    Sachi waffles a bit in her answer.
    Adam looks like he wants to talk and Kyle says, "Adam looks like he wants to pop out of his seat." (Williams Group Meeting 9.10.09)

In this case, Professor Williams first identified a group of experts ("the organic folks") who might be able to answer the presenter's question. She then focused her attention on Sachi, who seemed unwilling to speak to the issue. In contrast, Adam, a postdoc who was new to the group, was anxious to share his knowledge; however, given that Professor Williams knew a lot less about his knowledge base, she was much less likely to call upon him for advice in meetings.

Similar to Adriana's reluctance to speak up until called upon, Sachi was uncomfortable acting as the expert regarding a topic that was in her area of expertise. This type of reticence was not uncommon among the female members of the group. I noted multiple instances in which women in the group did not speak up about a topic, despite the fact that it was clear (usually through subsequent discussion or sometimes through quiet discussions that I overheard) that they were a qualified expert. Often, the women I observed seemed both less invested in expressing their expertise, as well as less confident in the level of knowledge they needed to have to speak up. In other words, similar to other educational contexts, men seemed much more confident speaking up with incomplete or incorrect answers, while women did not (Lundeberg, Fox, and Puncochar 1994). However, because women often waited to display their expertise until they were called upon, the gender balance of expressions of expertise was greatly affected.

It is clear from these results that one of the key ways that individuals are deemed experts is through interactions with others: people are told that a lab mate is particularly knowledgeable about a specific chemical or reaction; they learn who knows the most about instruments during group presentations and announcements; and principal investigators are often involved with identifying individuals' expertise during one-on-one exchanges and in larger group meetings. These interactive methods of expertise labeling are gendered in several ways, however. First, given the cultural association between technology and masculinity, it is not surprising that men were more likely than women to become the experts on new technologies within these lab spaces. However, given that knowledge about types of new instruments and machinery generally affords graduate students expertise beyond their principal investigators', the greater likelihood for men to gain these skills is an important gender difference in graduate students' training. Second, men graduate students and postdocs are more likely than their women peers to volunteer their chemistry knowledge in group contexts. More importantly, when others identify them as experts, they are more likely to accept others' definitions of their expertise.

Local Knowledge

When graduate students and postdocs were asked whom they commonly went to for help, many respondents discussed the importance of advice about the way that the lab worked, how to handle the PI, and getting a job in nearby chemical industries, all examples of local knowledge rather than specialized information about how to do chemistry techniques. These questions involve professional advice, support, and a level of mentoring beyond the kind of basic technical assistance that peers more commonly provide for one another. I found that women students were much more likely to be the ones whose expertise in these areas was requested by their peers. For example, Jennifer explained,

> People come to me for advice usually like when they're getting ready to graduate. So like I went through Sun Hee's CV [Curriculum Vita], and I gave her contacts at different companies and like, yeah, and like head hunters that I've worked with and said oh, you should contact this person, and this is how you get your stuff out there, and this is what you do if you wanna go into industry. I don't know a whole lot about academia. But I think that's typically my role.
> *Why did they think that was your role?*
> I think because I've done it. And for the position that I was in, it was pretty successful. And I think I still have a lot of contacts in that specific area. (Jennifer, West lab, white woman)

Jennifer had professional experience prior to her time in graduate school, but so had her colleague, Todd. While they were both often asked to comment about their time in industry during group meetings, in contrast to Jennifer, Todd was not approached for this type of help outside of group settings.

Women were also more likely to be asked to give advice about lab dynamics and interactions across multiple settings within the groups. These women students and postdocs were expected to give career and school advice, support others with their work, and provide insight into group dynamics. Lindsay explained that when she needed help with her science, she tended to go to one of the more advanced men in the group, Ahmed, but when she wanted to better understand group conversations, interactions, and jokes, she spoke with Carrie, a woman who sat near her. She described this dynamic:

> So I guess it's different aspects with different people. So in terms of like general where stuff is, explaining to me lab dynamics and conflicts, and more social things, the girl that sits next to me, her name is Carrie, she's been really great. . . .
>
> *What kinds of stuff did you need insight about that Carrie . . . ?*
>
> Oh, just like, "is that a joke?" [laughs]
>
> *So people would be teasing each other or something, and you'd say, "what's going on?"*
>
> Yeah. They're very, they had this thing, like especially Kira and Sean, where they'd try to say things as deadpan as possible. I'm not so good at . . . I'm like "are they kidding or not?" [laughs] (Lindsay, postdoc, Mitchell lab, white woman)

As a new member of the Mitchell group, Lindsay explained that it was difficult at times to adapt to the way that things worked differently than they had in her previous research group. She found that Carrie's help in interpreting the nuances of her colleagues' interactions helped her to feel more comfortable and less out of place overall. It was clear in our conversation that she valued this support nearly as much, if not more, than she did the scholarly help she received from the advanced men students in the group.

Several of the women students described relationships with other women that sounded as if they helped give each other guidance on how to successfully navigate the academic program as well. This mentorship between students occurred at times in mixed-gendered settings, but seemed to be most common, and most thorough, with woman-woman pairs. For example, when I asked who tended to come to her to ask questions, Zhi told me that a second year grad student who worked with her when she did her rotation goes to her "when she has questions, because she's doing all the things that I have done before, like candidacy, making posters for the conferences, and how to label things" (West lab, Asian woman). In this case, the supervisory role of mentor to a rotation student extended beyond simply teaching the younger student basic information about chemistry techniques, such as using instruments, to academic guidance. A similar form of mentorship was obvious in the Moore lab. When I asked Erica who she went to for help, she replied,

> Monica. I ask Monica for a lotta help and guidance. Yeah, 'cause she's the only one that has done it in our lab and the only one I can honestly look up to. I mean I can't look up to the guys in my other lab. [laughs] But like going through [the qualifying exam], Monica was willing to proofread my work and gave me suggestions. . . . [And] it was dead on. It was crazy. And so I'm kinda scared going through the thesis process next year 'cause she'll be gone. (Erica, Moore lab, white woman)

Erica's worry about who she will go to for help in the future was especially interesting given her experience as a support system for several men students in her other lab (she was a joint student and thus a member of two labs). Interestingly, while Erica did provide this support for the men in one lab, she chose to turn to a woman member in her other research group for the support and mentorship she needed. When that student graduated, she found herself with no one to help her out. Within these labs, it was clear that women were more likely than men to be approached by others for help dealing with issues pertaining to local knowledge, the information that applies specifically to interactions within their group, progression through their specific chemistry program, or information about functioning within their own specific laboratory context. While this type of expertise is immensely important to both graduate students and postdocs while they are in their particular training contexts, it will also be less valued in their future careers than the expertise associated with explicit and tacit knowledge that men students and postdocs were much more likely to both express and be associated with.

Conclusion

Chemists-in-training use several different factors to identify sources of peer support and expertise to guide them during their time in graduate school, including interactions with other group members and with their principal investigators. Unfortunately, women graduate students are far less likely to be viewed as, or to view themselves as, experts within these research groups. While men and women seem equally likely to turn to the peers that are near them for help, several explained that they sought out people with whom they had a closer bond because they felt more comfortable showing their lack of knowledge to them. There is also evidence from several studies that women may be more likely to use the latter strategy because they fear reinforcing negative stereotypes about women in science (Major and O'Brien 2005; Hirshfield 2010). Unsurprisingly, men and women often approach the most senior students in the lab for advice, because there is a strong belief among the members of these groups in the correlation between time in the program and skill and/or overall expertise. However, there are also several students in these groups who are known to be especially strong students. All but one of these students were men. Additionally, several women students expressed feelings of intimidation when comparing themselves with these "star" students. This is of particular note given academia's high-stakes system in which only the most successful secure faculty positions.

Men and women students' expressions of expertise also diverge in several ways. First, perhaps because of cultural associations between men and technology, men were more likely to become clear, obvious experts of new instruments in the group, and in the process, gain an expertise beyond that of even the principal investigator. Next, when PIs identify specific members within the group as experts, men tend to be more willing to speak up and embrace their knowledge and expertise. This is not surprising given previous studies that reported women feel less comfortable than men speaking up in group meetings in general (Fox 2001). However, as a consequence, women are not seen by others, including their principal investigators, as competent and confident. Finally, women are more likely to be expected to act as the experts in a variety of forms of local knowledge, including advising about lab interactions, proofreading work, and help with graduate school requirements.

These findings show that, in day-to-day interactions, men are more likely to be seen as experts in chemistry, both by their men and women peers. When they are asked to be experts by their peers and by their principal investigator, they are able to practice one of the most important skills of faculty members in their discipline: thinking through a question in their field, applying it to the topic at hand, and answering it with confidence. Women, on the other hand, are less frequently seen as experts by themselves or others. Consequently, they benefit from far less training and practice in the actual work of being a professor of chemistry. Additionally, because women are more likely to be seen as experts in local knowledge, they are also expected to shoulder more of the burden of this type of work within their research group. Just as this type of mentorship is not recognized or rewarded among faculty members (Joseph and Hirshfield 2011; Porter 2007; Olsen, Maple, and Stage 1995), it is also not rewarded among graduate students. Thus, women graduate students are more likely to use their time being asked to help their peers in ways that do not benefit their careers, while their men peers are being asked to help in ways that do.

The local versus tacit or explicit knowledge distinction that I describe is similar to the tension for university scientists between local and cosmopolitan orientations described by Hackett (1991). Specifically, Hackett explains that university scientists face seven "value tensions," one of which involves allegiance within the local sphere to their students, departmental colleagues, and to their universities, while at the same time experiencing more cosmopolitan commitments to disciplinary or other scientific collaborators (Hackett 1991). Hackett argues that financial ties are some of the most important contributions to the local orientation for some scientists, particularly marginal ones, whose position within the university may be less secure; as a result, marginal scientists may be forced to remain loyal to their local institution, rather than create more prestigious cosmopolitan relationships with collaborators in the broader scientific community. Likewise, my results suggest that scientists-in-training face a similar tension between local and "cosmopolitan" (explicit and tacit scientific) knowledge. If women's training is mainly focused on the former, they may miss out on the benefits of a more cosmopolitan orientation.

An additional consequence of my findings involves the relationship between graduate students, postdocs, and their PIs. As faculty advisors, PIs are given the task of offering mentorship, guidance, and references to their students and postdocs as they complete their doctoral programs or fellowships. The differences I have described in the way that men and women act and thus are likely to be perceived is likely to greatly impact the types of jobs that faculty believe are appropriate. Academic science depends greatly on the knowledge and expertise of its faculty. Therefore, if women do not gain the same amount of practice and training in engaging with and expressing their scientific expertise as their men peers, they may be at a disadvantage in their later careers. Further, time pressures associated with the expectations of being experts in local knowledge may be detrimental to their success. These elements have likely affected women's advancement in science and are a key feature of gender inequality in the STEM pipeline that calls for further study.

Notes

1. Please see Hirshfield (2011) for a more detailed description of my methods.

2. The professors' ranks ranged from assistant to full professor; however none of the professors had been at the university for more than ten years. Because of my

interests in group dynamics, this was an attempt to disentangle some of the effects of advisor prestige, money, and stability that I felt were likely to arise by comparing across well-established and very new research groups.

3. For the sake of ease, I have used pseudonyms that begin with the letter "M" to denote the professors who are men, and pseudonyms beginning with a "W" to denote professors who are women.

4. Other models include additional group meetings such as "literature meetings," which involve gatherings to discuss recent literature related to research explored by the group, practice talks given by group members preparing for qualifying exams or candidacy presentations, or "subgroup meetings," which are meetings that involve part or all of the group during which students discuss recent reactions, progress, and future research plans.

5. Please see Hirshfield (forthcoming) for a longer discussion of gendered interaction norms within this setting and their consequences.

PART IV

DIFFERENTIAL ON-RAMPS? HISTORICAL FORCES SHAPING THE SCIENTIFIC WORKFORCE

~

CHAPTER EIGHT

The Postdoc Pothole

The Changing Segmentation of the Biomedical Workforce, 1993–2008

Lisa M. Frehill

Recent growth in the biomedical sciences was planned: federal funding for the National Institutes of Health (NIH) doubled between 1998 and 2002 (Johnson 2013).[1] In 1995, NIH was appropriated $11.3 billion, which grew to just over $27 billion in 2003 ($21 billion in constant 1995 dollars). But with just a modest increase through 2013 to $30.7 billion (or a decrease in 1995 dollars to just under $17 billion), the long-term human resources consequences have been the subject of much debate in the biomedical research community.

Analysts' assessments of the impact of this change have ranged from the pessimistic conclusion that the United States has overproduced PhDs in the life sciences (Teitelbaum 2014) to the optimistic conclusion that the funding change enabled the expansion of the biotechnology industry and quickened innovation in the life sciences (Chatterjee and DeVol 2012). For example, in the midst of the doubling period, nearly one-third of R01-equivalent and Research Project Grant (RPG)[2] applications were funded by the NIH but in 2014, the success rates had declined to just 18 percent for RPGs and 18.8 percent for R01-equivalent awards. NIH R01s and RPGs have become crucial for researchers' career success (within academia for tenure and promotion); therefore, the increased competition for these funds presents a challenge to newer entrants to the biomedical research workforce (Daniels 2015; Garrison, Drehman, and Campbell 2014; NIH 2014b).

Postdoctoral researchers (postdocs) have been critical to the efficient use of funds allocated for biomedical research (see Garrison and Gerbi 1998; Miller and Feldman 2014). Between 1998 and 2002, during the period of expanded NIH funding, principal investigators (PIs) were able to recruit more postdocs to manage labs and supervise students in larger research enterprises. Postdocs occupy a transitional phase in the biomedical workforce: while they have completed formal education and earned a doctoral degree, the postdoc appointment is considered an additional training period during which postdocs are meant to acquire additional skills to become independent researchers (National Research Council [NRC] 2005a). The postdoc appointment also provides additional network connections and time to pursue their own research agenda while still reaping the benefits of supervision by a more experienced researcher.

However, in the post-doubling period (after 2003), questions have arisen about the attractiveness of traditional biomedical research career pathways, which have often been biased toward academia (Long, Allison, and McGinnis 1979; Smith-Doerr 2006), due to relatively flat wage trajectories, long hours, and lack of mentoring. Rather than serving as a bridge to independence, critics have found that many postdocs remain stuck in positions for longer periods (Stephan and Ma 2005) that are far from independent and, indeed, provide a source of inexpensive and highly skilled labor for university laboratories (NRC 2005b and 2014).

This chapter shows how the postdoc workforce, segmented simultaneously by gender and nativity, changed in three key time periods relative to the NIH doubling period. Using data from the Survey of Doctorate Recipients (SDR) I examine changes in the composition of the biomedical research postdoc workforce between 1993 and 1997 (pre-doubling); 1997 through 2003 (the doubling period); and 2003 through 2008 (post-doubling).

Trends in the U.S.-Trained Biomedical Science Workforce

Between 1981 and 2012, the U.S. PhD[3] biomedical workforce underwent significant change, more than doubling in size from 64,368 to 140,100 with a comparatively low unemployment rate of between 1.3 and 2.2 percent. The normative career trajectory for a PhD-trained biomedical scientist included a brief (one-two years) postdoc, after which (s)he would move into a faculty position and establish "research independence" (NRC 2005b). Analysis of data provided by Garrison and Campbell (2015) indicate that approximately two-thirds of PhD biomedical scientists were in academic employment, and 15 percent in industry employment in 1981. By 2012, after the rise of the biotech industry, just 48 percent were in academia and 36 percent worked in industry settings. As shown in table 8.1, approximately 34 percent of PhD-trained biomedical scientists were in a faculty position within five-six years of degree completion. Among those in academic positions, 51 percent were tenured faculty and another 18 percent were on the tenure track.

The Department of Energy and the National Institutes of Health kicked off the Human Genome Project in 1990. The "race" to decode the human genome spurred innovation in life sciences research. With advances in DNA sequencing technology, the project reached completion two years early in 2003. In some ways, the Human Genome Project was to the life sciences what the "Space Race" had been to the physical sciences and engineering in the 1960s: a large, publicly funded project that caught the imagination of young people. Table 8.2 shows that between 1981 and 1993, enrollment in doctoral-granting biomedical programs increased from 45,598 to 60,158, but

Table 8.1. Postdoc and Academic Employment of Biomedical PhDs, Selected Years 1981–2008

	1981	1993	NIH Funding Doubling Period 1997	2003	2008
Postdoc Employment					
Postdocs as a Percent of Biomedical PhD Workforce	9.6%	11.4%	11.5%	7.7%	9.0%
Postdoc Salaries (Level 1)	$14,040	$20,700	$21,420	$36,108	$38,976
Academic Employment— Biomedical PhDs					
Percent in a Faculty Position within 5-6 years of PhD	34.3%	22.6%	22.1%	19.3%	15.5%
Percent in Academic Tenured and Tenure Track Positions	45.8%	33.8%	31.0%	28.9%	25.6%
Among Academic Positions					
Percent—Tenured	51.3%	44.1%	40.5%	39.3%	39.0%
Percent—Tenure Track	18.0%	16.6%	16.6%	15.9%	16.2%

Sources:

Postdocs: 1981 data are authors' analysis of data derived from Garrison and Gerbi (FASEB 1998), remainder authors' computations from the 1993, 1997, 2003, and 2008 Survey of Doctorate Recipients.

Postdoc salaries: Authors' analysis of data from NIH "Stipend Levels" for the Kirchstein NRSA postdoctoral awards accessed at era.nih.gov/files/NRSA_Stipend_History.xlsx on March 5, 2015.

Academic employment: Authors' analysis of data derived from Garrison and Campbell (FASEB 2015).

Table 8.2.   Enrollments and Doctoral Degrees Awarded in Biomedical Fields, Selected Years 1981–2012

	1981	1993	NIH Funding Doubling Period		2008	2012
			1997	2003		
Enrollment in doctoral-granting departments	45,598*	60,158	60,698	73,819	82,601	88,249
Percent temporary residents	13.8%	24.9%	21.6%	24.7%	25.2%	23.8%
Doctoral Degrees	4,118	5,573	6,293	6,350	8,714	9,506
Percent women	28.9%	41.1%	44.1%	47.3%	51.8%	54.7%
Percent temporary residents	8.0%	25.2%	23.5%	24.7%	29.3%	25.6%

Source: Authors' analysis of FASEB 2015.

*Enrollment data are from 1982; 1981 data not available.

this growth was fundamentally level through 1997 (60,698), when the NIH doubling period began. During the 1997–2003 doubling period, doctoral enrollment once again increased (by 22 percent), and then in the 2003–2008 period PhDs grew from 6,350 in 2003 to 8,714 in 2008 on the heels of these earlier increased enrollments.

The composition of the biomedical PhD workforce also changed greatly over the last thirty years, even before the doubling period. Table 8.2 shows that in 1981, women accounted for 29 percent of PhD recipients and 41 percent by 1993. Steady increases in women's participation continued through 2012 when women accounted for over half (55 percent) of U.S. biomedical doctorate recipients. Yet, women's representation among life sciences faculty has lagged doctoral completion levels. In 1993, women accounted for just 28 percent of academically employed PhD life scientists and 24 percent of life sciences faculty. By 2006, women represented just 36 percent of full-time life sciences faculty (National Science Board 2008).

The number of international students in U.S. graduate programs also increased greatly in the 1990s. According to NSF analyses, up until 1985, the number of doctoral degrees earned by international students in the United States was relatively stable and increased slightly through 1990. The Immigration and Naturalization Act of 1990 provided new immigration categories that favored high-skilled immigration via the H-1B visa program (Wasem 2012; Lowell 2013). Further, starting in the 1980s, Asian nations such as China, India, and South Korea embarked upon institution building to develop science and engineering doctoral universities for which doctoral-trained faculty would be needed (NSF 1993). Together, the push from Asian countries seeking doctoral-trained human resources and the pull of potential post-graduation labor market entry in the United States led to an expansion in the number of degrees earned by temporary residents at U.S. universities. Table 8.2 shows that temporary residents accounted for 21.6 percent of students enrolled in doctoral-granting biomedical sciences departments in 1997, at the start of the doubling period. This number increased to 24.7 percent by the end of the doubling period and remained steady at the 24–25 percent level through 2012.

Employment outcomes for PhD biomedical scientists in the doubling period and beyond differ markedly from those of their predecessors. The Human Genome project and subsequent life sciences-based innovations have blossomed into a large, global biotechnology industry employing more than a third of U.S.-trained doctoral biomedical scientists (Garrison and Campbell 2015). Table 8.1 shows that only 14 percent of biomedical PhDs reported being employed in a faculty position within five-six years of completing their degree, versus 34 percent in 1981. Further, among those who work in academia, proportionately fewer are in the most prestigious tenured and tenure track positions (36 percent and 14 percent, respectively) compared to 1981 when over half of academically employed PhD biomedical scientists were tenured professors.

The competition for NIH funding is a key issue in many policy reviews of the biomedical PhD workforce (Alberts, Kirschner, Tilghman, and Varmus 2014, Daniels 2015; Garrison et al. 2014; NRC 2005b; NRC 2014; Stephan

Table 8.3. NIH Funding and Success Rates, Selected Years 1981–2012

| | 1981 | 1993 | 1997 | 2003 | 2008 | 2012 |
			NIH Funding Doubling Period			
NIH Funding ($ billions)	$3.60	$10.30	$12.70	$27.10	$29.30	$30.90
Success Rate—R01-Equivalent2	30.4%	23.0%	30.2%	30.2%	23.3%	18.3%
Success Rate—Research Project Grants (RPGs)	30.7%	23.5%	30.5%	29.9%	21.8%	17.6%
Average Age for First-Time R01-Equivalent Awardees	35.6	39.5	39.9	42.0	41.8	42.4

Source: Author's analysis of data from NIH Budget Office http://officeofbudget.od.nih.gov/approp_hist.html, access date March 21, 2015.

Source: NIH (2014), Table 218.

Source: FASEB (2014).

2012). Table 8.3 shows the steady decline in success rates for R01 and RPGs at NIH, from about 30 percent in 1981 to about 18 percent in 2012. Interestingly, though, during the doubling period the success rate remained unchanged, suggesting that even with the annual increases in funds, these additional awards merely kept pace with demand rather than increasing the chances of an individual researcher winning an award. Finally, the average age at which investigators win their first R01-equivalent award has increased by 19 percent since 1981, from 35.6 years to 42.4 years. Some observers suggest that this significant age increase is problematic for all early career biomedical scientists, but is particularly problematic for women in the field (Case and Richley 2013; Eaton 1999; NRC 2010; Smith-Doerr 2006).

Occupational Segregation and Change

Occupational segregation by race/ethnicity, nativity, and gender, is a consistent feature of the U.S. economy (Charles and Grusky 2004). Occupations vary greatly in terms of educational and experience requirements, rewards and benefits, and the conditions under which work is completed. The persistence of the gender gap in wages, for example, underscores the continued significance of gender as a mechanism of occupational segregation. Similarly, other studies point to the persistence of occupational segregation based on ethnicity and nativity (Mintz and Krymkowski 2011; Weeden 2002).

Queuing theories provide a framework for understanding how individual statuses impact occupational placement and how occupational composition changes over time (Lieberson 1980). In their classic work on mobility in the United States, Blau and Duncan (1967) found that white male upward mobility in the United States was enabled by immigration, which provided less advantaged new labor market entrants to occupy the lower rungs of the occupational structure so that the advantaged group (i.e., white males) could climb the ladder of opportunity. Looking more closely at gender, Reskin and Roos (1990) showed that changes in occupational characteristics such as prestige, autonomy, and wages impact the gender composition of occupations. Specifically, males flee occupations that have undergone negative changes in prestige, autonomy, and wages, while less advantaged workers—women and non-native workers—enter the vacuum created by these exits.

In sum, as the rewards of an occupation diminish (i.e., prestige, autonomy, wages), privileged workers within the labor market shun these negative conditions and move away from these occupations, creating openings for workers from lower-status groups to enter the field. Privileged workers move toward jobs that offer more rewards or engage in closure strategies to preserve their advantaged status by engaging in actions that limit occupational entry (Ignatiev 1995; Weeden 2002).

Government policies can also impact occupational composition, such as, Title IX in the late twentieth-century, which opened up previously restricted entry-points for women. Professions like medicine and law, which exercised control over women's participation by restricting access to higher education institutions in the pre-Title IX era, have experienced large transformations in gender composition. At the doctoral level, the late twentieth-century removal of *de jure* restrictions on women's entry to higher education resulted in increased women faculty in science and engineering fields in which they had previously participated—such as the life and social sciences—and slower movement into fields that had low historical representations of women such as engineering (Frehill 2006).

Data and Methods

I used the Survey of Doctorate Recipients (SDR) restricted-use data files for 1993, 1997, 2003, and 2008.[4] The SDR is a nationally representative survey of individuals who have completed doctoral degrees at U.S. colleges and universities. The sample is drawn from the Doctoral Records File, a large and ever-growing file in which information about nearly all research doctorate recipients from U.S. colleges and universities has been kept since the 1956–57 academic year. While these are considered excellent data, biomedical scientists who earned degrees at non-U.S. institutions are not included in these data. A number of publications have concluded that there are important shortcomings in the data available about postdocs (NRC 2000; NRC 2005a, 2014), with estimates that approximately half of all non-U.S. citizen postdocs have degrees from non-U.S. institutions. However, as questions persist about the quality of internationally trained doctoral scientists—especially those from Asian nations—the limitation of these data to those educated at U.S. universities provides a measure of control of this potentially important factor.[5] This exclusion also means that the findings herein are conservative, given the focus of this paper on the relative representation of international scientists among the U.S. PhD biomedical workforce.

Among its employment questions, SDR respondents are asked if their current position is a postdoc, which NSF defines on survey forms as "a temporary position awarded in academe, industry, or government primarily for gaining additional education and training in research." I selected biomedical postdocs based on respondents' reported doctoral field of study. Consistent with the NIH definition (NIH 2014a), biomedical postdocs were those who indicated one of the following eleven doctoral degree subfields: 1) Biochemistry and Biophysics, 2) General Biology, 3) Cell and Molecular Biology, 4) Ecology, 5) Animal and Plant Genetics, 6) Microbiology, 7) Human and Animal Pharmacology, 8) Human and Animal Physiology, 9) General Zoology, 10) Bioengineering and Biomedical Engineering, and 11) Other Biological Sciences. I am interested in the influence of respondents' gender and citizenship status[6] (particularly temporary status), hence the four groups of interest by gender and nativity are: U.S. women, U.S. men, international women, and international men.

I used shift-share analysis to distinguish between the different components contributing to change in the biomedical postdoctoral workforce.[7] The three components of interest are: 1) national growth effect; 2) subfield mix; and 3) competitive advantage. The *national growth effect component*, similar to that in the regional job growth models, represents the extent to which changes in the segregation of biomedical postdocs by nativity and gender is associated with general national-level postdoctoral growth. If there were no differences associated with nativity and gender, then the relative growth for each of the four groups would be similar.

The *subfield mix component* captures the extent to which each of the four gender-by-nativity groups are segregated into different biomedical degree subfields so that changes in group representation reflect the national-level changes in the mix of subfields. For example, if men are more likely to be in ecology but over a period of time ecology constitutes a declining share of the national distribution of biomedical postdocs, then the declining representation of men as postdocs would be an artifact of this change in the subfield mix. If there were no differences in the distribution of degree subfields across each of the four gender by nativity groups, then the relative change in subfields across groups would be similar.

Finally, the third component, *competitive advantage*,

indicates how much of the change in a given subfield is due to some unique (unmeasured) advantage that the subgroup possesses because the growth in biomedical postdoctoral employment cannot be explained by expected change. Here expected change is the sum of the subfield mix effect and the national growth effect. A positive competitive effect for a demographic subgroup in a subfield indicates the subgroup is outperforming national trends (both overall national trends and national trends in that specific industry). A negative effect means that subgroup in a subfield is underperforming compared to national trends. (Lee 2014)

Competitive advantage is a residual found when subtracting the change due to the national growth effect and the subfield mix effect from the known amount of overall change in the number of postdocs for each of the four groups. If no gender-by-nativity group (U.S. women, U.S. men, international women, and international men) possessed a competitive advantage, the residual would be zero and the change would be entirely associated with the distribution of gender and nativity groups across subfields (the subfield mix effect) or by general postdoctoral growth at the national level (the national growth effect).

Changes for each of the four gender-by-nativity groups were computed for the three periods under consideration: the pre-NIH funding doubling phase (1993 and 1997 SDR data); the NIH doubling phase (1997 and 2003 SDR data); and, finally, the immediate post-NIH doubling phase (2003 and 2008 SDR).[8]

Findings

Table 8.4 provides a snapshot of the general U.S. PhD biomedical workforce and the postdoc biomedical workforce at the four time points in our analyses. A majority of international recipients of biomedical sciences U.S. PhDs are in postdoc positions but the proportion declined by the end of the doubling period in 2003. Less than 9 percent of U.S. men in the biomedical workforce were in postdoc positions at all four time points; they were the least likely of the four groups to be in these relatively disadvantaged positions. U.S. women were second least likely to be in postdoc positions; in the three doubling period time points (1993, 1997, and 2003), U.S. women were about twice as likely as U.S. men to be in postdocs—but by 2008, this gap had narrowed.

These data fit the queue framework in that by 2008, just 6.6 percent of U.S. men but a statistically significantly greater percentage of U.S. women (9.5 percent) were in postdocs, with both of these proportions far lower than those of either international men or women (~50–52 percent, not significantly different). The results suggest that the PhD biomedical postdoc workforce is primarily segregated by nativity then secondarily by gender.

Prior to the start of the NIH doubling period, a majority of international women and men (about 70 percent of both sexes) in the U.S. doctoral-degreed biomedical workforce were in postdoc positions. By 1997, at the start of the doubling period, proportionately fewer international men and proportionately more international women in the biomedical research workforce were postdocs. Similar to U.S. women and men, though, as the doubling period drew to a close in 2003, the relative percentage of international mem-

Table 8.4.   U.S. Degreed PhD Biomedical Workforce, Number and Percent of Postdocs by Gender and Nativity, Selected Years 1993–2008

		U.S. Men	International Men	U.S. Women	International Women
1993	Total PhD Workforce	70,908	1,110	23,667	386
	Number Postdocs	6,262	776	3,690	269
	Percent Postdocs	*8.8%*	*69.9%*	*15.6%*	*69.7%*
1997	Total PhD Workforce	80,320	1,010	30,656	497
	Number Postdocs	7,069	666	4,814	362
	Percent Postdocs	*8.8%*	*65.9%*	*15.7%*	*72.8%*
2003	Total PhD Workforce	90,037	2,186	42,856	1,257
	Number Postdocs	5,011	999	3,936	613
	Percent Postdocs	*5.6%*	*45.7%*	*9.2%*	*48.8%*
2008	Total PhD Workforce	97,464	3,221	54,194	1,910
	Number Postdocs	6,399	1,608	5,156	991
	Percent Postdocs	*6.6%*	*49.9%*	*9.5%*	*51.9%*

Source: Authors' analysis of NSF restricted-use SDR data. Use of NSF data does not imply NSF approval of methods, findings, or conclusions.

bers of the biomedical research workforce who were postdocs had declined to around 50 percent.

Shift-share analyses results are summarized in table 8.5, with figure 8.1 comparing these results to components of growth for the most advantaged workers, U.S. men, and the least advantaged workers, international women. In the pre-doubling period, 1993–1997, the majority of growth in the number of U.S. men postdocs was associated with the overall expansion of the postdoc workforce during that period, while for U.S. women and international women, the growth in the number of postdocs was associated with both overall growth and competitive advantage. So that while overall growth would mean generally expanding opportunities (needs) for postdocs, competitive advantage suggests that certain demographic groups were more likely than others to be in these positions. The decline in the number of international men among U.S.-trained biomedical postdocs would have been larger based on the large negative competitive advantage component shown in table 8.4, but the national and field-specific growth of postdocs moderated this effect.

During the doubling period, 1997–2003, the results shown in table 8.5 and more clearly illustrated in the second panel of figure 8.1 show a more complicated picture. NIH funding increased from $12.7B to $27.1B with no change in the success rate of applicants, which remained stable at 30.2 percent, as shown in table 8.3. The number of both U.S. men and women postdocs declined during the period (total growth), while the number of

Table 8.5. Shift-Share Results of the Analysis of Gender and Nativity on Employment in the PhD Biomedical Workforce

	Men		Women	
	U.S.	International	U.S.	International
1993–1997				
National growth	928	115	547	40
Field-of-degree growth	104	79	101	0
Competitive advantage	−225	−304	476	53
Total growth	807	−110	1,124	93
1997–2003				
National growth	−1,575	−148	−1,072	−81
Field-of-degree growth	171	44	291	18
Competitive advantage	−654	437	−97	314
Total growth	−2,058	333	−878	251
2003–2008				
National growth	1,273	254	1,000	156
Field-of-degree growth	354	36	420	103
Competitive advantage	−239	−26	−199	120
Total growth	1,388	264	1,220	378

Source: Authors' analysis of NSF restricted-use SDR data. Use of NSF data does not imply NSF approval of methods, findings, or conclusions

international postdocs increased. Looking at the components of change, the declines for both U.S. men and women were associated with the national declines—perhaps due to the increased NIH funds availability, which enabled more postdocs to make the transition to independence—and to their competitive advantage (i.e., nativity).

The relative importance of competitive advantage was larger for U.S. men, with competitive advantage accounting for ~32 percent of the decline, than U.S. women, for whom competitive advantage accounted for just 11 percent of the decline in the number of postdocs between 1997 and 2003. Field-of-degree impacted growth by exercising a "breaking effect" on the decline in the number of U.S. women and men postdocs, suggesting that biomedical scientists in some fields were less likely than those in others to be in a postdoc.

International men's and women's postdoc growth during this same period (1997–2003) was due to competitive advantage, in spite of the overall national decline in the number of postdocs. As with the 1993–1997 period, field-of-degree was a less important component of growth in the number of international postdocs, although slightly more important for men than women. These results also fit a queuing framework by showing that interna-

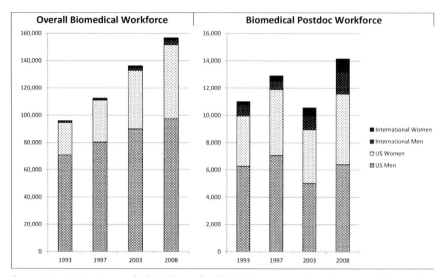

Figure 8.1.   U.S. Degreed PhD Biomedical Workforce Number of Workers by Gender and Nativity, Selected Years, 1993–2008.
Source: Enobong Hannah Branch. Authors' analysis of NSF restricted-use SDR data. Use of NSF data does not imply NSF approval of methods, findings, or conclusions.

tional workers may have entered positions left open by the departure of U.S. workers in the same occupational niche. It should be noted that postdoc salary rates increased by nearly 69 percent during this NIH funding growth period, substantially larger than the 3.5 percent salary level increase between 1993 and 1997.[9]

Finally, in the post-doubling period, the number of postdocs expanded among all four demographic categories. The national-level demands for postdoc workers in biomedical science drove the increases for U.S. women and men and for international men, but competitive advantage for these three demographic categories had a negative impact on this growth. Field-of-degree accounted for about one-fourth of U.S. men's but just over one-third of the growth in the number of postdocs among U.S. biomedical scientists. International women's growth was due to the effects of national growth (41 percent), field-of-degree (27 percent), and competitive advantage (32 percent). Indeed, international women were the only group here to have an increase in biomedical postdoc participation due to competitive advantage, meaning that as these positions became less attractive to more privileged workers (U.S. women and men as well as international men), openings were available for the least privileged workers (international women).

Discussion

Between 1998 and 2002, NIH funding was doubled, resulting in varied interpretations of the "fall-out" associated with this change in publicly funded research. On the one hand, some analysts claim the over-production of doctoral-trained scientists is a waste of public resources (Alberts et al. 2014; Daniels 2015, and Teitelbaum 2014) while others cite the expansion of the biotech industry as a desirable outcome of this expenditure of public funds and advocate for expanded public investment in the biomedical scientific workforce for economic and health benefits (Alberts et al. 2014; Battelle 2014; Garrison et al. 2014).

Consistent with the queue model of economic segregation, changes in the three time periods under consideration, pre-doubling, doubling, and the immediate five-year post-doubling period from 2003 to 2008, revealed that the U.S. biomedical postdoc workforce was segmented primarily by nativity and secondarily by gender. U.S. men were the most privileged group, followed by U.S. women, and then international men and women.

The shift-share analyses demonstrated the importance of the intersection of nativity and gender in the demographic changes in the postdoc workforce net of both overall national growth effects and group differences in fields of study. Specifically, as postdoc opportunities expanded but the rewards associated with these positions declined, more privileged groups were less likely and less privileged groups were more likely to be in postdoc positions, consistent with the queue model, as shown by the "competitive advantage" of international women as the least privileged group of biomedical PhDs.

For much of the fifteen-year period considered, there were few differences between international men and women, but, notably, there were competitive advantage differences. For international women, competitive advantage was consistently positive and accounted for a substantial portion of growth in the number of international women postdocs in the biomedical sciences. Among international men, however, competitive advantage was only positive during the NIH doubling period, when postdoc salary levels increased by nearly 69 percent. Consistent with the queuing model, international postdocs occupied "slots" left open by U.S. workers (both men and women), whose competitive advantage contributed to the declining numbers of U.S. postdocs during this same period.

That competitive advantage was negatively associated with international men's postdoc growth in both the pre- and post-doubling periods, while international women's was positive across all three periods is intriguing. The higher salaries during the doubling period may have exerted a strong migratory pull for international men, which became less lucrative in the post-doubling period. International men may also have had expanding options for employment beyond U.S. academic and industry positions, which could also have served as a pull factor.

The biotech industry has grown in many Asian nations due to both public expenditures and globalization processes (Battelle 2014; Ernst and Young 2014; Heimeriks and Boschma 2013). Asian nations also continued to build their own doctoral-granting university programs in line with the trend first noted by the 1993 NSF publication "Human Resources for Science and Technology: The Asian Region." Recent research by Hur, Ghaffarzadegan, and Hawley (2015) found that permanent resident biomedical postdocs' productivity increased during the post-doubling period, while there were no such increase for U.S. citizen biomedical postdocs, which may provide the former with a human capital advantage in the increasingly global knowledge workforce. Further, Corley and Sabharwal's (2007) analysis of SDR 2001 data found that international scientists and engineers had lower salaries (overall) and were less satisfied in their jobs than were their U.S. peers. The possible pull of opportunities at home and push of comparatively lower salaries, lower satisfaction, more robust research productivity, and more substantial competition for NIH funding may have had differential impacts on U.S. versus international postdocs who graduated from U.S. universities.

While these push-pull factors affected both international men and women, the role of gender in understanding migration of doctoral-trained scientists needs to be better understood. Finn's (2014) ongoing research on stay rates of international[10] doctoral scientists and engineers using SDR data, for example, has shown that international women have been increasingly likely to remain in the United States as compared to international men. In 1997, there was a negligible 2 percentage point gender gap in stay rates, which widened to 6 percentage points with the 2009 and 2011 cohorts. Furthermore, while there was no substantial difference directly after PhD completion—about 65–66 percent of international men and women stay in the United States—gender differences emerge over the life course. A higher percentage of international women (66 percent) than men (60 percent) remained in the United States as long as sixteen years after PhD completion; the extent to which improving opportunities for international men outside the United States contributes to this trend needs to be more closely studied.

Do international women realize other benefits by remaining in the United States versus returning to home countries? Or, like their U.S. counterparts, are international women more likely to be "place-bound" by family ties in the same labor market in which they earned their doctoral degree? Anecdotal evidence suggests that despite critiques of gender bias in U.S. academe (e.g., Preston 2004; and Stewart, Malley, and LaVaque-Manty 2007), international women suggest that U.S. institutions offer a more welcoming environment than those in their home country, enabling a fulfilling career in science. Additional research is needed to understand these issues, especially since international women now outnumber international men among U.S.-trained doctoral biomedical scientists.[11]

Turning to U.S. PhDs in biomedical sciences, the doubling period appears to have been a boon, seemingly providing the means by which this expanding population moved to research independence, consistent with the disciplinary norms. However, many of these PhDs did not move into academic faculty positions but, rather, into the burgeoning biotech industry. Despite the pro-academic bias articulated in the policy literature about postdocs, industry offers more favorable working conditions for women (Case and Richley 2013; Eaton 1999; Smith-Doerr 2004) and international PhD biomedical scientists (McQuaid, Smith-Doerr, and Monti 2010).

While academic labor forces have been characterized by stagnation, with a decline in the relative availability of tenured faculty positions, the biotech industry is undergoing continued U.S. and global expansion (Ernst and Young 2014; Battelle 2014). Most observers note the growing need for graduate students trained to meet employers' skills needs for continued expansion (Alberts et al. 2014; and NRC 2011). Other commentators suggest entrepreneurship as a viable non-academic option for talented doctoral scientists (Thon 2014), the benefits of which have been especially noted for international biotech entrepreneurs (McQuaid et al. 2010).

Many solutions, such as those presented in the Alberts et al. 2014 perspective piece, fail to account for the hierarchy of academic biomedical programs (Smith-Doerr 2006). The one-size-fits-all approach characteristic of this literature, therefore, is unlikely to meet the diverse labor market needs for highly trained life scientists, which includes preparing faculty for teaching-oriented positions at the vast majority of institutions that are not in the limited "top-10" and for the biotech industry. The evidence in table 8.2 indicates that market-clearing forces already appear to be operating within biomedical graduate education. During the 1997–2003 period, graduate enrollments increased by nearly 22 percent; with the consequence that this large cohort generally completed their PhDs in the post-doubling period, contemporaneous with policy concerns about more and longer postdoc periods (Stephan and Ma 2005; NRC 2014). However, in the immediate five-year post-doubling period, graduate enrollment continued to grow, but by a more modest 12 percent and then by only 7 percent from 2008 through 2012.

Conclusion

The data used represent both a strength and a weakness. On the one hand, the SDR is widely recognized as a high-quality, representative dataset about U.S.-trained doctoral scientists and engineers, an important, but relatively small segment of the U.S. workforce of about 144 million people. Sample surveys from the Bureau of Labor Statistics, therefore, are often inadequate for studying the doctoral-degreed workforce. The important weakness: these data are limited to those who earned a PhD in the United States. While this served as a control for potential perceived differences in institutional quality as contingent on world region, by some estimates, the SDR captures about 40–60 percent of the U.S. postdoc workforce (NSB 1998; NRC 2000; NRC 2005a, 2014). It would be important to develop estimates of the relative importance of non-U.S.-trained postdocs at various times to better understand the possible impact of this limitation on the findings presented herein.

While the 1993 NSF report (Johnson 1993) provided a somewhat optimistic prognosis for the development of doctoral programs and educational infrastructure in Asian nations, with the exception of China,[12] these programs have not yet surpassed U.S. degree production. Our findings about competitive advantage suggest that with the more modest increase in postdocs' salary levels[13], internationally trained women may fill the less lucrative postdoc openings left vacant by the dwindling number of U.S.-trained biomedical postdocs. Further, immigration policy discussions need to account for the gender differences noted by Finn (2014), that international women are more likely than men to stay in the United States. The extent to which postdocs are able to obtain greater rewards in staying versus leaving, and whether women and men have similar access to these rewards, needs further research.

As women's presence—regardless of nativity—increases in the biomedical sciences, to what extent will women be able to shape the field and to what extent will existing status hierarchies about work location persist? Eaton noted as early as 1999 that half of biomedical scientists in industry were women, suggesting that industry forms of work organization may provide useful models for other biomedical science workforce sectors (most notably, academia). However, if the demographic trends noted persist, it is possible that the biomedical workforce may be horizontally segregated by economic sector, with men continuing to be in high-prestige, tenured academic positions and women in industry. This has implications for the allocation of public funding of biomedical science, as academic elites are able to shift the burden to the public to protect their interests in maintaining research infrastructure that are not available to those in industry (Ehrenberg and Rizzo 2003).

Finally, this chapter has not addressed the implications of changes in racial/ethnic segregation of the biomedical workforce, largely due to small cell sizes and large standard errors for U.S. African Americans, Latinos/as, and American Indians and Alaska Natives. The timing of entry of different groups to this workforce, given the funding dynamics, holds implications for long-term career success. The queue model suggests that disadvantaged workers move into positions that are left vacant by advantaged workers seeking better opportunities when those positions experience declines in status, prestige, and economic rewards. To what extent are the changes in the participation of U.S. women and men in the biomedical postdoc workforce further influenced by race/ethnicity? As "late comers" to the biomedical workforce, and at a time when there are significant concerns about the health of the biomedical funding infrastructure, will biomedical workplaces ever achieve a modicum of parity with the diversity of the United States? Or will growing numbers of African American and Latino/a postdocs experience diminished career opportunities? While this chapter has only scratched the surface of these issues, it offers important insights into how policy interventions are related to workforce changes that have long-term implications for group participation.

Notes

1. Acknowledgments: The author greatly appreciates comments from Margaret Usdansky and Katie Seely-Gant on earlier drafts and the invaluable assistance provided by Enobong (Hannah) Branch. This research was initially supported as a part of work on a grant to Marlene Lee of the Population Reference Bureau from the National Institutes of Health, National Institute of General Medical Sciences (NIGMS), to whom I am grateful for her formative guidance on the project. Additional research was completed while the author was serving at the National Science Foundation. Any opinions, findings, conclusions, or recommendations expressed in this chapter are those of the author and do not necessarily reflect the views of the National Science Foundation or the Population Reference Bureau.

2. There are several types of Research Project Grants available at NIH. The R01 is the award sought by most principal investigators, considered to be the fundamental individual-level grant and indicative of "research independence." Investigators can request funding for up to five years, with no upper limit on the request. Additional budget justification is necessary to support requests of more the $250,000 a year, therefore, a single PI could secure over $1M (NIH 2012; Richardson 2013).

3. This chapter focuses on the U.S.-trained PhD biomedical workforce. Therefore, workforce size estimates in table 8.1 were taken from the Federation for Societies of Experimental Biology (FASEB), which uses a set of degree fields similar to those

included in our analyses. Biotechnology industry groups and analysts use alternative definitions of the workforce and typically do not focus explicitly on the doctoral-degreed workforce.

4. The SDR is not administered annually, hence the somewhat irregular data years used for this chapter. While the NIH doubling period is formally considered to be 1998 through 2002, the SDR datasets' frequency permits sufficient overlap with this time specified. Throughout the text, our references to data and findings use the years associated with each SDR administration.

5. Race/ethnicity was not included in these analyses because of the very low representation of groups other than Asians and whites. When the nativity, sex, postdoc status, field, and race/ethnicity crosstab is constructed, small cell sizes and large standard errors make analysis problematic. A majority of international women and men in all years were of Asian descent.

6. Citizenship status was dichotomized to match NSF, NIH, and FASEB reporting. Those who indicated they were on temporary U.S. resident visas constituted one nativity group ("international") while those who were U.S. citizens or on permanent resident visas constituted the second nativity group (U.S.).

7. Shift-share analysis is most commonly used to partition regional job growth into components associated with national trends and those associated with unique regional factors (e.g., Esteban-Marquillas 1972; LaFaive and Hohman 2009). In the traditional application to regional change, the total growth is partitioned into three components: national growth effect; industry mix effect; and local share effect, a residual interpreted as a location competitive advantage effect, which is generally a valuable means by which a region can attract businesses. While I retain this term consistent with this literature, the "reward" associated with having a competitive advantage in the postdoc labor market is a position that has become less attractive to privileged workers.

8. In equation (1), the total growth in postdoc employment of sex group i and nativity group j (i.e., TGi,j) is the sum of three components of growth:

$$TG_{i,j} = NG_{i,j} + FG_{i,j} + C_{i,j} \qquad (1)$$

The first term, NGi,j, is the effect of national growth, the second term, FGi,j, is the field-of-degree effect, and the final term, Ci,j, is the competitive advantage of the sex group i and nativity group j. Equations for each of these components are as follows:

$$NG_{i,j} = E_{i,j}\, r_{00} \qquad (2)$$

$$FG_{i,j} = E_{i,j}\, r_{i,0} - E_{i,j}\, r_{o,o} = E_{i,j}\, (r_{i,0} - r_{0,0}) \qquad (3)$$

$$C_{i,j} = E_{i,j}\, r_{i,j} - E_{i,j}\, r_{i,o} = E_{i,j}\, (r_{i,j} - r_{i,0}) \qquad (4)$$

Ei,j is the postdoc employment of women and men. The r terms reference growth rates associated with the subscript indexes (where 0 references national, i sex and j ethnicity).

9. In 1981, postdoc salaries were $14,040. They rose to $20,700 in 1993 then skyrocketed to $36,108 in 2003 (a 69 percent increase since 1997). (See "Stipend Levels" accessed at era.nih.gov/files/NRSA_Stipend_History.xlsx on March 5, 2015.)

10. Finn's (2014) gender analyses formed the "foreign-born" category, referred to in this chapter as "international," to include both permanent residents and those on temporary visas. Some of his analyses used the same aggregation we used, consistent with NSF, NIH, and FASEB. Finn did not simultaneously control for field-of-degree and gender.

11. I analyzed Integrated Postsecondary Education Data System (IPEDS) data accessed via the NSF WebCASPAR data tool (March 27, 2015) to find that within the two detailed fields of "Biological sciences" and "Medical sciences," U.S. doctoral awards to temporary resident women first surpassed those of men in 2009 (1,276 women and 1,249 men). In 2013 (the most recent available data), 1,350 temporary resident women and 1,239 temporary resident men earned PhDs from U.S. institutions. As a point of comparison, among U.S. citizens and permanent residents, women earned 4,038 and men 3,065 doctorates in these fields in 2013; U.S. women surpassed men's participation in 2005.

12. The most recent edition of Science and Engineering Indicators, 2014, provides trend data on doctoral degree production by broad fields in China, India, Japan, South Korea, and Taiwan. The level of aggregation, whereby physical and biological sciences are included in one category, means that the data in the relevant table (i.e., Appendix Table 2-42) do not differentiate the biomedical fields discussed in this chapter to permit more meaningful comparisons.

13. Postdoc salaries continued to rise in 2008 and 2012 to $38,976 and $41,364, respectively, but these were modest salary increases compared to those during the doubling period (see "Stipend Levels" at era.nih.gov/files/NRSA_Stipend_History. xlsx on March 5, 2015).

~

CHAPTER NINE

The Long Shadow
of Immigration Policy

"Appropriate Work" and
Wage Inequality in U.S. Tech Work

Sharla Alegria and Cassaundra Rodriguez

International workers make up a large and important segment of the tech work force, which includes all occupations related to computer hardware, software, and networks. These workers are often missed in conversations about the "science pipeline," particularly when considering obstacles to broadening participation for women and minorities. Unlike domestic workers, international workers must navigate complex and interconnected systems of migration policy, ethnic and racial stereotypes, and legal commitments to their employers, in addition to typical workplace challenges. Each year we "pipe" tech workers to the United States from all around the world, but some countries are more heavily represented than others. U.S. immigration policy, particularly since 1965, has selected for certain kinds of immigrants, depending on the sending countries. Thus, we argue there is not one "science pipeline" that may contain blockages or leaks, but multiple paths into tech work that are shaped by local, national, and transnational processes.

In this chapter we explore the intersections between immigration policy and workplace inequalities. Specifically, we compare the histories of immigration policy and work affecting Mexican and Chinese workers, demonstrating that U.S. understandings of "appropriate work" for racial/ethnic groups and immigration policy have shaped one another with lasting consequences for the racial/ethnic minority groups we examine. We find that the participation and wages in tech work for Chinese and Mexican workers reflects racialized associations, demonstrating that immigration policy and longstanding discourses about migrant workers help shape pathways and potholes to tech work.

A Global Labor Force

Asian and Latino workers make up a considerable part of the U.S. workforce. In 2013, about 13 percent of U.S. workers were Latino, while nearly 6 percent were Asian (American Community Survey 2013). Although Chinese and Mexican ethnic groups are often subsumed into larger pan-ethnic groups, U.S. relations, and thus immigration policies, with countries throughout Asia and South and Central America are not the same. For example, the majority of Chinese immigrants came to the United States voluntarily, while many Hmong and Cambodian immigrants came as refugees attempting to escape Pol Pot's "killing fields" (Newbold 2002; Sakamoto and Woo 2007). Thus, a careful examination of the relationship between immigration policy and work requires a country-level, rather than a continent-level, focus.

Mexican and Chinese workers represent the largest subgroups, 62 percent and 23 percent, respectively, of full-time employed Latino and Asian workers in the United States (American Community Survey 2008–2013). Both Mexican and Chinese workers in the United States are relatively likely to be first generation immigrants, among full-time employed workers, 49 percent and 78 percent, respectively (American Community Survey 2008–2013). However, among tech workers, 23 percent of Mexicans were born in Mexico and 82 percent of Chinese workers were born in China.

Highly skilled international workers now make up large shares of the most educated STEM (science, technology, engineering, and math) workforce. In 2011, international students earned 51 percent of computer science doctorates, 56 percent of engineering doctorates, 60 percent of economics doctorates, and about a third of all doctorates in STEM fields (National Science Board 2014). In 2009, 50 percent of the 85,000 H-1B visas approved were used to recruit computing and electrical engineering professionals (GAO 2011). H-1B visas are temporary work visas issued to companies to recruit skilled workers, particularly STEM workers.

Not only do international workers form a critical mass among highly skilled professionals in the United States, national economic and science policy makers argue that these workers make the United States more globally competitive (Branch and Alegria forthcoming). In 2005, Congress charged the National Academies with identifying challenges and making specific recommendations "to ensure that the United States maintains its leadership in science and engineering to compete successfully, prosper, and be secure in the 21st century" (National Academies 2007: X). Among the committee's recommendations was, "*Make the United States the most attractive setting in which to study and perform research so that we can develop, recruit, and retain the best and brightest students, scientists, and engineers from within the United States and throughout the world*" (National Academies 2007:9).

Echoing the recommendations of the committee, Microsoft CEO Bill Gates testified before Congress in 2008 to plead the tech industry case for increasing the number of U.S. tech workers. He also told Congress that there were 100,000 new tech jobs in the United States annually but in 2006 only 15,000 college graduates with tech degrees (Competitiveness and Innovation 2008). Like the National Academies report, Gates argued that the future of the U.S. position as a global leader in innovation was at risk because the tech industry faces a labor shortfall that could be ameliorated if the United States encouraged immigration (Competitiveness and Innovation 2008).

Despite the consensus among tech industry insiders about the importance of immigration for the tech industry, U.S. immigration policy is fraught with controversies. On one hand, international workers, particularly skilled workers, make important contributions to the U.S. economy, but on the other hand, American workers fear that increasing numbers of international workers will depress wages (Matloff 2013). Consequently, we have seen deportation of low-skilled undocumented workers rise dramatically, while senators, policy advisers, and industry insiders call for loosening restrictions on immigration for skilled workers (Schumer and Graham 2012; Competitiveness and Innovation 2008; National Academies 2010). At the same time that Senators Schumer (D-NY) and Graham (R-SC) called for easier access to high-skilled international workers they also want to take steps that would effectively prevent those who are undocumented, and often low skilled, from working in the United States at all. They write, "ensuring economic prosperity requires attracting the world's best and brightest," yet only a few sentences later call for legislation requiring employers to check bio-encrypted social security cards to document the work status of all new hires (Schumer and Graham 2012).

Debates about immigration in the United States suggest a bi-furcated system with one set of hopes and fears shaping high-skilled immigration and another shaping low-skilled immigration. These concerns are also racialized, with the largest share of H-1B visas going to Asian workers (GAO 2011), while most of the punitive immigration policy is focused on the Mexican border. Media portrayals reflect the ways in which Latino migrants are commonsensically assumed to participate in low-wage labor, often as service workers. When Latino characters occupy other kinds of jobs in popular culture, it is common for other characters to mistake them for "the help" (Brayton 2008). On the other hand, media portrayals of Asian characters as highly skilled workers, such as scientists, are ubiquitous.

Media coverage about the alleged births of Chinese American babies born to Chinese maternity tourists precipitated comments about how important Chinese brains are for the U.S. economy (Medina 2011). Building on stereotypes of Chinese individuals as mathematically inclined and hard working (Ho and Jackson 2001), some public responses to Chinese maternity tourism were celebratory because Chinese children were seen as future brilliant tech or STEM workers. While the representation and responses to Mexican and Chinese workers vary, they both ultimately rely on understandings about the suitability of racialized groups for low-skilled or high skilled work. In addition to the legal hurdles all international workers face, Mexicans also contend with the additional obstacle of powerful associations between Mexicans in the United States and low-skill manual and domestic work.

"Appropriate Labor"

Despite considerable shifts, particularly after the Civil Rights Act of 1964, one of the most durable and researched features of the labor force is its segregation by both gender and race (Branch 2011; Reskin and Roos 1990; McTigue, Stainback, and Tomaskovic-Devey 2009; Stainback and Tomaskovic-Devey 2012). An extensive literature in sociology demonstrates that many jobs are "sex-typed," that is, typically associated with masculine or feminine labor (Reskin and Roos 1990; Acker 1991; Williams 1992; Budig 2002). The gendering of work is so common that we refer to some jobs as "blue collar" and others as "pink collar" in reference to the assumed gender of the workforce.

A smaller but growing literature also shows how jobs can be racialized as "brown collar jobs" which are jobs with a high concentration of Latino workers (Catanzarite 2000). As Waldinger and Lichter (2003) argue, "In a racialized society like the United States, entire ethnic groups are ranked according to sets of socially meaningful but arbitrary traits; these rankings determine fitness for broad categories of jobs" (8). Wooten and Branch (2011) describe the conditions under which members of racial/ethnic and/or gender groups are tracked into particular jobs as "appropriate labor." They write,

appropriate labor conveys the notion of a negotiated ideal indicating who has been collectively defined as suited for a particular type of work. Importantly, these negotiations provide a justification for why a group is represented in one occupation as opposed to another. (292)

The logic of appropriate labor and the relationship between racial ideology and policy, particularly immigration policy, provides a point of entry to understand the barriers to tech work that some groups face.

Glenn (2002) argues that the relationship between race and gender and certain jobs is part of a social process occurring at the level of representation, micro-interaction, and the social structure (12). The consequences of past policies did not simply disappear when they ended. Rather, they are part of a social landscape that shapes the kinds of work and workers that seem like a natural fit. In part, this process implicates the different migration policies for Mexican and Chinese workers going back to the 1800s. The history of Chinese immigration is mostly of exclusion then selective migration, while Mexican immigrants experienced limited inclusion, largely as agricultural workers in the southwest. In the following sections, we examine the different immigration policies governing Mexican and Chinese migration to the United States and show that these policies have different implications for the kinds of labor deemed "appropriate" for these two groups.

Chinese Migration and Exclusion

In the mid-nineteenth century, early Chinese migrants were recruited to perform the unskilled labor needed to build the nation's railroads. Industry and government heads initially welcomed these laborers as a source of cheap labor for the Central Pacific Railroad (Calavita 2000). However, as Chinese laborers became part of the racial landscape, fears of "Yellow Peril" grew (Lyman 2000). In congressional spaces, comments about the Chinese explicitly marked them as unwanted others, noting that the "Chinese are peculiar in every respect" (Congressional Record 1882). White workers also feared that Chinese laborers would take American jobs and reduce wages (Lyman 2000). In line with these sentiments, popular media at the time depicted the Chinese as villains (Rajgopal 2010). Chinese migration was severely limited by the Chinese Exclusion Act of 1882. This act also stipulated that Chinese migrants already on U.S. soil would be ineligible for citizenship (Takaki 1989). It was not until 1952 that Asian immigrants in the United States could even become naturalized citizens (Kilty 2002).

Policies for, and depictions of, Chinese migration changed over the course of the twentieth century. During World War II, the United States and China became allies against Japan, likely influencing a change in anti-Chinese sentiment. Representations of the wartime era reflected this shift as Chinese migrants stopped being cast as villains in films (Rajgopal 2010). Chinese exclusion ended in 1943, and in 1952 the McCarren-Walter Naturalization and Immigration act repealed the remaining Asian exclusions and allowed Asians to become naturalized U.S. citizens. Importantly, the act also introduced preferences for family reunification and for individuals with particular skills. A decade later the Hart-Cellar Naturalization and Immigration Reform Act of 1965 removed the country-based quota system and continued to prioritize family reunification and highly skilled workers. As a result, the 1965 Act, with its preferences for skilled workers, dramatically increased migration pathways for Asians (Kilty 2002).

Selective migration of highly skilled workers is consistent with contemporary representations of Asians as particularly appropriate for high-tech work. Part of this representation rests on the construction of Asians as "model minorities" (Hirschman and Wong 1986; Kilty 2002). The concept of the model minority was popularized by the mainstream media during the Civil Rights movement, and cast some Asian-descendent groups as hard working and well equipped to out-compete white Americans (Zhou 2009). The model minority characterization stood in direct contrast to views about African Americans and Latinos (Kilty 2002). This may explain why, for instance, Americans do not report Asian migration as damaging to the United States (Timberlake, Howell, Grau, and Williams 2015).

Shaped by this model minority construct, Asians have been depicted as hard working and math or science oriented (Espiritu 1997). Following this logic, Asians are believed to be, and depicted as, naturally technologically savvy. For example, in a study of magazine advertisements depicting Asian Americans, Paek and Shah (2011) found that this group is depicted as having strong technological skills. While the Asian category is broad and heterogeneous, Ruble and Zhang (2013) found that undergraduates specifically think of Chinese international students as smart and gifted at math and science. The Asian model minority trope was constructed by selective immigration policy. Chinese laborers were first recruited then excluded from immigrating to the United States; their exclusion meant that very few low-skilled Chinese workers came to the United States between 1848 and 1943. When policies for Chinese immigration changed in the mid-1900s the new policies gave preference to highly skilled workers.

Mexican Immigration

The association between Mexicans and low-skilled labor has been shaped by a very long history involving immigration policy and the coercive outcomes of landowning systems. Restrictive policies on Asian immigration in the mid to late 1800s limited the supply of low-skilled laborers in the west and southwest. Consequently, employers shifted their attention to Mexican labor (Glenn 2002; Massey 2007). At the same time, following the Treaty of Guadalupe Hidalgo in 1848, many Mexican landowners lost the right to their lands when the United States ceded it from Mexico and were subsequently employed doing low-paid agricultural work on the land they used to own (Glenn 2002; Gómez 2007). Regardless of previous land ownership or class privilege, Mexicans as a group quickly became disenfranchised and largely coerced to do hard, manual labor, subject to the demands and restrictions of wage work (Zamora 1993).

Soon enough the labor hierarchy of the Southwest was characterized by Anglo men occupying the best jobs, whereas the dirtiest, most manual and low-skilled jobs were deemed "Mexican work" (Glenn 2002). In the early 1900s, there was effectively no border patrol to speak of—no regulation of Mexican immigration to the United States—and Mexican citizens fled to the United States to escape starvation and the civil war, taking jobs in agriculture, urban industry, and the railroads (Takaki, 1993). Mexican workers were exploited for their cheap labor and migration remained only loosely regulated, arguably, until the establishment of the Border Patrol in 1924 (Ngai 2004).

While informal mechanisms continued to mark low-skilled jobs as "Mexican work" this association became especially formalized in the 1940s. The Bracero Program, for instance, was a U.S. program implemented from 1942 to 1964 that established a temporary Mexican agricultural workforce for the United States. The term Bracero, derived from the Spanish word *brazos*, translates to *arms*, which highlights how Mexican migrant workers were specifically recruited for their bodily labor. The Bracero program was an option only available to Mexican migrant men; informal and formal mechanisms also tracked Mexican women into low-paying arduous labor before, during, and after the program. For instance, in the Southwest at the turn of the century, it was understood that paid household labor was "Mexican women's work" (Romero 1988:326). Mexican women in the Southwest were actively recruited into domestic work training programs so that they could supply low-wage labor to white households (Sánchez 1995). These immigration policies made low-skilled Mexican workers the solution for labor demands. They not only encouraged continued flow of migration (both legal and unauthorized) but also entrenched an association between low-skilled migration and Mexicans or Latinos (Massey 2007).

Contemporary Immigration Context

The history of Chinese immigration is one of largely explicit exclusion, while the history of Mexican immigration is one of conditional incorporation for low-wage workers. Chinese workers were excluded almost completely until the 1950s, when quotas and eventually caps ensured that Chinese workers who emigrated would be disproportionately highly educated.

The legacies of these policies and informal mechanisms that tracked Mexicans into low-wage labor still live on today. Latinos as a group remain concentrated in "bad jobs" that are unstable, lack benefits, and pay low wages (Maldonado 2009; Canales 2007). Mexicans, in particular, especially compared to their peers from Central and South America, are highly concentrated in precarious jobs (Canales 2007). To some extent, it appears that Mexicans' access to good jobs is limited even in the second generation (Waldinger, Lim, and Cort 2007).

While education is part of the explanation for why Mexicans are concentrated in bad jobs, employers play a remarkable role in tracking this group and associating them with low-wage labor. Indeed, researchers have found that employers often rely on social markers of suitability for jobs, among them race, gender, and/or immigrant status (Neckerman and Kirschenman 1991; Kennelly 1999; Moss and Tilly 2001; Shih 2002; Browne and Misra 2002; Maldonado 2009). As a result of contemporary hiring practices and migration policy, Mexican workers are still tracked in low-paying jobs that require little education.

Contemporary migration policy has shifted somewhat since 1965, but still provides additional paths to migration for the world's educated elite. If anything, newer immigration policies double down on this principle with the creation of the H-1B visa program in 1990, which allows employers to hire international workers with specialized skills temporarily to fill labor shortages in specialty occupations (GAO 2011). The H-1B visa is especially important in the tech industry; 40 percent of H-1B visas issued from 2000 to 2009 were used to bring in workers in tech occupations (GAO 2011). Employers must sponsor H-1B visas, which means that in order for a worker to get an H-1B visa, a company must be willing to hire them, apply for, and hold the visa on their behalf. Employers are also required to make efforts to hire someone who is already eligible (i.e., a U.S. citizen or permanent resident) to work in the United States before applying for an H-1B visa. While employers are required to pay workers on H-1B visas prevailing market wages, in the tech industry workers on these visas tend to be paid slightly lower wages (GAO 2011).

While H-1B visas do not have country requirements more than half of H-1B visas granted from 2000 to 2009 went to workers from Asia, 8.9 percent to workers from China specifically (GAO 2011). Mexican workers did not receive enough H-1B visas during this time to even merit their own category in the Government Accountability Office report. These H-1B visa patterns make it clear that when tech companies intend to hire international workers, Asian workers, including Chinese workers, are an obvious choice. This choice is made even easier by staffing companies in Asian countries, who file for and hold the visas for workers that they contract out to American tech companies (Banerjee 2006; GAO 2011). Possibly because the infrastructure of staffing agencies is not in place, or because companies do not tend to think of tech work as "appropriate work" for Mexican immigrants, for all intents and purposes tech companies are not bringing Mexican workers to the United States on H-1B visas.

The Long Shadow of
Migration Policy: An Analytical Approach

We have outlined immigration policies of the past in order to show that the United States specifically selected for workers with different skill sets from China and Mexico. We argue that these policies are part of the puzzle for understanding differential pathways for Chinese and Mexican workers in the tech industry. Using data from the most recent five-year period (2008–2013) of the American Community Survey (ACS) we are also able to examine the differences in education[1] and income, defined as average hourly wages,[2] for Chinese and Mexican international tech workers.

Importantly, our analysis shows that despite Mexico's proximity to the United States less than 1 percent of tech workers in the United States between 2008–2013, were born in Mexico compared to the nearly 3.5 percent who were born in China. We expect the immigration policies of the past, and the practical application of the current H-1B visa program, to suggest that Mexican workers will be less prepared for careers in tech compared to Chinese workers. Since H-1B visas require that workers have narrow specialization and immigration laws favored highly educated Chinese workers, but low-skilled Mexican workers, we would expect Mexican workers in tech to have lower levels of education generally, to be less likely to have a computer science or related degree, and to work in occupations that pay less on average. Moreover, if employers view Chinese workers as more "appropriate" for tech work, we may even see wage inequality between Mexican and Chinese workers with equivalent qualifications.

We also examine differences in college major (also called degree field), grouped into four categories: computer science, math, or engineering, other STEM fields, non-STEM fields, and no bachelor's degree. We consider workers with degrees in computer science, math, or engineering to have specialized in a tech field. Those who hold degrees in other STEM fields are not specialists, but we expect that their skills are more closely related than the skills of those who majored in a non-STEM field.[3] Finally, we define tech workers broadly using the occupational categories specified in the ACS.[4]

Mexican and Chinese
International Workers in Tech Occupations

Table 9.1 clearly shows that Chinese workers are more educated than their Mexican counterparts. The majority of Chinese workers, 58 percent, who came to the United States prior to 1965 possessed a high school or equivalent degree compared to only 24 percent of Mexican workers. After 1986, 76 percent of Chinese workers had a high school or equivalent degree (not shown). And even though Mexicans after 1965 were better educated than their earlier counterparts, the majority, nearly 69 percent, still lacked a high school education.

Historical immigration policies and practices had a clear effect on the education levels of workers. Although workers may have entered the United States prior to the repeal of the Chinese Exclusion Act, it is likely that most entered in 1943, when the exclusion technically ended, or later. Even pre-1965 immigration is likely to be skewed by the selection for educated Asian workers made possible by the 1957 immigration act. Nineteen sixty-five marked a turning point in immigration policy when new immigration laws both dramatically loosened restrictions and selected for high-skilled Asian immigrants.

Among current international tech workers, Chinese workers are more likely than Mexican workers to have at least a college degree and to have majored in a tech-related field (see table 9.2). Ninety-five percent of Chinese

Table 9.1. Percentage of Mexican and Chinese International Workers with a High School or Equivalent Degree, 1960–2013

	Immigrated before 1965	Immigrated after 1965
Chinese	58.1	76.2
Mexican	23.8	31.5

Source: American Community Survey 1960–2013.

Table 9.2. Mexican and Chinese International Tech Workers Degree Attainment by Field, 2008–2013

	Chinese	Mexican
No Degree	4.5%	42.9%
Computer Science, Engineering, and Math	62.5%	33.9%
Physical, Biological, Psychological, and Social Sciences	10.0%	2.3%
Non-STEM	23.5%	21.0%

Source: American Community Survey 2008-2013.

tech workers have at least a bachelor's degree compared to about 57 percent of Mexican tech workers. The majority of Chinese tech workers, 62.5 percent, have a degree in a field closely related to computing, computer science, engineering, or math, compared to only 33.9 percent of Mexican tech workers. We expect this difference in educational preparation to have important implications for earnings among Mexican and Chinese tech workers.

Chinese workers are more likely than Mexican workers to be employed in the best paying tech occupations and those where workers have the most education (see table 9.3). Data in this table are restricted only to Chinese and Mexican workers.[5] The top two occupations for Chinese workers in tech are: 1) software developers and engineers (39 percent) and 2) computer programmers (13 percent), where the median income per hour and years of education is $48.44 (18) and $41.67 (17), respectively. The top two occupations for Mexican workers are: 1) computer support specialists (15 percent) and 2) software developers and engineers (15 percent), where the median income per hour and years of education is $29.41 (16) and $48.44 (18), respectively. While software developers and engineers are one of the highest paying occupations, and they are in the top two for both groups, Mexican workers are considerably less concentrated in this job than their Chinese counterparts. The majority (56 percent) of Chinese workers work in the five highest paying occupations compared to only 33 percent of Mexican workers.

Our descriptive wage analysis shows considerable differences between Chinese and Mexican workers by occupation and education. But do these wage differences between groups persist once we systematically account for differences in education, experience, occupation, and other demographic characteristics?

Accounting for Group Differences

We use ordinary least squares regression to answer this question taking into account demographic, work, and education characteristics. The demographic

Table 9.3. Distribution of Mexican and Chinese Tech Workers by Occupation Wages, and Education

Tech Occupations	Median Hourly Wage	Mean Years of Education	Mexican (in percent)	Chinese (in percent)
Computer Network Architects	$52.37	17.0	1.2	1.5
Electrical Engineers	$49.74	17.8	6.9	8.7
Information Security Analysts	$48.76	16.7	0.7	0.4
Software Developers and Engineers	$48.44	17.7	14.9	39.1
Computer and Information Systems Manager	$47.32	16.9	9.8	6.4
Computer and Information Research Scientist	$46.39	18.9	0.3	0.5
Computer Hardware Engineers	$46.06	17.6	1.1	3.0
Database Administrators	$44.13	17.2	3.1	3.4
Computer Programmers	$41.67	16.9	10.9	12.8
Computer Scientists and Systems Analysts	$39.92	16.7	4.9	3.5
Network Systems and Data Communications	$39.78	16.8	1.3	1.1
Computer Systems Analyst	$39.22	16.8	8.4	5.5
All other computer occupations	$35.29	16.0	7.2	3.2
Network and Computer Systems Administrator	$34.09	16.2	6	2.9
Web Developers	$33.42	16.3	1.7	1.7
Computer Support Specialists	$29.41	15.6	15.2	5.5
Computer Operators	$17.77	13.5	6.3	0.85

Source: American Community Survey 2008–2013.

characteristics of interest are gender, marital status, having children, age at immigration,[6] U.S. citizenship, geography, English fluency, and potential experience.[7] Geography indicates the U.S. region where the respondent lives, Northeast, South, Midwest, and West. We subtract years spent in education from age to compute a measure of potential experience.[8]

The work characteristics of interest are occupation and industry. Tech workers are employed in virtually every U.S. industry, from programming machines in the manufacturing industry, to writing the programs that financial analysts use. Some industries have higher wage structures than others, thus workers who have equivalent jobs in retail compared to financial services, for example, may earn different wages. Therefore, we account for industry in our wage analysis. As table 9.3 demonstrates there are notable differences in pay across tech occupations; thus we account for occupation as well.[9]

The education characteristics of interest are: education in the United States, degree type, and degree field. Education in the United States tells whether or not the respondent completed at least their final year of education in the United States; for most respondents this would mean they hold their highest degree from a U.S. institution. Degree field is grouped into four categories: computer science, math, or engineering (omitted), other STEM fields, non-STEM fields, and no bachelor's degree. Finally, degree type is defined as less than high school, high school, associates, bachelor's (omitted), masters or professional degree.

Table 9.4 shows the regression coefficients from the OLS regression with logged average hourly wage as the dependent variable,[10] which can be interpreted approximately as percent differences from the omitted group (Chinese workers). For example, the coefficient for Mexican workers in the baseline model is –0.483. The negative sign indicates that Mexican workers earn less than Chinese workers. To estimate how much less simply multiply the coefficient by 100 to arrive at a percent. Mexican men earn about 48 percent less than Chinese men on average.

The baseline model shows the average wage difference between groups with no controls. The demographic model includes all individual character-

Table 9.4. Results of OLS Regression Predicting Average Hourly Wage by Nativity and Gender for Tech Workers, 2008–2013

	Baseline Average	Demographic Controls	Demographic and Work Controls	Demographic, Work, and Education Controls
Nativity/Gender Group (Chinese Workers omitted)				
Mexican Workers	–0.4828***	–0.3983***	–0.3033***	–0.1341***
Women		–0.1087***	–0.0862***	–0.0775***
Intercept	3.7505***	2.2261***	2.5052***	2.7177***
Adjusted R²	0.0887	0.2183	0.289	0.3331
N	8,342	8,213	8,213	8,213

Source: American Community Survey 2008–2013.

istics. The demographic and work model adds the occupation and industry characteristics. The final model adds the education variables. Between group differences (demographic model) explained some of the pay gap between Chinese and Mexican tech workers. The wage gap drops about 8 percentage points from 48 percent to 40 percent. Adding work characteristics explained more of the difference in wages indicating that Chinese workers are more likely to work in occupations and industries that pay better wages. The final model, which adds the education controls, reduced the wage gap between Chinese and Mexican workers to about 13 percent.

Figure 9.1 graphically represents the decomposition of the wage gap into portions explained by demographic characteristics, work characteristics, educational characteristics, and the remaining gap that is unexplained. The large decrease in the gap for Mexican workers suggests that much of the lower pay they receive is the result of differences in the characteristics that matter for wages—they work in lower-paying occupations, have less education, majored in fields unrelated to computing, etc. Yet, even after accounting for work and human capital characteristics, education, and degree field, Mexican tech workers earn about 13 percent less than Chinese tech workers. The pay gap may reflect differences in employers' perceptions of the groups' appropriateness for technical work. We do not examine the interaction be-

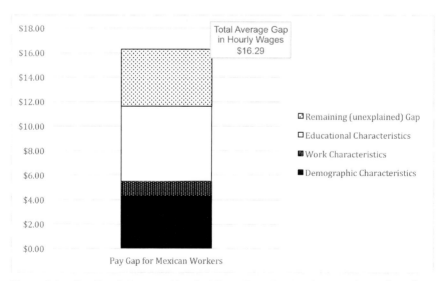

Figure 9.1. Predicted Average Hourly Wage Gaps for Mexican Tech Workers from OLS Regression by Demographic, Work, and Educational Characteristics, 2008–2013.
Author's analysis. Created by author, using data from American Community Survey 2008–2013.

tween race and gender in this analysis, however, it is noteworthy that women experience an average pay gap of about 8 percent that is virtually unaffected by the controls in the models.

Conclusion

There are two different immigration debates—one on immigration from Mexico concerning restricting undocumented migration, and the other on immigration from Asian countries, including China, where the concerns are primarily about speeding up and loosening restrictions on migration. These contemporary debates ignore the legacy of past policy that selected for highly skilled Chinese workers and Mexican agricultural workers that can still be seen in the human capital differences between these groups, even among tech workers.

We argue that the wage discrepancy we observed reflects this differential legacy of immigration policy that shaped the paths into the United States for these two groups of workers. For Chinese workers, higher levels of education eased the path to migration. More recently the popularity of H-1B visas for Asian workers in the tech industry has meant greater access to immigration for Chinese workers with specialized computing skills. The immigration policies that select for highly educated Chinese workers, for all intents and purposes, have not applied to Mexican workers—instead the large-scale immigration policies for Mexican workers selected for agricultural workers with low levels of education. Even though the H-1B visa program is theoretically available for Mexican workers, employers are not using the program to bring Mexican workers to the United States.

It is not at all surprising, given the paths to the United States, that there are considerable differences in the preparation and occupations of Mexican and Chinese tech workers that account for a considerable wage gap. We would expect Mexican tech workers to have lower educational attainment, to work in occupations that require fewer specialized skills, and thus pay less. What is surprising, however, is that a large wage gap persists even after accounting for differences in individual, work, and educational characteristics. This gap suggests that employers value Asian workers more highly even when their positions are roughly equal. It is possible that these pay differences reflect unmeasured differences in productivity, yet the trend remains informative.

Immigration policies are bound up in imagined portraits of groups and they give those imagined portraits lives of their own. They make "Yellow Peril" actionable by ending Chinese and most Asian migration to the United States, they also allow for associations between ethnic groups and certain kinds of work. Asians would not be thought of as the "model minority" now had it not been for nearly a century of exclusion that ended with deliberate policies to create a "brain drain" where immigration to the United States was easiest for Asia's educated elite. Had only Chinese laborers been allowed to immigrate to the United States, or only Mexico's educated elite, we would have entirely different associations about "appropriate labor" for these groups. The histories of Mexican and Chinese immigration to the United States are both histories of fear and restriction; however, the nuances of Chinese immigration, more recently selecting for high levels of education and technical skills in particular, meant that Chinese labor could be seen as "appropriate labor" for tech work.

The legacies of immigration policy reinforce and reproduce the idea that Chinese labor is "appropriate" for tech work while Mexican labor is more "appropriate" for agricultural and domestic work. When Mexican workers make it into tech work with all the skills to be successful they are met with lower wages than their Chinese counterparts. Immigration policy may have been shaped by fears from the past, but they cast long shadows that help form obstacles to participation in tech work for groups whose history of access to work in the United States has centered on their physical labor rather than their intellect. Therefore, discussions about the science pipeline need to consider how historical immigration policies have laid the groundwork for entry and economic success for certain workers, and not for others. At the intersection of migration policy and the inequalities in the tech work force, we find that an understanding of how groups have been racialized as (in)appropriate for tech work contributes to our understanding of challenges to establishing equity and for the recruitment and retention of a diverse tech workforce.

Notes

1. We use years of education to compare the average number of years of education among workers in particular tech occupations, but highest degree in our income models.

2. Hourly wages is a common measure of income in stratification research.

3. We use the NSF categories to determine STEM fields, which classifies psychology and social sciences as STEM fields but health sciences, arts, and humanities as non-STEM (https://www.lsamp.org/help/help_stem_cip_2010.cfm).

4. A full list of all the occupations we included is in table 9.3.

5. If we had included all tech workers in this analysis the averages wages may have been different.

6. Age at immigration indicates the age when a respondent moved to the United States.

7. Marital status, having children, English fluency, and U.S. citizenship are all binary indicators each coded 1 if respondents are married, have at least one child, speak English fluently, and are U.S. citizens and 0 otherwise.

8. We include experience squared to account for the downward pull of retirement on wages.

9. The occupation categories in the ACS did change slightly in 2010, primarily this added detail to the existing occupation categories. We coded occupations based on the year of interview, practically this means that some occupations only existed in the later years of the survey data.

10. Logged average hourly wage as the dependent variable.

PART V

CREATING A ROAD MAP:
STRATEGIES FOR PERSISTENCE

CHAPTER TEN

~

Pathways for
Women in Global Science

Kathrin Zippel

Global science is rapidly evolving. Academic scientists and engineers are increasingly expected to participate in international networks. The United States has long been attracting academic talent from all over the world, but universities in Asia and Europe, in particular, are becoming competitors and collaboration partners. International research collaboration and investment have increased in importance for U.S. faculty (Adams 2013). More than one-third of articles published by U.S. scientists in science and engineering (S&E) journals had co-authors from non-U.S. institutions in 2012, an 83 percent increase from 2002 (National Science Board 2014). For U.S. scholars these internationally co-authored publications pay off: they are more likely to be placed in high-impact factor journals and get cited more frequently (Larivière, Ni, Gingras, Cronin, and Sugimoto 2013; Hsiehchen, Espinoza, and Hsieh 2015).

Furthermore, because the United States has been a magnet for international graduate students, postdocs, and faculty, over 20 percent of the technical workforce, and about 30 percent of STEM faculty in postsecondary universities and colleges are international workers (National Science Board 2014). In some countries, internationalization is growing even faster than in the United States. The European Union, for instance, has been offering funds for large collaborations to spur new research. How these important opportunities are structured affects whether women and minorities have access to them.

Universities, funding agencies, professional associations, and governmental agencies shape the globalization of the work and the transnational flows of scientists and engineers. Funding agencies act as gatekeepers, and university resources, policies, and practices support mobility and collaboration (Zippel 2011). By failing to consider the gendered dimensions of international mobility, institutions risk reproducing inequalities among scientists. For example, expectations of "excellence" that ask faculty to demonstrate international reputation and collaboration may put those who are less mobile at a disadvantage (Ackers 2004; Costas, Camus, and Michalczyk 2013; Leemann 2010).

Because academia is increasingly internationalized, the underrepresentation of women in STEM fields has global as well as national dimensions. Global science, as the new frontier for women and men from underrepresented minority groups, offers important opportunities and challenges that I discuss in this chapter.[1] I conclude with a set of recommendations of policies and practices for researchers, universities, and funding agencies to promote international collaboration and level the playing field for women and minorities. I suggest ways to design the globalization process to be more inclusive for women scientists, and to "internationalize" gender equality policies in science and academia.

The .edu Bonus

For U.S. scientists, research experiences abroad can be particularly encouraging because of the .edu bonus (Zippel 2016). Only U.S. institutions of higher education have email and worldwide web addresses ending with .edu. Such an affiliation with an U.S. institution carries status in global academia. My concept of the .edu bonus describes how being abroad renders status as a U.S. scientist important and gender and race less salient. Cultural schemas for U.S. scientists reveal an .edu bonus that depicts U.S scholars as particularly competent. U.S. women scientists as well as men from minority groups report they are seen and treated foremost as U.S. scientists, with their gender and/or racial/ethnic status less important, and the cultural beliefs about U.S. scientists overshadow stereotypes of women and underrepresented minorities as less competent.

Being a woman and/or man of color and a foreigner thus becomes a positive combination, not an accumulation of disadvantages. In interactions with international colleagues, U.S. women and men from minority groups gain status and a sense of being desirable collaborators because of their affiliation with U.S. academic institutions. They do not feel they must live according to local gender and/or racial/ethnic norms; instead they find a sense of freedom in not being expected to fit in. Hence, international experiences might be particularly empowering for women and for men from underrepresented minority groups.

At the same time though, (global) science continues to be organized in gendered and racialized ways (Zippel 2016). While specific research and collaboration experiences, of course, are likely to differ from setting to setting (country, continent, etc.), they also depend on who the U.S. scholars are: their age, gender identity, sexual orientation, class background, racial/ethnic/national backgrounds, etc. These characteristics can create what I call "glass fences," which are gendered obstacles that affect participation in these opportunities (Uhly, Visser, and Zippel 2015; Zippel 2016).

Access to global science, considered "elite" in U.S. universities, intensifies challenges for U.S.-based women because burdens and barriers are amplified at the international level. For example, balancing family and work creates additional hurdles, notably for dual-career couples, when work takes researchers abroad (Lubitow and Zippel 2014). However, my research also shows that diverse families and family commitments can affect both men and women, and families can also serve as motivators and supports (Zippel 2016).

What Does Focusing on the Pipeline Miss? The Globalization of Academia

The "leaky pipeline" refers to the steady attrition of girls and women over the course of education and academic careers, all the way to leadership positions. However, the statistics commonly used in the United States to illustrate the pipeline across education and career steps are misleading because the pipeline contains scientists and engineers born or educated in both the United States and abroad (Xie and Shauman 2003). The pipeline concept in its simplest form focuses narrowly on leakages within countries and ignores influx across countries due to international mobility. This is illustrated by the influx of international scientists and engineers in the last forty years (Stephan 2012; and Teitelbaum 2014).

Further, the pipeline provides a myopic view of the national scientific workforce. Policy debates and the literature on gender and science often implicitly assume that U.S.-based scientists work primarily in the United States and that U.S. norms, values, and behaviors for science are universal. Yet, those assumptions do not hold true. Career paths and academic workplaces

are increasingly "internationally" organized through mobility and collaborations across national borders. As a result, the U.S. scientific enterprise is
more porous than it is imagined. Engaging in international experiences,
mobility, and collaboration for U.S. scientists can provide opportunities to
increase research capacity and range.

My research on international collaborations and mobility of faculty in
STEM fields shows how international study and research can fuel the U.S.
pipeline in the long run. International experiences can provide opportunities for U.S. women and individuals from minority groups to build research
capacities, create networks, and access important resources and facilities. International training, research positions, and engagement with collaborators
can also provide crucial opportunities to circumvent exclusionary networks
at home, particularly important for women and men from underrepresented
minority groups. Women who go abroad for some career steps, for example,
may find their experiences act as catalysts for their domestic careers. U.S.
scientists and engineers, especially women and individuals from minority
groups, can benefit from these international opportunities that can help
faculty avoid pitfalls in the national pipeline and circumvent blockages in
national career paths.

However, international options also constrain "choices" for both women
and men. These developments are reconfiguring gender relations in global
science. Yet, the intersecting changes in gender relations and the globalization of science have garnered surprisingly little attention from sociologists
and researchers of higher education.

Methods

I draw from data collected through multiple methods in my extensive study
on international research collaboration and mobility (see Zippel 2016 for
further detailed information). Data on the experience of U.S. science faculty
include a survey of 100 principal investigators of NSF-funded international
STEM projects (2009); interviews with more than 100 university STEM
faculty (2007–10); and 8 focus groups with 18 STEM faculty (2009–10)
with and without experience of international collaboration and mobility. To
study institutional contexts, I conducted interviews with thirty department
chairs and university administrators, seventeen funding agency personnel,
sixteen policy makers, and thirteen academic experts in the United States
and Europe (2007–11) about international opportunities and barriers. Finally, I draw from results of an international expert workshop on international research collaboration I organized at the National Science Foundation
in 2010 (with Lisa Frehill).

Global Pathways in Science

Many fields today rely on extensive international collaborations and some geographic mobility. Some disciplines and subfields absolutely require international engagement. For example, for particle physicists, the European Organization for Nuclear Research, known as CERN, operates a laboratory in Geneva, Switzerland, and the Deutsches Elektronen-Synchrotron (DESY) research institute resides in Hamburg, Germany. These are key places to obtain data and meet international colleagues. Geophysicists and astronomers cooperate with colleagues around the world to conduct observations and collect as well as analyze data because the phenomena they study are abroad. Even those whose research is confined to the United States increasingly find that the world of science is organized through global exchange of knowledge. International engagement offers opportunities to present research, get new ideas for one's own work, and meet contacts for future collaborations. Informal discussions with colleagues from different research traditions and experiences are crucial to test ideas and frameworks (Jöns 2007, 2009; Fox and Faver 1984).

U.S. academics that encounter closed doors at home because their research topics and approaches in innovative fields are not considered mainstream may find support for their original ideas abroad. Academics facing dead-end career paths or exclusionary networks find that international experiences can help circumnavigate them. International collaborations and mobility can also provide important pathways to academic careers through experiences in early career steps, including intellectual stimulation and research capacity building. For example, undergraduate students' research experiences abroad can pique their interest in academic careers.

When reminiscing, professors described fondly their experiences as research assistants abroad as breakthroughs that confirmed they were on the right track toward a scientific career (see Rosser 2004). These experiences can be catalysts for graduate students and postdoctoral fellows by providing opportunities to set up longer lasting networks (Martinez, Epstein, Parsad, and Whittaker 2012a, 2012b). In fields where U.S. research has been less developed or even fallen behind, students and postdocs can learn cutting-edge research approaches and methods that they can bring back, providing career advantages. Working environments that, at first sight, seem minimally conducive to high quality research can be particularly valuable training sites. For example, a professor found that his graduate students learned problem solving and how to be innovative in laboratories in Eastern Europe where the research infrastructure was less than perfect, and they had to improvise.

Internationalization provides opportunities from which white women and individuals from minority groups can especially benefit, enjoying the ".edu" bonus.[2] We might expect that being a woman *and* a foreigner would compound disadvantages, but I find that U.S.-based women benefitted from a ".edu" bonus. They are perceived as competent and highly desirable collaboration partners because being a scientist *from the United States* is more salient than being a *woman* scientist. For example, one of my interviewees, Martha, a full professor of geology, felt highly valued and respected by her international collaborators who did not want to share her with anyone else: "There's a protectiveness of the goose that lays the golden egg, and they don't want to lose it by developing intellectual relationships with anyone else" (Zippel 2016: page). U.S. women scientists report they are seen and treated foremost as U.S. scientists, with their gender status less important, and the cultural beliefs about U.S. scientists as competent overshadow stereotypes of women as less competent. Being a woman and a foreigner thus becomes a positive combination, not an accumulation of disadvantages.

This .edu bonus also works for men from minority groups, for example, the former president of the American Chemical Society, Joe Francisco, an African American chemist, credits the support of the international community in facilitating his career success. He explains that long before he received any acknowledgment for his work in the United States, international colleagues recognized his work and collaborated with him. W. E. B. Du Bois, an American sociologist and historian, did graduate work at the University of Berlin before he was the first African American to receive a doctorate at Harvard University in 1891. Similar to gender becoming less salient, for U.S. men of color, race can become less salient when they are perceived foremost as a U.S. scientists abroad, thus helping them to advance their academic careers. In addition, U.S. women of color can also benefit from being away from constraining U.S. gender and racial expectations. For example, in one of my interviews, a Latina woman professor of physical sciences discussed how she "passed" in several Southern European countries while still carrying the status as a U.S. scientist.

The .edu bonus can be crucial for professional advancement, helping scientists and engineers move to the "fast lane" by circumventing roadblocks in traditional national career paths. U.S. women scientists and men of color can gain important research opportunities abroad; they are sought after collaboration partners and highly respected. Abroad they have access to networks in which no local women or racial/ethnic minorities hold equal positions of power, as constraining norms and expectations for local women or racial/ethnic minorities do not apply to them as U.S. scholars.

Pipeline Spillover Effects:
Internationalization's Disadvantage and Promise

Women and men from minority groups may drop out of the pipeline, or not advance as others do, if they do not have access to international collaborations and their benefits. Several spillover effects between national and international career opportunities demonstrate disadvantages for scientists who cannot engage in research internationally. First, small expert workshops organized in other countries provide visibility and networking opportunities with top national scholars in the field. Graduate students and junior faculty can benefit from creating international networks, as well as, ironically, from meeting U.S. senior faculty. Exchanges with top U.S. professors over breakfast at small all-paid workshops or international research facilities can create important ties back home. Similarly, international workshops and conferences bring visibility abroad as well as in the United States; this shows how practices of academic work and networks are increasingly intertwined, and international engagement can contribute to international *and* national network building.

A second spillover effect allows professors to attract top talent from abroad, including graduate students and postdocs, who are less inclined to work with scholars who do not have an international reputation. Third, a national and international reputation is taken for granted in many countries, and while this is less so in the United States, international visibility is often expected for promotion to full professor. Some universities and colleges in STEM fields expect evaluation letters from international colleagues, in addition to domestic letters. Leadership in one's field is also measured by speaking invitations and panel participation at internationally organized conferences, and by winning international research awards.

Finally, research shows that internationally co-authored publications get cited more; even with the metrics for U.S. careers, successful researchers will be those who engage with researchers in other regions and build an international reputation. A full professor of chemistry, for example, considered his trips to present his work around the world good investments to increase citation counts for his work; he was already established and cited among U.S. colleagues and there was potential to expand his citation counts abroad.

International engagement also provides personal benefits that can keep academics in the pipeline. Faculty in our interviews and focus groups discussed how inspiring they find intellectual exchange with colleagues abroad. They cherish building friendships, and find time in a different cultural and language setting to be stimulating to their personal growth. Many faculty members consider international collaborations a perk in their U.S. careers (Zippel 2016).

International opportunities thus can provide positive experiences that benefit academic careers and keep academics in the pipeline (even if not always visible in U.S. statistics).[3] They can serve as career catalysts, "fast lanes" that may allow skipping career steps in the United States, thus potentially circumventing roadblocks and slowdowns in the national career path. Lack of possibilities to engage internationally can hinder the development of professional visibility and reputation in both national and international networks. Being less known to international colleagues means lower citation counts, less opportunity to collaborate on high profile, high impact papers, and fewer colleagues who can be asked to write letters for promotion and other evaluations. Because of these important stakes, we need to further understand the glass fences for U.S. academics engaging in the international worlds of science.

Challenges and Constraints: Glass Fences[4]

U.S. academics engage less in global science than colleagues in other countries for many reasons. The large size of the U.S. academic community itself is a factor, and disciplines or research fields may be U.S. focused. I argue that obstacles embedded in the organization of academia create additional barriers for U.S. academics to be involved in communities around the world. Obstacles for all academics can have material, bureaucratic, social, and cultural dimensions that funding agencies and academic institutions reproduce through formal and informal rules and practices. For example, international funding can be complicated, and visa and other rules constrain collaborations across countries. Institutions often do not value international research and collaborations themselves, but only the publishable products in U.S.-recognized journals and grants that they produce (Zippel 2016). Such obstacles apply to everyone, but can have different implications for all women and for men from underrepresented minority groups who tend to be located in resource-poor institutions with less time and financial and administrative resources to support their international work. When these obstacles are gendered, I call them glass fences.

Moreover, glass fences make international research and collaborations particularly cumbersome for women because some of the gendered barriers at the national level are amplified in global academia. Global academia is organized in elitist ways, in that it is limited to faculty with access to institutional administrative resources and large overhead accounts, who can afford to pay for their own travel or receive invitations by international colleagues. Furthermore, international meetings often take the shape of small, invitation-only, expense-paid workshops that continue traditions of "old-boy" networks and restrict access for women and others with less status in academia and professional networks.

These meetings often do not offer child care possibilities, because the expectation is that attendees have no care obligations. Balancing family and work can create obstacles for both fathers and mothers, particularly in dual-career couples, as well as anyone with care obligations, particularly when the work takes researchers abroad. Women and men with children use a variety of strategies to handle this and related burdens (Lubitow and Zippel 2014). My research shows, however, that diverse families and family commitments can affect both men and women, and that families can also serve as motivators and supports as well as barriers abroad.

Finally, glass fences can emerge from cultural assumptions, myths, and stereotypes about academic cultures as open to women, and cultures can be more or less open to those who wish to build a career in that country. Particular concerns about hostile environments due to sexism, racism, and homophobia, in both academic and societal cultures, may pose barriers. Language skills, cosmopolitan "cultural" capital, familiarity with travel abroad, and cross-cultural competences aid collaborations and mobility across national boundaries. These skills are not equally distributed across all academics, especially those who have grown up in working class or poor families with less access to these opportunities.

Thus a variety of glass fences exist that affect access to mobility and research collaborations, particularly for women and also for men from underrepresented minority groups. Both individuals and academic institutions can take steps to dismantle or circumvent these glass fences, and help to climb over them.

What Can Women and Men of Color Do?

Interestingly, women as students tend to be more internationally mobile than men, while women professors participate in international science at lower rates than men. Women and minority men should view the global scientific world as an opportunity for both career advancement and personal growth and enrichment. International opportunities can provide a range of options to pursue training, research, and academic careers. NSF postdocs and faculty report overwhelmingly positive experiences and outcomes (Frehill and Zippel 2011; Frehill, Vlaicu, and Zippel 2010; Martinez et al. 2012a,

2012b). As we have seen, these networks can help scholars expand beyond home departments, universities, and national circles, potentially circumventing local or national career stoppages. Therefore, women and minority men should consider promising international collaborations as part of their research and find out how these collaborations can also be compatible with their private lives.

Administrators, colleagues, and faculty themselves view family commitments, particularly for mothers, as a key glass fence that can block involvement in international research and collaborations. However, studies are not clear on whether families actually keep women from participating in global science. In my research we found that parents use various strategies to handle family responsibilities and mobility when work takes them abroad, including taking the children with them, leaving the children at home, or adjusting their research by shortening trips (Lubitow and Zippel 2014; Tripp 2002). Amid American ideologies of intensive mothering that promote the phenomenon of "helicopter parenting," it might be worthwhile to explore alternative short-term options involving other caregivers.

International research settings vary in how supportive they are to parents with children. Some countries, universities, and research settings provide better quality, less expensive child care and school settings than the United States, making longer research stays financially feasible for families (Lubitow and Zippel 2014; Tripp 2002). For example, good quality public child care and opportunities for family-friendly job arrangements exist in Scandinavian countries, the Netherlands, and France, while private arrangements for child care might be less expensive in Latin America and Asian countries. Parents may take friends, grandparents, or other relatives on international travel for child care. Some (international) fellowships pay for child care costs and dependents' travel. Many parents also approach living in a different country as an opportunity for children to broaden their view with cosmopolitan values, be exposed to a different language and culture, or reconnect with their home country in the case of faculty with foreign backgrounds. Colleagues or hosts with experiences in these countries can supply family-related information, and some universities have welcome centers that can help locate these facilities.

Considering alternatives to traveling abroad if mobility is limited is important. For example, data can be exchanged online, collaborative online spaces can be used, and regular video conferencing through Skype and other providers can be set up. It may even be worthwhile to invite foreign colleagues or their students to one's home institution (U.S. funding agencies and visa regulations have strict policies regarding paying international guests, but faculty with overhead accounts can sometimes use these funds to accommodate foreign guests or provide private solutions by hosting guests in their own homes, etc. without violating these laws).

What Institutions Can Do[5]

Academic institutions and funding agencies, as well as professional associations that seek to recruit and retain women and men from underrepresented minority groups into science, should support international collaborations and academic mobility in more inclusive ways. They risk reproducing (gendered) inequality in hierarchically stratified and structured universities when they maintain gendered and racial/ethnic inequalities that result from the accumulation of disadvantages. For example, if men encounter fewer obstacles for international collaboration and mobility and have more resources to overcome them, over time they are more able to take advantage of paths that lead abroad while women have less access due to glass fences.

Institutions should take into account that global science is a new frontier for both women and men, and they should work toward taking down obstacles and glass fences while integrating concerns about diversity into internationalization strategies. Efforts to promote gender equality in universities should thoughtfully include international opportunities. I focus here primarily on support for collaborations, in particular, that can keep scholars in science. Therefore, I suggest several areas where institutions can promote more inclusive participation in global science: mentoring, resource distribution, helping create networks, and dealing with family commitments.

- Mentoring and career-advice structures should provide information for international funding opportunities, provide cultural competency, language and other soft skills, and increase transparency in universities' and funding agencies own administrative procedures and policies.
- International programs should be highly flexible, for example, with multiple deadlines throughout the year. The timing as well as lengths of stays should be as flexible as possible, for example, instead of one twelve-month visit, multiple shorter trips over two-three years.

Women and others excluded from internal networks benefit most from transparent procedures of resource distribution and information. Women faculty have comparatively less access to administrative support (NRC 2009), therefore taking down or easing administrative barriers, such as complicated regulations for international travel and collaborations, as well as offering compensation to overcome these barriers, will particularly benefit women and others with reduced access to these resources.

- Institutions should keep data on how resources are distributed and provide more financial resources to faculty to fund international collaborations.
- Internationalization strategies should include transparent policies and practices to provide institutional supports for international conferences and hosting international visitors, such as information, housing, and office space.

Since establishing and maintaining networks requires intense effort, institutions should support all women and men from underrepresented minority groups in building networks. If they are oriented toward integrating diversity concerns through partnerships, institutional cooperation can decrease risks for individual faculty members and potentially benefit those with fewer resources.

- At the graduate level, students benefit if they do not have to initiate contacts themselves, but can apply to an integrated program that allows them to gain research capacity and develop their networks abroad.
- For example, instead of relying exclusively on individual faculty to initiate and maintain international networks, institutional cooperation that is inclusive for women scientists can offset some structural disadvantages, and reduce costs and risks for all.

Policies also need to recognize the diverse ways international engagement manifests itself, as well as the diversity among women, men, and families, which means that a variety of supports are needed.

- Programs should be supportive of couples; in particular, dual-career academic couples, and should create family-friendly options for international mobility, including financial supports, health insurance, child care, school fees, etc. for dependents to accompany faculty members.
- Policies and programs should enable faculty to bring caretakers beyond partners.

Finally, internationalization strategies should be developed to diminish obstacles and glass fences and aid women in overcoming barriers to international research, but do not place an undue burden to succeed at any cost.

Equating mobility with excellence in research as promoted by the European Union is an exclusionary rather than inclusionary strategy. International activities should not be required of faculty, but rather supported in ways that do not disadvantage those with limited mobility. Studying the Marie Curie Mobility Schemes, Louise Ackers (2005) argues that mobility as a requirement is discriminatory to those who are less mobile for multiple reasons. When institutions raise the bar by setting expectations for faculty to demonstrate international reputation and collaboration, anyone with limited mobility will be disadvantaged.

Conclusion

We need to reconsider the pipeline as a national concept for the U.S. scientific community. Since the metaphor is nationally focused, it renders invisible how international experiences, collaboration, and mobility can and do open doors for women as well as men from minority groups at various levels to excel in scientific careers, and how important these networks are for national career paths. My frameworks of the spill-over effects between national and international careers, the .edu bonus, and glass fences, highlight how gender and the globalization of scientific work are systematically intertwined, allowing us to see the challenges and benefits of integrating women and minorities into the globalizing scientific world. These experiences, including innovative research skills, can serve academics on their path and be catalysts to help faculty get into the "fast lane." Institutions such as universities, funding and state agencies, and professional associations are actively shaping processes of globalizing scientific work through policies and organizational practices with profound implications for the integration of women into science. They have created opportunities to take down obstacles and glass fences and create a more diverse and open global world of science.

However, by failing to take the gendered dimensions of international collaboration into account, institutions can inadvertently reproduce existing inequalities between women and men scientists. Instead of telling women it's too risky to go abroad, we should focus on how we can change organizational practices, cultures, and climates to make scientific workplaces more conducive to women's satisfaction and success both at home and abroad. The good news is that policies and practices that take into account academia's deeply stratified structure, as well as international mobility as a gendered phenomenon, will create opportunities to build a more inclusive globalized world of science, encouraging all academics to draw their circles wider.

Notes

1. The emphasis of this volume is pointing us in promising directions for the retention of women in science, synthesizing existing scholarship, and sharing our knowledge in a manner that is accessible to a wide audience. To that end this chapter introduces some new ideas but it is in part based on data and written work that has appeared elsewhere: see Hogan, Zippel, Frehill, and Kramer 2010; Lubitow and Zippel 2014; Uhly, Visser, and Zippel 2015; Zippel 2010 and 2016.

2. For more discussion of the .edu bonus, see Zippel 2016.

3. See, for example, Rosser (2004) who discusses in her work how women look back at their careers and point to research stays abroad as particularly stimulating. See also Zippel 2016.

4. For more discussion on the concept of glass fences see Zippel 2016 and Uhly, Visser, and Zippel 2015.

5. For more extensive suggestions particularly for funding agencies, see also Hogan, Zippel, Frehill, and Kramer 2010; http://nuweb.neu.edu/zippel/nsf-workshop/ and Zippel 2016.

CHAPTER ELEVEN

Agency of Women of Color in STEM

Individual and Institutional Strategies for Persistence and Success

Maria Ong, Lily T. Ko, and Apriel K. Hodari

Women of color—women who self-identify as black, Latina, Native American, and Asian American—are increasingly identified as untapped domestic talent who can fill critical positions in the U.S. science, technology, engineering, and mathematics (STEM) workforce (Committee on Equal Opportunities in Science and Engineering [CEOSE] 2009; National Academies 2010).[1] Despite some increases in degree attainment over the past three decades, underrepresented minority (URM) women (black, Latina, and Native American) still remain scarce in almost all STEM disciplines in higher education and careers (CEOSE 2009; National Science Foundation [NSF] 2015). In 2010, they represented 13 percent of the U.S. population (ages twenty-five–sixty-four), but only 4.5 percent of the PhD recipients in STEM who were U.S. citizens or permanent residents (NSF 2015).

The proportion of URM women in STEM faculty positions in the same year was even lower, 2.1 percent (Hess, Gault, and Yi 2013). In higher-level positions in STEM, such as full professorship and executive positions, Asian American women have been as scarce as, or even scarcer than, their women of color counterparts (Burelli 2009; Ong, Wright, Espinosa, and Orfield 2011; Wu and Jing 2011). The current underrepresentation of all women of color in STEM is cause for national concern because it withholds STEM role models from today's increasingly diverse youth (Hess, Gault, and Yi 2013) and it deprives the country from fully benefitting from a diverse STEM workforce that might offer new perspectives toward innovative and transformative solutions in science, technology, and engineering (National Academies 2011; Kachchaf, Ko, Hodari, and Ong 2015; Page 2007).

Our past research (Ong 2005; Ong et al. 2011; Ko, Kachchaf, Hodari, and Ong 2014) and other studies (e.g., Brown 2000; Carlone and Johnson 2007; Johnson 2007; Johnson, Brown, Carlone, and Cuevas 2011; Joseph 2012; Justin-Johnson 2004; MacLachlan 2006) have focused on the reasons for the unnecessary loss of potential STEM talent. Overwhelmingly, the studies report that women of color leave STEM because they experience social isolation; lack of a sense of belonging; lack of mentoring; low expectations from others; and difficult interpersonal relationships with peers, faculty, and supervisors. They leave STEM at every stage of education, particularly at critical transition points such as entering college or graduate programs, and they sometimes leave even after they have earned PhDs and developed careers in STEM (Brown 2000).

The "leaky pipeline" is a metaphor commonly used to describe the loss of underrepresented groups, including women of color, along the STEM educational and career trajectory (Blickenstaff 2005; Espinosa 2011). In general, the idea is that they enter the pipeline at the beginning of their education and then leak out of the pipe at every stage along the way. Recently, this metaphor has come under scrutiny for its allusion to passivity of women of color (Branch 2013; Johnson et al. 2011; Malcom and Malcom 2011). Further, as Malcom and Malcom (2011) point out, the model often emphasizes inherent student characteristics, such as interest and preparation, over the role of institutions, thus placing any blame for leaking out squarely on the women themselves.

An alternative metaphor of a roadway better accounts for the ways in which women of color, far from being passive victims, are innovative agents as they navigate and persist in STEM (Branch 2013; Reyes 2011). Complete with exits, pathways, and potholes, the roadway metaphor acknowledges a broader array of personal experiences, decisions, and actions; it also does a better job of recognizing the "road conditions" of institutional environments, which play a crucial role in shaping the educational and career experiences of women (Malcom and Malcom 2011). Our study is better aligned with the roadway metaphor, as we found that women of color, while affected by their environments, use a number of agentic strategies for persisting and succeeding in STEM.

Very few empirical pieces exist on agency for women of color in STEM. In this chapter, we address the question, "What agentic strategies are enacted by women of color to persist and succeed in STEM education and careers?" In an earlier paper (Ko et al. 2014), we outlined eight strategies of agency enacted by women of color, but the analysis was limited to participants in physics and astronomy. In this chapter, we highlight and elaborate upon five of these strategies: *choosing to learn and work in safe, welcoming places; participating in STEM diversity conferences; building alternative academic and professional networks; temporarily leaving the STEM realm;* and *engaging in activism.* In addition to drawing on data from physics and astronomy, we include data from our more recent studies of women of color in computer science and engineering. This chapter concludes with a list of recommendations for institutions interested in addressing their "road conditions," which could lead to greater recruitment and persistence of women of color and broadened participation in STEM.

Data

Our data were drawn from three interconnected National Science Foundation-sponsored projects: *Beyond the Double Bind,* a four-year project in which we studied women of color in physics, astronomy, computer science, and engineering; *Computing Beyond the Double Bind,* a three-year project aimed at deepening the knowledge base about the experiences of women of color in computing; and *Engineering Beyond the Double Bind,* a 2.5-year study on women of color in engineering. Though data collection consisted of a variety of sources, this chapter will focus on the data derived from two sources: extant texts and interviews.

Extant texts are defined as publicly available documents, such as autobiographies and news articles, which were not produced for the purposes of our study, but were treated as data to address the research question (Charmaz 2006). The interviews, which were semi-structured and open-ended, were conducted by team members and focused on women's experiences in their STEM education and careers. All interviews were audio recorded and transcribed. To date, across the three projects, we have gathered 330 pieces of data from, or about, 135 women: 281 extant texts on 97 women of color (some women had multiple texts written about them); and 49 interviews with 38 women of color (some women were interviewed more than once). The participants were either students in higher education or professionals; they were in physics, astronomy, computer science, or engineering. All data were entered into Nvivo 9 coding software and then analyzed using methods of narrative analysis (Riessman 2004). (For more details on our methods, please see Ko et al. 2011:176–78; and Kachchaf et al. 2015:177–78.)

Findings

This chapter highlights five strategies of agency utilized by women of color to persist and succeed in STEM. The strategies were usually enacted in response to prior experiences of isolation or negative interactions in the STEM realm (see Ong 2005; Ko et al. 2014). These strategies include: choosing to learn and work in safe, welcoming places; participating in STEM diversity conferences; building alternative academic and professional networks; temporarily leaving the STEM realm; and engaging in activism.

Choosing to Learn and Work in Safe, Welcoming Places

One agentic strategy women of color in our research used was proactively seeking and choosing places to learn and work that were welcoming and safe. For some, having such "counterspaces" (Solórzano and Villalpando 1998; Solórzano, Ceja, and Yosso 2000; Yosso, Smith, Ceja, and Solórzano 2009) felt critical to their sense of belonging. For example, Melissa, a black college junior in engineering, explained that she chose her school based on the strong sense of "family" that the school's STEM diversity program offered. She recalled the impression that a visit to the program made on her as a high school senior: "Coming to [visitors' weekend], I was able to see the nurturing family structure of the program. And I really liked that, because that's how my family [is], they support me in everything that I do. And I thought that would help me a lot when I was at school." Similarly, Nell, a black senior also in engineering, described the same STEM program as "home":

> I love that it's like a home away from home. So that when I come in the [program] office I don't feel like a visitor. I feel like I belong. And that I have a little bit of everyone's story and they have mine. So it's like we really are a family and I appreciate that because I don't get to go home that often.

Some women who did not have that sense of belonging in their undergraduate career sought it out later in their graduate programs or careers. For example, Jami Valentine,[2] a black woman, carefully selected a PhD physics program that enrolled more women and minorities compared to the very low numbers in her undergraduate program, in order to ensure different social and cultural experiences. Several women of color proactively *avoided* situations that did not seem welcoming or supportive. For instance, in conducting a search for a graduate program, Nina, an Asian American graduate student in astronomy and astrophysics, considered an opportunity that would allow her to work in a new subfield with a renowned male professor. However, upon speaking with current students in the program, she realized that this professor's lab was sometimes not a safe space in terms of professional growth, especially for women:

> When I visited and I talked to [the professor's] graduate students, they actually warned me away from him. They told me that it's very stressful working for him, because he was very stingy with his money and would make his students pay out of their own pocket to go to conferences and stuff. And sometimes he wouldn't credit his students' work. And his male students actually told me that it happened more frequently with his female students. And as much as this guy has done, and as much as I wanted to try theory, I honestly just don't want to put up with crap like that. That's not why I'm in grad school. (Originally cited in Ko et al. 2014:179)

Nina's proactive approach enabled her to avoid being in a situation where she might have been entrenched in a relationship with an unsupportive, and potentially undermining, advisor. She then sought out schools that offered advisors with reputations of being good mentors, as well as departments that were understanding, and supportive, of gender issues. When visiting schools, she studied the gender balance of the students, took note of the number of women faculty, and asked about whether or not the female faculty were actively supportive of the women students. In the end, Nina enrolled in a graduate program where she felt welcome, and where she had the company of several female peers and faculty.

Participating in STEM Diversity Conferences

A majority of the women of color in our study used the agentic strategy of participating in STEM diversity conferences. Regional and national STEM diversity conferences can offer critical counterspaces for those who often do not feel they belong in their own programs (Ko et al. 2014). A comment by Lexie, a black and Asian American graduate student in computer science, succinctly illustrates this notion:

> I think towards the end [of my undergraduate career], I would go to more diversity conferences, like the Richard Tapia conference or the Grace Hopper conference, where I got to see a huge ballroom full of women in computer science, or a huge ballroom full of minorities in computer science. I just didn't feel like I fit [into my former home department]. . . . And there's something special, too, right, about connecting with people that are similar in a way that most people aren't . . . going to the Richard Tapia conference, the last time

I went there it was a blast, it was fantastic. . . . I felt like I belonged at that conference. I felt like I was supposed to be there, like anyone else there, and it was really great meeting them all. And just knowing that they probably go through some of the same stuff I do, and just, it felt really cool.

In this comment, Lexie contrasts the lack of fit within her former home department, with a strong sense of belonging and connecting with other underrepresented persons in computing at these diversity conferences. Furthermore, diversity conferences can allow women of color and members of other underrepresented groups to feel that they can be "whole," bringing together at once all of their social, cultural, and professional identities. Chloe, a postdoctoral fellow in physics, spoke about the importance of attending the National Society of Black Physicists as a student: "It was a safe space where I can actually be a person of color and be a physicist at the same time and not have anyone question my commitment to either identity" (partially quoted in Ko et al. 2014:184). Jade, a black undergraduate in computer science, also commented on her experience at the ACM Richard Tapia Celebration of Diversity in Computing, comparing it to her recent experience at a more mainstream conference in her subfield:

[Tapia is] very relaxed socially, it's not tense. At [the mainstream conference] everyone was rushing around and it was just a lot. [At Tapia] it's more laid back, you don't feel like anybody is thinking, "Oh, we didn't know Black people did computing!" Everybody is walking around trying to learn something so it's a very laid-back atmosphere. It's not a bad thing to have fun, everybody is laughing, talking, smiling. You don't have to be so serious at Tapia.

At a counterspace like Tapia, especially in contrast to the mainstream conference, Jade felt consistently recognized by others as a black female computer scientist; she did not have to worry about others' perceptions of her, and her joint social and academic identities were not questioned. The absence of worrying about others' perceptions of her, or feeling the need to monitor or manage these perceptions, contributed to her sense that the Tapia computing conference was "laid back." Jade's comment underscores the importance for women of color to be in a space where their intellectual abilities and belonging in STEM are readily accepted, instead of second guessed. We believe that the opportunity to feel "whole" in a STEM diversity conference like Tapia crucially contributed to Jade's sense of comfort.

Building Alternative Academic and Professional Networks

As mentioned above, research studies have documented the experiences of isolation, exclusion, and negative interactions that women of color have in their STEM environments; these alienating experiences can lead to anemic academic and professional networks that could negatively impact their abilities to persist and succeed. In our study, we found that rather than passively lamenting their diminished networks, women of color proactively, and thoughtfully, built their academic and professional networks using alternative means. For many of them, this meant leaning more heavily on minority peers or advanced colleagues in the same field. For example, Serena, an Asian American postdoctoral fellow in computer science education, spoke of how, as an undergraduate, she and other minorities were excluded from most study groups in computer science. She and two of the other minority undergraduates, a Black man and a Black woman, formed their own study group and helped one another throughout the rest of their undergraduate careers:

> In my computer science class, a lot of the projects were group [work] and so I found two . . . [minority] teammates who were heaven-sent. And we stuck by each other and actually, after we found each other, planned all of our schedules in sync with each other, so we took the same classes in order to get through the undergraduate experience together. Because a part of being a minority is that people don't want to work with you. They don't look at you and sense that you are a smart person they want to work with. So finding people who believe in you and [whom] you believe in, and then sticking together, was really important. (Originally quoted in Ong 2011:33)

While some women of color, like Serena, chose to work closely with peers, others reached out to advanced members of their field. Valencia, a Native American and Latina graduate student, recounted struggling academically and feeling isolated as an upper division undergraduate in engineering. Fearing that she might confirm any perceived notions of intellectual inferiority, she felt that she could not reveal to her peers or professors that she was close to failing. Instead, Valencia took action in reaching out to a Latina postdoctoral student, and this relationship likely changed the course of her schooling:

> So it was [in] my junior year as an undergrad that I finally just reached out to a Latina who was a post-doc at the time. . . . I didn't know her that well, but I just emailed her and I was like, "Look, no one knows I'm doing bad, but I'm doing bad and I need help and I don't know who to turn to. And I'm afraid I

might have to drop out." And so she emailed me back: "Call me." She's like, "Okay, let's meet." And so we met and she was just like, "Look, it's not that you aren't good enough to be here. You are. It's just that you need some"—she would always say this—"tools in your toolbox. It's like you want to build a house and you can have all the desire and effort to build a house, but if you don't have the right tools, you're not going to get anywhere." So she really helped me clarify a lot what was going on internally. I was like, "Am I just messing up? I've been working so hard but yet I'm still getting bad grades. I'm busting my butt but I'm not getting anywhere." So she was really the one to teach me these kinds of tools in [my] toolbox. Like, time management or goal planning. You know, just looking at the long-term things and which resources to go to.

Rather than quietly and passively "leaking out" of the STEM pipeline, Valencia took the proactive measure to reach out and find help from someone who identified with her and who supported her academically as well as socially. The Latina postdoctoral fellow made herself immediately available and re-casted Valencia's experiences of "doing bad" as simply an absence of "tools in [her] toolbox." Then she took time to teach Valencia these missing tools. Through her actions, the postdoctoral mentor, who sustained a relationship with Valencia over the years, served as a critical support that ultimately kept Valencia on the engineering path.

When support is not available nearby to women of color, STEM diversity conferences and organizations, such as those described above, can serve as resources for alternative network building, especially for junior scholars. Chloe credited her persistence and success in physics to her alternative network of senior black scientists, whom she met through the National Society of Black Physicists: "A good professional relationship with people who took an active interest in making sure that I get through the field was incredibly important."

Temporarily Leaving the STEM Realm

The STEM realm perpetuates the myth that, in the single-minded pursuit of scientific truth, the ideal worker is one who is always thinking about and doing STEM, is always present and available in the workplace, and is always ready to travel for the sake of STEM. Additionally, there is a tacit expectation that the ideal worker will readily sacrifice personal time and time with family in order to meet the demands of work (AstroBetter 2012; Ceci and Williams 2010; Kachchaf et al. 2015). While the ideal worker norm may be an ideal or a myth, in our research, we came across many stories that illustrated the "all work all the time" practice, such as the extreme example of one participant's supervisor who missed the birth of his child to collect routine data (Kachchaf et al. 2015). Such high expectations may be stifling and unappealing to many, but they are especially so to women of color in STEM, who are often isolated and encounter frequent negative interactions with peers and supervisors in their learning and work environments (Kachchaf et al. 2015). To persist in STEM, one agentic strategy that women in our study employed was to temporarily leave the STEM realm.

Some women surreptitiously pursued hobbies, often not sharing or downplaying these outside enjoyments with their STEM colleagues and supervisors. Hobbies included reading fiction, gourmet cooking, traveling, bird watching, learning how to dance, exercising (one participant became a yoga instructor on the side), and participating in musical activities, such as choir or a Native American drumming circle. Valencia explained how critical it was for her to discover and participate in a Native American drumming circle on her campus: "Even if I am that one person in that one [engineering] class, I'll at least have a group somewhere on campus, even if they're in a different field, knowing that I could relate to them and go to them and feel that same sense of community." Luz Martinez-Miranda, an engineering professor with degrees in music performance and physics, espoused the values of having time to devote to non-STEM activities:

> I've spent most of my life playing the piano. In fact, I received my bachelor's degree in music [and physics] while at the University of Puerto Rico. I know for me, having another interest was nice because it got my head out of just doing science-related studies. I don't believe that one's life can always be about work! (Originally cited in Ko et al. 2014:186)

The majority of women of color in our study who discussed outside activities echoed Martinez-Miranda's claim. Rejecting the pervasive "all STEM, all the time" myth enabled them to persist and succeed when they were focused on their STEM work (Ko et al. 2014).

Engaging in Activism

More than half the women in our sample reported participating in activism, which our projects defined as "STEM-related volunteer work." Our prior work (Ko et al. 2014; Ong 2005) and the research of others (e.g., Baez 2000; Ceglie 2011) found that activism aided women of color in persisting in STEM, changing departmental culture, and giving back to their communities. Additionally, past studies have shown that minorities and women often enter faculty positions with a stronger commitment to social justice compared to their white, male majority counterparts (Park 1996) and that community members, and the institutions themselves, expect them to be involved as leaders and advocates (Foster-Fishman and Stevens 2002). Indeed, our study participants reported that they engaged in activism for social justice purposes—to increase the numbers of girls and women, minorities, and girls and women of color in STEM—but they also did it as a way to keep *themselves* persisting in STEM.

Activism manifested in activities such as giving motivational talks, teaching, and serving as role models. As an example of giving motivational talks, Diana Garcia-Prichard, a Latina physicist, often spoke to high school girls to encourage them to explore non-traditional careers and to get experience in project-based physics. Joan Robinson Berry, a black engineer, said, "I have used my own experience to convince young people that math and science are not as hard as they think and that engineers are not nerds. . . . I want to open doors and help people to reach their potential, especially young people who come from underrepresented groups." Robinson Berry has often told young people: "If I can become an engineer, so can you." Sandra Begay-Campell, a Native American engineer, has also used her life experiences to help guide young women of color:

> I began with a clear academic plan to become an engineer, but it was a rocky road of challenges. I can speak only from my experiences, which can teach other women of color, particularly American Indian women, that you may stumble and fall from your life's path yet still get back up and continue on.

Teaching others was an agentic strategy of activism that led to greater confidence and a sense of making a difference. Chloe reflected on how teaching more junior students increased her confidence and helped her realize her own STEM knowledge base: "It's actually very heartening when you realize, 'Well, at least somebody in the room thinks I know what I'm talking about'" (originally cited in Ko et al. 2014:188). Ashley, a black undergraduate in engineering, had plans to teach as a form of activism in her future. She said:

> I feel like more people should love math, like I do. And I think if I was to teach it, I could express my love to more people. And hopefully they would catch on and love it. Because I tutor and I just see the bad foundation that a lot of teachers give their students. And it makes them hate math. I think if they could love it, then we would have more people in the science and STEM fields. You know? I want to give back in that sense.

Serving as a role model was another type of activism. Nell, a black senior in engineering, illustrated the responsibility she felt was placed upon her to serve as a role model. When she struggled in her studies and thought about quitting STEM and school, she was motivated to persist by thoughts of her younger relatives: "All my other siblings weren't in college yet, so it was like, 'Nell, this wouldn't be a good look. Disappointing all your cousins and your siblings [who will] think that, "Oh no, I can't do college because Nell can't do college."' I think that was a big push."

Activism was usually found to be a positive, enjoyable, and agentic way for women of color to increase diversity and persist in STEM; however, the institutions that employed these women did not always reward it. For instance, we found for women of color in careers, activism was not typically considered as a significant contribution for promotion or tenure and therefore did not always assist in career advancement (Ko et al. 2014; also Baez 2000). Nevertheless, we found that almost without exception, the women in our study who participated in activism had no regrets and aimed to continue engaging in activism.

Conclusion

In this chapter, we have brought into high relief the ways in which women of color can be active agents on their own respective STEM roadways. The women described in our study were agents and advocates for their own persistence and success through the ways that they chose to learn and work in safe, welcoming STEM environments; sought out counterspaces in STEM diversity conferences; built alternative academic and professional networks; temporarily left STEM; and participated in activism. Their narratives, which profoundly illuminate their agentic strategies, allow us to forcefully reject any allusions to passivity suggested by the "leaky pipeline" metaphor. Instead, the evidence of our research fits much better into Branch's (2013) roadway model, as the model acknowledges that outcomes are dependent upon the women of color's agency as well as environmental conditions (Malcom and Malcom 2011).

By striving to understand the experiences and agentic strategies of women of color, many leaders of STEM departments and workplaces can identify gaps in the support structures and begin to fill them. Some steps they may take, drawing directly from the work presented in this chapter, include:[3]

- Create and maintain an environment that is welcoming to all. Increase diversity at all levels, including students, faculty, administrators, and staff. Nurture a local culture that affirms all participants' STEM abilities and has a zero tolerance for any acts of racism, sexism, or other biases.

- Support the participation of women of color in campus, regional, and national STEM diversity organizations and events. Be aware of upcoming events and encourage them to attend. Fund their membership fees to STEM diversity organizations and fund their attendance at STEM diversity conferences.
- Model and promote a more balanced lifestyle that includes a healthy mix of outside-of-STEM activities. Prohibit punishment of those who reveal outside-of-STEM activities. Create policies that allow for non-STEM time and flexibility in work schedules.
- Support women of color who participate in activism. Make activism a part of the institutional mission and create institutional opportunities for STEM-related volunteerism. Eliminate career-advancement penalties related to activism. Instead, value activism as an institutional service and/or scholarship-as-outreach component of the promotion and tenure package. Be specific and clear about what types of activism will count, or not count, toward promotion and tenure (e.g., leading an afterschool science program for underresourced girls vs. sitting on an advisory board). As with any other part of a career portfolio, outreach will need to be documented, with descriptions and evidence about its significance and goals, context, new scholarship, and other outcomes, including impact on the community, the institution, and the woman of color herself (see Foster-Fishman and Stevens 2002).

In spite of the challenges that women of color in our research faced, they each exercised agency and actively influenced the journeys on their STEM roadways. However, it is not fair, nor is it reasonable, to expect that individual women of color should put forth all of the effort in their promotion and success in STEM. Institutional leaders committed to diversifying their organizations and increasing the quality of STEM through diversity must change the environmental climate—STEM's roadway conditions—to ensure that all feel supported and that they belong.

Notes

1. We thank Mindy Anderson-Knott, Enobong Hannah Branch, Jodut Hashmi, Patricia Wonch Hill, Mary Anne Holmes, Nuria Jaumot-Pascual, Rachel Kachchaf, Irene Liefshitz, Julia McQuillan, and Janet Smith for supporting us in the overall

project and for providing feedback on earlier drafts of this chapter and helping in its development. We are also very grateful to the participants in our research who provided both inspiration and thoughtful responses, and to our project advisors who critically guided the development of our projects. This material is based upon work supported by the National Science Foundation under Grant Nos. NSF-DRL 0909762, NSF-CNS 1451341, and NSF-EEC-1427129. Any opinions, findings, and conclusions or recommendations expressed in this material are those of the authors and do not necessarily reflect the views of the National Science Foundation. Please send all correspondence regarding this chapter to Maria Ong, maria_ong@terc.edu.

2. Subjects from extant texts—public documents—are referred to by their real names. Interviewees are referred to by pseudonyms. A full reference list of our extant texts can be found at https://www.terc.edu/display/Library/Extant+text+references+for+Narratives+of+the+Double+Bind.

3. In an earlier paper, we provided detailed advice to women of color who wished to persist in STEM and to STEM departments and organizations that wished to increase their numbers of women of color and to broaden participation in STEM. Some of these ideas are mentioned here. For those seeking more ideas, we refer them to Ko, et al. 2014.

~

CHAPTER TWELVE

Smooth Roads to Promotion

Creating Data-Guided and Community-Generated Changes for Eliminating Bumps and Potholes

Julia McQuillan, Mary Anne Holmes,
Patricia Wonch Hill, and Mindy Anderson-Knott

How can universities improve the roads, road signs, and maps to help recruit, retain, and promote women in science, technology, engineering, and math (STEM) departments? There are no easy answers (Dean and Koster 2014). The National Science Foundation (NSF) ADVANCE program institutions have been working on the challenge of increasing women in STEM fields since 2001. Our university (the University of Nebraska-Lincoln) joined the community of NSF ADVANCE-Institutional Transformation (IT) funded programs in 2008. ADVANCE-IT awards are designed to transform STEM departments and institutional practices and policies to reduce the known barriers to success for STEM women faculty.

ADVANCE awards are wide-ranging and complex, with many elements designed to transform different parts of the institution while engaging key stakeholders in the transformation (e.g., Holmes 2014). To obtain, successfully carry out, and evaluate our ADVANCE-Nebraska project, we developed a theory of change based on Risman's (2004) model of gender at the individual, interactional, and institutional level (described in more detail below). Our logic model detailed levers for change at each level and ways to assess whether interventions were achieving desired increases in the numbers of STEM women faculty. We also assessed whether interventions led to unintended negative consequences. We adjusted our interventions and logic model based upon formative evaluation results.

We conceptualize the process as similar to making a map to guide efforts to increase satisfaction and a desire to stay and be successful in our STEM departments. As with map making, when our understanding of the terrain changed we changed our map. Our process involved self-study, an honest assessment of the study results, and ongoing formative evaluation to adjust course on the road to an equitable, enjoyable workplace.

Creating a Roadmap

How did we create and follow our roadmap? As described in our earlier chapter, "Does the Road Improve in the Land of the Tenured?" (see chapter 4), we held informal gatherings with STEM women faculty to learn their perspectives and needs, consistent with community-based participatory research practices. Based upon those conversations, we were concerned that the few (N=19) full professor women in STEM fields were isolated and several had rocky processes (e.g., having to sue to get tenure). Few had mentors or explicit guides in their careers. Follow-up surveys of men and women STEM faculty showed that for women faculty, positive department culture and intention to stay scores are lower at higher rank (assistant, associate, full).

There are two possible explanations for this: 1) that as rank increases, dissatisfaction increases over time or 2) that the surprising decline in a desire to stay with higher rank reflects an historical artifact. The first indicates that there is something about either the duration of time in the academy, or within the process of promotion and tenure, that is associated with dissatisfaction for women more than men. Conversely, because this is not longitudinal data, it may be that we are seeing a cohort effect. Women who are now full professors were often the first or only women in their department, and therefore the pattern could be an anachronism that will disappear with new cohorts even if departments make no changes. The low numbers of women in academic positions in the past has slowly begun to change, but as recently as 2013 the Association of American Universities (Carr 2013) reported that only one-third of full professors in the United States are women; in STEM fields, women comprise only 13 percent of full professors (2010–2012 cohort), barely an increase from 10 percent in the 2004–2006 cohort.

Data and reports of the negative department cultures for STEM women from a variety of institutions abound; explanations vary from explicit discrimination to implicit bias (e.g., Monroe, Ozyurt, Wrigley, and Alexander 2008; Roos and Gatta 2009; Valian 1998). But are things better now? Do the processes of obtaining tenure and promotion continue to disadvantage women? Does the process itself traumatize those who go through it? We find more evidence for ongoing challenges, but acknowledge that when many current full professor women, particularly in STEM, began their careers department and institutional climates were much worse.

Acknowledging, analyzing, and attempting to improve department cultures to support all faculty could result in improved satisfaction. Alternatively, examining and reporting problems could increase dissatisfaction because of more clarity that things could be better (Seigel 1996). We conceptualize the process of digging up information on problems and constructing new routes, signs, and guides as the necessary price for long-term improvements.

Reviewing prior studies as well as our surveys and focus groups, we identified several "bumps" in the road that might explain why higher ranked women might have lower satisfaction than their male peers:

1. Women perceive that they need to have exceptional promotion files in order to overcome the assumption that women are not as good as men in STEM fields;
2. Women face increased implicit bias as status inconsistency increases (at higher ranks the disparity between "woman" and "professor" becomes larger);
3. Women are often given higher service and teaching loads than men, which take more time and receive less recognition;
4. No longer perceived as "little sisters," women tend to experience more isolation with higher rank (see chapter 4);
5. Often family demands (e.g., school-aged children, aging parents), which disproportionately impact women, overlap with transitions to associate and full professor.

The Tenure and Promotion Processes

It is possible that the tenure and promotion process itself creates stress and frustration among women more so than for men. Because women often do not fit the "ideal worker" model of faculty (Williams 2000), they could try harder and worry more about additional scrutiny. Some women described having "scars" from the process of putting together their files and criticism from their colleagues about their records. Similar reports of feeling "beat up" by the promotion review process are consistent with data from other institutions (Roos and Gatta 2009; Monroe et al. 2008).

There are several actions that institutions and departments can take to reduce unnecessary stress from promotion processes. An ambiguous "line" that faculty have to clear to earn promotion opens up more room for implicit biases to influence the process. *Having more clear expectations* allows faculty creating promotion packages to have a sense of their likelihood of obtaining promotion. Second, *providing annual feedback and discussing plans toward full professor* should help faculty have a realistic sense of their chances of earning promotion and reduce the likelihood of "surprises." Third, *having university-wide sessions for creating promotion files* has several benefits. All of the attendees will get the same information, helping to produce a level playing field. In addition, attendees should feel less alone in the process of putting together their file. Any other practices and processes that can help make the promotion process routine, professional, and gender neutral should help minimize the likelihood of "scars" from the process.

Status Inconsistency and Continuing Implicit Bias

Implicit associations between STEM disciplines and (white) men often means that women are "framed" more by gender than by their status as faculty (Ridgeway 2011). The associations are usually automatic and implicit, leading to dynamics of status inconsistency. STEM faculty, particularly full professors, occupy a high status position. Yet because men are the presumed "ideal worker" (Williams 2000; Williams, Phillips, and Hall 2014), women must work harder to be seen as worthy of the respect afforded their full professor status, rather than their lower status as a woman. The difference between their self-perception (full professor) and perception by others (woman) creates status inconsistency, thus contributing to perceptions of disrespect (Berger, Blackwell, Norman, and Smith 1992).

Status inconsistency can lead to lower job satisfaction, because experiencing more respectful treatment is associated with higher job satisfaction (Henry 2011). Status inconsistency can also create discomfort in the faculty who must reconcile how to interact with someone who simultaneously occupies a low and high status, thus possibly leading to avoidance (see the section on isolation). Recent research by Kasumovic and Kuznekoff (2015) found evidence that in highly competitive environments where women are in the minority (in this case, online gaming) women were more likely to be treated with hostility by underperforming men than their male counterparts in identical scenarios. The authors suggest that "low-status males increase female-directed hostility to minimize the loss of status as a consequence of hierarchical reconfiguration resulting from the entrance of a woman into the competitive arena" (Kasumovic and Kuznekoff 2015).

Ridgeway (2011) points out the importance of status—differences in esteem and respect—as well as money and power, in trying to unwrap gender inequality. Holleran, Whitehead, Schmader, and Mehl (2011) found that both men and women are less likely to discuss research with women "around the water cooler" in STEM departments resulting in "isolation" and lack of information dissemination. When such conversations did occur, both men and women perceived the woman speaker as less competent than men, indicating the ongoing influence of implicit bias in the lives of STEM faculty women. Rhoton (2011) found that "successful" women faculty in STEM disciplines consider sacrifice, toughness, and out-manning men to just be a part of the process of a successful career. Yet they may face dashed hopes if they think that the process of having to prove one's self over and over ends with tenure (Williams et al. 2014). STEM women report that their departmental colleagues perceive them as less productive than the men in the department even when women are equally productive (Riffle, Schneider, Hillard, Polander, Jackson, DesAutels, and Wheatly 2013).

Riffle et al. (2013) further reported that STEM women perceive themselves as having less influence on their department and experience less collegiality. Women particularly perceive greater exclusion from academic departments with a low representation of women (Maranto and Griffin 2011). Several STEM departments in our institution contained only one or two women. The common suggestion that faculty should self-promote to advance their careers often results in more success for men but backlash for women (Moss-Racusin and Rudman 2010). Having more women in a department can help to reduce the salience of gender, normalize women in the field, and make the faculty, rather than the gender, status more dominant in interactions. Cluster hiring is one way to quickly increase the number of women in a department; a shorter-term plan may involve bringing in several women as colloquium speakers.

Isolation

Isolation may persist or increase for women at the full professor rank, since there are fewer women in leadership positions in academia (Currie, Thiele, and Harris 2002), but evidence suggests that having more women in leadership positions at a given institution leads to a tendency to having more women at higher ranks among the faculty (Bilen-Green, Froelich, and Jacobson 2008). The opposite may also be true, however, a lack of women at the top leads to fewer women in the pipeline to join or replace them.

Maranto and Griffin (2011) report that women feel a chillier climate when there are fewer women in the department. Malcom and Malcom-

Piqueux (2013) discuss the importance of "critical mass" in achieving diversity in STEM fields and that a mindful effort must be made to achieve self-sustaining diversity. Holmes, O'Connell, Frey, and Ongley (2008) found that simple numbers did not affect gender parity: the types of lifestyles represented mattered too. Some of the women in our focus groups described greater isolation from colleagues with each promotion. Departments could find ways to create more connections among associate and full professors, such as assigning mentors, or creating opportunities for "group" mentoring in which the full professors meet collectively with associate professors about roles and expectations.

Disproportionate Workloads

There is a well-documented tendency in the workplace to associate women with "housekeeping" and "motherly" roles, such as undergraduate advising and curriculum, certification programs, every woman student graduate committee, etc. (Pyke 2011). Service is, in fact, faculty governance, and must be appropriately valued, rewarded, and equitably shared (Gappa, Austin, and Trice 2007). Pyke (2011) describes how "gender equity" work at academic institutions overloads women and people from underrepresented groups with service work to serve as the requisite "woman" or "minority."

Many studies have documented the disproportionate service load, without disproportionate compensation, among faculty women (e.g. Bird, Litt, & Wang 2004; West and Curtis 2006; Britton 2012; Pyke 2011). Several of the women in our focus groups described disproportionate service for women. One woman said: *"They [men] are not asked to do as much service. And when they refuse to do service they are allowed to refuse to do it. And when I say I can't do it I am told I am really not doing enough."* Yet not all of them wanted less service. Some described enjoying service work and seeiing it as important; their frustration was that the department and their colleagues did not value and appreciate the service contributions.

There are several ways that universities and departments can value service work. First, some institutions provide service pathways to promotion. Second, at the associate and full professor level, allowing faculty to change their apportionment to reflect greater service demands should contribute to better evaluations and raises. Third, nominating faculty for service-related awards promotes a sense that service contributions are recognized and appreciated. Fourth, if departments report "kudos" for teaching and research, they should also report "kudos" for service contributions.

Family Demands and Promotion Demands Often Overlap

Combining family and lab work is more difficult for women than for men because promotion often overlaps with higher family care demands and the gendered division of labor assigns care work to women (Fox 2010; Monroe et al. 2008). Many academic women report that managing the household, lack of personal time, and the demands of child care as well as elder care are sources of stress for them (Gappa et al. 2007). Borland and Bates (2014) found that only family responsibility differences by gender could explain lower job satisfaction for women faculty at predominantly undergraduate institutions, because service loads, networks, and mentorship appeared equivalent between men and women. Although a higher proportion of men than women faculty in at least one research-intensive institution are parents (Wonch Hill, Holmes, and McQuillian 2014), the care of young children interferes with research time more for women, thus inhibiting the central route to promotion (Misra, Lundquist, and Templer 2012). Across all ranks, women more than men report academic and family stress with little institutional support for work-life balance (O'Laughlin and Bischoff 2005). Creating and supporting work-life policies, therefore, are important for retaining women through full professorship.

Newer generations of faculty, often dual career couples, may find both partners engaging in care work and thus work-life policies could become more relevant for men as well. Less than 10 percent of male faculty, at one research-intensive Midwest institution, have full-time stay-at-home wives (Wonch Hill et al. 2014). On-site, affordable child care, stipends for child care for conference travel, resources for elder care options, and recognition that dependent care responsibilities can slow the work necessary for promotion to full professor, are all ways that institutions can change to reflect contemporary faculty realities.

The only metric where women at full professor scored higher than men is for having enough department resources. The ADVANCE toolkit requires an extensive analysis of the resources that faculty have. Our evaluation team found no significant differences in resources between men and women faculty; therefore we expect that perception matches reality in our case. Yet each institution should do their own analysis; for example, an MIT (1999) report found that among the faculty at MIT, women had fewer resources than men. Monitoring salaries, space, and resources, and asking for an accounting of discrepancies between men and women, is a powerful way to encourage departments to ensure that faculty are compensated and supported based upon performance, not gender.

There are many factors that we did not fully explore with our limited data. For example, we could not specify discipline. We did observe, however, that some faculty reported departmental climate challenges, while others described a positive climate with supportive department members and chair. Particular contexts likely contribute to differences in perceptions of culture and satisfaction (Sabharwal and Corley 2009). We also do not know which faculty had access to formal mentoring pre-tenure, but such support should contribute to higher satisfaction among assistant professors (Blau, Currie, Croson, and Ginther 2010). Because we were particularly interested in women who are full professors and this is a very small group (N=19), we did not do multivariate analyses. Combining the survey results with the focus group results did, however, help to illuminate some of the factors that contribute to lower satisfaction for higher rank women STEM faculty.

Strategies for Institutional Change

At the end of the description of each "bump" or "pothole" described above, we provided some specific strategies for improving the roads for faculty across gender and rank. Here we describe our ADVANCE team strategies for institutional change. Beginning with the third round of NSF-ADVANCE IT grants, programs were required to have a social science conceptual framework for their projects. The goal was to make interventions with successful impacts potentially transferrable to other institutions, even non-academic institutions. We used Risman's (2004) "gender as a social structure" model, plus insights from social psychological theories of social networks and implicit biases, to guide our project.

Risman's model conceptualizes gender at three levels: individual, interactional, and institutional. The individual component addresses how individuals identify their capabilities and expectations of gender. The interactional level addresses how people "do gender" in interaction with others through gendered lenses, and incorporates the impact of implicit assumptions about how people should behave based on sex category. The institutional component arises from interactions that form and evolve with the institution, including practices and policies that can have differential impacts on men and women.

Guided by the gender as a social structure framework, we provided professional development activities to address the individual component. For the interactional component and the low hiring rates of women, we addressed the search process by using the University of Michigan's STRIDE (Stewart, La Vaque-Manty, and Malley 2004) and the University of Wisconsin's

WISELI programs as models (Sheridan, Fine, Pribbenow, Handelsman, and Carnes 2010). We promoted informal networking via luncheons (as per the University of Washington) to reduce women's sense of isolation and promote informal peer mentoring across the campus (Yen, Quinn, Carrigan, Litzler, and Riskin 2007). We provided workshops and trainings for search committee members and department chairs/heads to address the interactional component. Our STEM faculty committees as well as our leadership team created our program "Best Practice Documents" to help implement new policies and procedures to address the institutional component.

We did not, at first, devise different efforts by rank. Yet reviewing our evaluation reports from prior activities, surveys of department chairs, surveys of faculty, focus groups, and input from faculty on ADVANCE committees, we decided to try and rank specific programs. We first created a "conversation series" that included topics relevant to faculty at all ranks and ones for specific career stages. We chose the label "conversation" rather than "workshop" to make the events more collegial and collaborative. We invited faculty who had success in an area (e.g., starting a lab, mentoring relationships, working with graduate students, international collaborations) to lead the conversations.

In the spirit of community-based participatory research, we invited department chairs to "data breakfasts" to review the data we had compiled on specific departments and on faculty overall, and asked for their ideas about the most effective ways to increase women in their departments. We also asked how they thought faculty satisfaction could be improved, particularly for associate professors and full professor women. We had a luncheon with just the full professor women (seventeen of nineteen attended) and asked them their thoughts on our findings and what the university and their departments could do to improve work satisfaction.

The data gathering and conversations produced many ideas. We were not able to act on all of them, but have encouraged ongoing units (e.g., the Chancellor's Commission on the Status of Women) to continue to work for change. For example, one participant explained that in her department everyone reads and discusses the tenure file, but only the tenured faculty vote. This level of inclusion and transparency helps the pre-tenure faculty to know what is expected and what they need to do to earn tenure. We could offer this approach to department chairs, but could not require such practices unless the University Regents decided to change university level policies.

Faculty also described how at different times in the history of the university, teaching, service, or research has been more or less valued. The heavier service burdens with promotion, particularly when they take away from research and do not seem to be valued, are particularly discouraging to faculty. But many did not ask for less service work; rather, they wanted higher value for the work and more equitable distribution of service demands, for example by more rotation of leadership roles.

The UNL STEM Women Focus groups also led to a series of specific recommendations for the senior administrative team at the university (e.g., provost and deans). We recommended paying attention to committee assignments so that women faculty are asked to serve on committees and in positions that build careers (e.g., executive committees, Tenure and Promotion committees, Graduate Advisor), not only those that do university "housekeeping." Encouraging deans to ask department chairs to review the service loads of faculty at regular intervals will help hold departments accountable for rotating more and less career-building assignments and not systematically letting those who try to avoid service roles "off the hook. " We recommended, but have not yet succeeded, in adopting the "Equity Advisors" approach to paying attention to diversity on search committees. Because equity advisors are trained to focus on processes that interrupt implicit bias they should have more positive influence on search processes than having token members of groups (e.g., "a woman" and/or "a racial/ethnic minority") on committees. Equity advisors may be men or women, minority or majority, and thus provide a way to have greater sharing of the responsibility to focus on excellence through diversity.

At the departmental/interactional level, strategies include having regular faculty meetings (e.g., every three years) to discuss and clarify tenure requirements, including all faculty in discussion of promotion files (but only the promoted vote), and clear, written expectations. At the university or college level, it is valuable to host annual workshops on the promotion process with examples of dossiers and binders with all of the sections that should be included in the dossier. At our university, all departments are currently required to include documents that explain their promotion and tenure procedures and criteria in their academic program reviews (every seven years); these documents could be reviewed more often and made available to all department faculty annually.

In addition to general promotion and tenure workshops, hosting annual "Pathways to Promotion" workshops in each college, for chairs and faculty who are associate professors, will help clarify the process to and benefits of timely promotion to full professor, and encourage chairs to support faculty on their path. The benefits of promotion serve the faculty member (e.g., recognition, increased salary) and the department (e.g., additional role models, additional mentors, eligibility for more awards and leadership roles).

Many departments need reminders about how to appropriately review candidates for promotion. Universities should provide clear guidelines about what can and cannot be discussed (e.g., our policies require the discussion to focus only on what is in the file). In addition, because work-life balance policies such as stop-the-clock are more recent, departments need reminders about how to consider faculty who have had family-related leaves. Universities could also include language in the standard letters to external letter writers that describes how they should consider work-life balance leaves. Providing guidance to department chairs about what components of a file should be evaluated and in what way, as well as what are appropriate and what are inappropriate discussion points, will also be helpful. Exemplar departments use formal "rubrics" for evaluation of promotion to make expectations very clear and to minimize the impact of implicit bias

We expect that there are even more possible changes that our institution could make, and that similar data gathering would reveal ideas unique to other places. Recognizing that the way that work is organized often reflects implicit assumptions about who will occupy the position (Acker 1990), we assumed that the changing characteristics of faculty (e.g., more women, more elder care responsibilities, more dual-career faculty, more mobile faculty) should be reflected in changes to the way that universities organize and support faculty work (Gappa et al. 2007). The ideas provided here reflect the themes from the survey and focus group data at our institution. We have borrowed solutions from others as well as developing our own. We hope that other institutions can gather data on the experiences of their faculty so that they can better assess the practices and procedures that facilitate or inhibit faculty satisfaction.

~

References

Abbiss, Jane. 2008. "Rethinking the 'Problem' of Gender and IT Schooling: Discourses in Literature." *Gender and Education* 20(2): 153–165.

Acker, Joan. 1990. "Hierarchies, Jobs, Bodies: A Theory of Gendered Organizations." *Gender and Society* 4(2): 139–158.

Acker, Joan. 1991. *Doing Comparable Worth: Gender, Class, and Pay Equity*. Philadelphia: Temple University Press.

Ackers, Louise. 2004. "Managing Relationships in Peripatetic Careers: Scientific Mobility in the European Union." *Women's Studies International Forum* 27(3): 189–201.

Adams, Jonathan. 2013. "Collaborations: The Fourth Age of Research." *Nature* 497 (7451): 557–560.

Aguirre, Adalberto Jr. 2000. *Women and Minority Faculty in the Academic Workplace: Recruitment, Retention, and Academic Culture*. ASHE-ERIC Higher Education Report, Volume 27, Number 6. Jossey-Bass Higher and Adult Education Center.

Alberts, Bruce, Marc W. Kirschner, Shirley Tilghman, and Harold Varmus. 2014. "Rescuing US Biomedical Research from its Systemic Flaws." *Proceedings of the National Academy of Sciences* 111(16): 5773–5777.

Allen-Ramdial, Stacy-Ann A., and Andrew G. Campbell. 2014. "Reimagining the Pipeline: Advancing STEM Diversity, Persistence, and Success." *BioScience* 64(7): 612–618.

Alstete, Jeffrey W. 2000. *Posttenure Faculty Development: Building a System for Faculty Improvement and Appreciation*. San Francisco: Jossey-Bass.

Anderson, Melissa S., Karen Seashore Louis, and Jason Earle. 1994. "Disciplinary and Departmental Effects on Observations of Faculty and Graduate Student Misconduct." 65(3): 331–350.

Arbesman, Samuel, and K. Brad Wray. 2012. "Demographics and the Fate of the Young Scientist." *Social Studies of Science* 43(2): 282–286.

Aronson, Joshua, Michael J. Lustina, Catherine Good, Kelli Keough, Claude M. Steele, and Joseph Brown. 1999. "When White Men Can't Do Math: Necessary and Sufficient Factors in Stereotype Threat." *Journal of Experimental Social Psychology* 35(1): 29–46.

Astin, Helen, and Linda J. Sax. 1996. "Developing Scientific Talent in Undergraduate Women." In *The Equity Equation: Fostering the Advancement of Women in the Sciences, Mathematics, and Engineering*, edited by C. S. Davis, A. Ginorio, C. Hollenshead, B. Lazarus, and P. Rayman. San Francisco: Jossey-Bass.

AstroBetter. 2006. "Not What We Want." Retrieved June 25, 2013 (http://www.astrobetter.com/not-what-we-want/).

August, Louise, and Jean Waltman. 2004. "Culture, Climate, and Contribution: Career Satisfaction Among Female Faculty." *Research in Higher Education* 45(2): 177–192.

Austin, Ann E. 2002. "Preparing the Next Generation of Faculty: Graduate School as Socialization to the Academic Career." *The Journal of Higher Education* 73(1): 94–122.

Austin, Ann E., and Melissa McDaniels. 2006. "Preparing the Professoriate of the Future: Graduate Student Socialization for Faculty Roles." In *Higher Education: Handbook of Theory and Research*, vol. XXI, edited by J. C. Smart. Netherlands: Springer.

Awando, Maxwell, Ashley Wood, Elsa Camargo, and Peggy Layne. 2014. "Advancement of Mid-Career Faculty Members: Perceptions, Experiences, and Challenges." In *Gender Transformation in the Academy*, vol. 19, *Advances in Gender Research*, edited by V. Demos, C. W. Berheide, and M. T. Segal. Bingley, UK: Emerald Publishing Group Limited.

Babbie, Earl R. 2009. *The Practice of Social Research*. Belmont, CA: Wadsworth Publishing.

Baez, Benjamin. 2000. "Race-related Service and Faculty of Color: Conceptualizing Critical Agency in Academe." *Higher Education* 39(3): 363–391.

Bailyn, Lotte. 2003. "Academic Careers and Gender Equity: Lessons Learned from MIT." *Gender, Work and Organizations* 10(2): 137–153.

Baldwin, Roger, Deborah DeZure, Allyn Shaw, and Kristin Moretto. 2008. "Mapping the Terrain of Mid-Career Faculty at a Research University: Implications for Faculty and Academic Leaders." *Change* 46: 55.

Baldwin, Roger G., Christina J. Lunceford, and Kim E. Vanderlinden. 2005. "Faculty in the Middle Years: Illuminating an Overlooked Phase of Academic Life." *The Review of Higher Education* 29 (1): 97–118.

Balka, Ellen, and Richard Smith. 2000. *Women, Work, and Computerization: Charting a Course for the Future.* Boston: Kluwer.

Bandura, Albert, Claudio Barbaranelli, Gian Vittorio Caprara, and Concetta Pastorelli. 2001. "Self-Efficacy Beliefs as Shapers of Children's Aspirations and Career Trajectories." *Child Development* 72(1): 187–206.

Banerjee, Payal. 2006. "Indian Information Technology Workers in the United States: The H-1B Visa, Flexible Production and the Racialization of Labor." *Critical Sociology* 32(2–3): 427–447.

Barker, Lecia J., Charlie McDowell, and Kimberly Kalahar. 2009. "Exploring Factors that Influence Computer Science Introductory Course Students to Persist in the Major." *ACM SIGCSE Bulletin* 41(2): 282–286.

Battelle. 2014. "Battelle/BIO State Bioscience Jobs, Investments and Innovation 2014." Retrieved on March 21, 2015. (https://www.bio.org/sites/default/files/Battelle-BIO-2014–Industry.pdf).

Beaton, Ann, Francine Tougas, Natalie Rinfret, Nathalie Huard, and Marie-Noelle Delisle. 2007. "Strength in Numbers? Women and Mathematics." *European Journal of Psychology of Education* 22(3): 291–306.

Becher, Tony. 1987. "The Disciplinary Shaping of the Profession." In *The Academic Profession: National, Disciplinary, and Institutional Settings*, vol. 15, edited by Burton R. Clark. Berkeley: University of California Press.

Beede, David, Tiffany Julian, David Langdon, George McKittrick, Beethika Khan, and Mark Doms. 2011. *Women in STEM: A Gender Gap to Innovation.* Washington, D.C.: U.S. Department of Commerce Economics and Statistics Administration.

Berger, Joseph, James W. Blackwell, Robert Z. Norman, and Roy F. Smith. 1992. "Status Inconsistency in Task Situations: A Test of Four Status Processing." *American Sociological Review* 57(1): 843–855.

Berheide, Catherine White, and Cay Anderson-Hanley. 2012. "Doing It All: The Effects of Gender, Rank, and Department Climate on Work-Family Conflict for Faculty at Liberal Arts Colleges." In *Social Production and Reproduction at the Interface of Public and Private Spheres*, vol. 16, *Advances in Gender Research* edited by M. T. Segal, E. N. Chow, and V. Demos. Bingley, UK: Emerald Group Publishing Limited.

Berheide, Catherine White, Lisa Christenson, Rena Linden, and Una Bray. 2013. "Gender Differences in Promotion Experiences at Two Elite Private Liberal Arts Colleges in the United States." *Forum on Public Policy* 1: 1–19.

Berheide, Catherine White, and Rena Linden. 2015. "Do Work/Life Policies Matter? The Importance of Work/Life Policies for Reducing Faculty Intentions to Quit." In *Family Friendly Policies and Practices in Academe*, edited by C. R. Solomon and E. Anderson. Lanham, MD: Lexington Books.

Berheide, Catherine W., and Susan Walzer. 2014. "Processes and Pathways: Exploring Promotion to Full Professor at Two Liberal Arts Colleges in the United States." In *Gender Transformation in the Academy*, vol. 19, *Advances in Gender*

Research, edited by V. Demos, C. W. Berheide, and M. T. Segal. Bingley, UK: Emerald Publishing Group Limited.

Berryman, Sue. 1983. "Who Will Do Science? Trends and Their Causes in Minority and Female Representation Among Holders of Advanced Degrees in Science and Mathematics." New York: Rockefeller Foundation.

Bilen-Green, Canan, Karen A. Froelich, and Sarah W. Jacobson. 2008. "The Prevalence of Women in Academic Leadership Positions, and Potential Impact on Prevalence of Women in the Professorial Ranks." Women in Engineering ProActive Network. Retrieved on March 21, 2015 (http://journals.psu.edu/wepan/article/viewFile/58533/58221).

Bilimoria, Diana, Susan R. Perry, Xiangfen Liang, Eleanor Paolo Stoller, Patricia Higgins, and Cyrus Taylor. 2006. "How Do Female and Male Faculty Construct Job Satisfaction? The Roles of Perceived Institutional Leadership and Mentoring and Their Mediating Processes." *Journal of Technology Transfer* 31:355–365.

Bilimoria, Diana, and Xiangfen Liang. 2012. *Gender Equity in Science and Engineering: Advancing Change in Higher Education*. New York: Routledge.

Bird, Sharon R. 2011. "Unsettling Universities' Incongruous, Gendered Bureaucratic Structures: A Case-study Approach." *Gender, Work and Organization* 18(2): 202–230.

Bird, Sharon, Jacquelyn S. Litt, and Yong Wang. 2004. "Creating Status of Women Reports: Institutional Housekeeping as 'Women's Work.'" *NWSA Journal* 16(1): 194–206.

Blau, Francine D., Janet M. Currie, Rachel T. Croson, and Donna K. Ginther. 2010. "Can Mentoring Help Female Assistant Professors? Interim Results from a Randomized Trial (No. w15707)." National Bureau of Economic Research.

Blau, Peter Michael, and Otis Dudley Duncan. 1967. *The American Occupational Structure*. New York: Wiley.

Blickenstaff, Jacob Clark. 2005. "Women and Science Careers: Leaky Pipeline or Gender Filter." *Gender and Education* 17(4): 369–386.

Borland, Elizabeth, and Diane C. Bates. 2014. "Emerging Gender Parity and Persistent Differences: Cultural Shifts among Faculty Cohorts at a Primarily Undergraduate Institution." In *Gender Transformation in the Academy*, vol. 19, *Advances in Gender Research*, edited by V. Demos, C. W. Berheide, and M. T. Segal. Bingley, UK: Emerald Publishing Group Limited.

Bozeman, Barry, and Monica Gaughan. 2011. "Job Satisfaction among University Faculty: Individual, Work, and Institutional Determinants." *The Journal of Higher Education* 82(2): 154–186.

Branch, Enobong Hannah. 2011. *Opportunity Denied: Limiting Black Women to Devalued Work*. New Brunswick: Rutgers University Press.

Branch, Enobong Hannah. 2013. "A Road Instead of a Pipeline? Incorporating Agency and Constraint into Our Understanding of Women in Science." Paper presented at the Women in Science Mini-Conference at the Eastern Sociological Society Meeting, March 23, Boston, MA.

Branskamp, Larry, and John Ory. 1994. *Assessing Faculty Work: Enhancing Individual and Institutional Performance*. San Francisco, CA: Jossey-Bass.

Brayton, Sean. 2008. "'Mexican Labor in the Hollywood Imaginary." *International Journal of Cultural Studies* 11(4): 459–476.

Brewer, Marilynn B., and Rupert J. Brown. 1998. "Intergroup Relations." In *The Handbook of Social Psychology*, vol. 15, edited by Daniel T. Gilbert, Susan T. Fiske, and Gardner Lindzey. New York: McGraw-Hill.

Britton, Dana M. 2010. "Engendering the University through Policy and Practice: Barriers to Promotion to Full Professor for Women in the Science, Engineering and Math Disciplines." In *Gender Change in Academia: Remapping the Fields of Work, Knowledge, and Politics from a Gender Perspective*, edited by B. Riegraf, B. Aulenbacher, E. Kirsch-Auwärter, and U. Müller, 15–26. Weisbaden, Germany: VS Verlag für Sozialwissenschaften.

Britton, Dana M. 2012. "Keeping Rank." *Contexts* 11(4): 66–67.

Brown, Shirley V. 2000. "The Preparation of Minorities for Academic Careers in Science and Engineering: How Well Are We Doing?" In *Access Denied: Race, Ethnicity, and the Scientific Enterprise*, edited by G. Campbell, R. Denes, and C. Morrison. New York: Oxford University Press.

Browne, Irene, and Joya Misra. 2003. "The Intersection of Gender and Race in the Labor Market." *Annual Review of Sociology* 29: 487.

Buch, Kimberly, Yvette Huet, Audrey Rorrer, and Lynn Roberson. 2011. "Removing the Barriers to Full Professor: A Mentoring Program for Associate Professors." *Change: The Magazine of Higher Learning* 43(6): 38–45

Budig, Michelle J. 2002. "Male Advantage and the Gender Composition of Jobs: Who Rides the Glass Escalator?" *Social Problems* 49(2): 258–277.

Bunton, Sarah A., and April M. Corrice. 2011. "Perceptions of the Promotion Process: An Analysis of U.S. Medical School Faculty." *Analysis in Brief* 11: 1–2. Washington, D.C.: Association of American Medical Colleges.

Burke, Ronald J., and Mary C. Mattis (eds.). 2007. *Women and Minorities in Science, Technology, Engineering, and Mathematics: Upping the Numbers*. Northampton, MA: Edward Elgar Publishing.

Burrelli, Joan. 2009. "Women of Color in STEM Education and Employment." Paper presented at the Mini-Symposium on Women of Color in STEM, October 27, Arlington, VA.

Calavita, Kitty. 2000. "The Paradoxes of Race, Class, Identity, and 'Passing': Enforcing the Chinese Exclusion Acts, 1882–1910." *Law and Social Inquiry* 25(1): 1–40.

Callister, Ronda Roberts. 2006. "The Impact of Gender and Department Climate on Job Satisfaction and Intentions to Quit for Faculty in Science and Engineering Fields." *Journal of Technology Transfer* 31: 367–375.

Cambrosio, Alberto, and Peter Keating. 1988. "'Going Monoclonal': Art, Science, and Magic in the Day-to-Day Use of Hybridoma Technology." *Social Problems* 35(3):244–260.

Canale, Anne Marie, Cheryl Herdklotz, and Lynn Wild. 2013. "Mid-career Faculty Support: The Middle Years of the Academic Profession." Rochester, NY: Faculty Career Development Services, the Wallace Center, Rochester Institute of Technology. Retrieved on March 21, 2015 (https://www.rit.edu/academicaffairs/facultydevelopment/sites/rit.edu.academicaffairs.facultydevelopment/files/images/FCDS_Mid-CareerRpt.pdf).

Canales, Alejandro. L. 2007. "Inclusion and Segregation: The Incorporation of Latin American Immigrants into the U.S. Labor Market." *Latin American Perspectives* 34(1): 73–82.

Canes, Brandice, and Harvey Rosen. 1995. "Following in Her Footsteps? Faculty Gender Composition and Women's Choices of College Majors." *Industrial and Labor Relations Review* 48: 486–504.

Carli, Linda L. 2006. "Gender Issues in Workplace Groups: Effects of Gender and Communication Style on Social Influence." In *Gender and Communication at Work*, edited by M. Barrett and M. J. Davidson. England: Ashgate Publishing Limited.

Carlone, Heidi B., and Angela Johnson. 2007. "Understanding the Science Experiences of Successful Women of Color: Science Identity as an Analytic Lens." *Journal of Research in Science Teaching* 44(8): 1011–1245.

Carr, Jennifer Z., Aaron M. Schmidt, J. Kevin Ford, and Richard P. DeShon. 2003. "Climate Perceptions Matter: A Meta-Analytic Path Analysis Relating Molar Climate, Cognitive and Affective States, and Individual Level Work Outcomes." *Journal of Applied Psychology* 88(4): 605–619.

Carr, Rebecca. 2013. "Women in the Pipeline for Science, Technology, Engineering and Math: Nationally and at AAUDE Institutions." Association of American Universities Data Exchange. Retrieved on March 21, 2015 (http://aaude.org/system/files/documents/public/reports/report-2013–pipeline.pdf).

Carroll, Wendy, and Albert Mills. 2006. "Gender Identity, the Culture of Organizations, and Women's IT Careers." In *Encyclopedia of Gender and Information Technology*, edited by E. M. Trauth. Hershey, PA: Idea Group Reference.

Case, Susan S., and Bonnie Ann Richley. 2013. "Barriers to Women in Science: Examining the Interplay between Individual and Gendered Institutional Research Cultures on Women Scientists Desired Future." In *Gender in Organizations: Are Men Allies or Adversaries to Women's Career Advancement?* Cheltenham, UK: Edward Elgar.

Catanzarite, Lisa. 2000. "Brown-Collar Jobs: Occupational Segregation and Earnings of Recent-Immigrant Latinos." *Sociological Perspectives* 43(1): 45–75.

Cech, Erin, Brian Rubineau, Susan Sibley, and Caroll Seron. 2011. "Professional Role Confidence and Gendered Persistence in Engineering." *American Sociological Review* 76(5): 641–666.

Ceci, Stephen J., Wendy M. Williams, and Susan M. Barnett 2009. "Women's Underrepresentation in Science: Sociocultural and Biological Considerations." *Psychological Bulletin* 135(2): 218–261.

Ceci, Stephen J., and Wendy M. Williams. 2010. *The Mathematics of Sex: How Biology and Society Conspire to Limit Talented Women and Girls.* New York: Oxford University Press.

Ceci, Stephen J., and Wendy M. Williams. 2011. "Understanding Current Causes of Women's Underrepresentation in Science." *Proceedings of the National Academy of Sciences* 108(8): 3157–3162.

Ceglie, Robert. 2011. "Underrepresentation of Women of Color in the Science Pipeline: The Construction of Science Identities." *Journal of Women and Minorities in Science and Engineering* 17(3): 271–293.

Chalabaev, Aina, Brenda Major, Phillipe Sarrazin, and Francois Cury. 2012. "When Avoiding Failure Improves Performance: Stereotype Threat and the Impact of Performance Goals." *Motiv Emot* 36: 130–142.

Charles, Maria, and David B. Grusky. 2004. *Occupational Ghettos: The Worldwide Segregation of Women and Men.* Stanford, CA: Stanford University Press.

Charmaz, Kathy. 2006. *Constructing Grounded Theory: A Practical Guide through Qualitative Analysis.* Sage Publications Limited.

Chatterjee, Anusuya, and Ross C. DeVol. 2012. "Estimating Long-Term Economic Returns of NIH Funding on Output in the Biosciences." *The Milken Institute.*

Cheryan, Sapna, Benjamin J. Drury, and Marissa Vichayapai. 2013. "Enduring Influence of Stereotypical Computer Science Role Models on Women's Academic Aspirations." *Psychology of Women Quarterly* 37: 72 29.

Cheryan, Sapna, Paul Davies, Victoria Plaut, and Claude Steele. 2009. "Ambient Belonging: How Stereotypical Cases Impact Gender Participation in Computer Science." *Journal of Personality and Social Psychology* 97(6): 1045–1060.

Cheryan, Sapna, and Victoria C. Plaut. 2010. "Explaining Underrepresentation: A Theory of Precluded Interest." *Sex Roles* 63: 475–488.

Cheryan, Sapna, Victoria C. Plaut, Caitlin Handron, and Lauren Hudson. 2013. "The Stereotypical Computer Scientist: Gendered Media Representations as a Barrier to Inclusion for Women." *Sex Roles: A Journal of Research* 69: 58–71.

Choo, Hae Yeon, and Myra Marx Ferree. 2010. "Practicing Intersectionality in Sociological Research: A Critical Analysis of Inclusions, Interactions, and Institutions in the Study of Inequalities." *Sociological Theory* 28(2): 129–149.

Clegg, Sue, Deborah Trayhurn, and Andrea Johnson. 2000. "Not Just For Men: A Case Study of the Teaching and Learning of Information Technology in Higher Education." *Higher Education* 40: 123–145.

Cohen, Phillip N., and Matt L. Huffman. 2007. "Working for the Woman? Female Managers and the Gender Wage Gap." *American Sociological Review* 72(5): 681–704.

Cohoon, J. McGrath, and William Aspray. 2006. "A Critical Review of the Research into Women's Participation in Postsecondary Computing Education." In *Women and Information Technology: Research on Under-Representation*, edited by J. M. Cohoon and W. Aspray. Cambridge, MA: The MIT Press.

Colatrella, Carol. 2011. "Gender Equality, Family/Work Arrangements, and Faculty Success in Danish Universities." *The Journal of the Professoriate* 4(2): 23–46.

Collaborative on Academic Careers in Higher Education (COACHE). 2006. "COACHE Highlights Report." Cambridge, MA: Harvard University.

Collins, Harry M. 1974. "The TEA Set: Tacit Knowledge and Scientific Networks." *Social Studies of Science* 4(2): 165–185.

Collins, Harry M. 1992. *Changing Order: Replication and Induction in Scientific Practice.* Chicago: University of Chicago Press.

Collins, Harry M. 2001. "Tacit Knowledge, Trust and the Q of Sapphire." *Social Studies of Science* 31(1): 71–85.

Collins, Harry M., and Robert Evans. 2002. "The Third Wave of Science Studies: Studies of Expertise and Experience." *Social Studies of Science* 32(2): 235–296.

Collins, Harry M., and Robert Evans. 2007. *Rethinking Expertise.* Chicago: University of Chicago Press.

Collins, Patricia Hill. 1986. "Learning from the Outsider Within: The Sociological Significance of Black Feminist Thought." *Social Problems* 33(6): S14–S32.

Collins, Patricia Hill. 1990. *Black Feminist Thought: Knowledge, Consciousness, and the Politics of Empowerment.* Boston, MA: Unwin Hyman.

Collins, Patricia Hill. 2004. *Black Sexual Politics: African Americans, Gender, and the New Racism.* New York: Routledge.

Committee on Equal Opportunities in Science and Engineering. 2009. *Broadening Participation in America's STEM Workforce.* Arlington, VA: National Science Foundation. Retrieved March 1, 2015 (http://www.nsf.gov/od/oia/activities/ceose/reports/2008CEOSE_BiennialReport.pdf).

Congressional Record. 1882. 47th Congress, 1st Session. Washington, D.C. "Full Committee Hearing—Competitiveness and Innovation on the Committee's 50th Anniversary with Bill Gates, Chairman of Microsoft." 110th Cong., March 12th, 2008. (Written Testimony of William H. Gates Chairman, Microsoft Corporation and Co-Chair, Bill & Melinda Gates Foundation Before the Committee on Science and Technology United States House of Representatives).

Cooke, Donna K., Randi L. Sims, and Joseph Peyrefitte. 1995. "The Relationship Between Graduate Student Attitudes and Attrition." *The Journal of Psychology* 129(6): 677–688.

Cooper, Joel. 2006. "The Digital Divide: The Special Case of Gender." *Journal of Computer Assisted Learning* 22: 320–334.

Corley, Elizabeth A., and Meghna Sabharwal. 2007. "Foreign-Born Academic Scientists and Engineers: Producing More and Getting Less than Their U.S.-Born Peers?" *Research in Higher Education* 48(8): 909–940.

Correll, Shelley J. 2001. "Gender and the Career Choice Process: The Role of Biased Self-Assessments." *American Journal of Sociology* 106(6): 1691–1730.

Costas, Ilse, Céline Camus, and Stephanie Michalczyk. 2013. "The Mobility Discourse as a New Public Management Strategy: Gender Impacts on Academics in German and France." In *Die unternehmerische Hochschule aus der Perspektive der*

Geschlechterforschung: Zwischen Aufbruch und Beharrung, edited by Kristina Binner, Bettina Kubicek, Anja Rozwandowicz, and Lena Weber, 137–151. Münster: Westfählisches Dampfboot.

Creswell, John. 2012. *Planning, Conducting, and Evaluating Quantitative and Qualitative Research*, 4th edition. Los Angeles, CA: Pearson Publications.

Crosby, Faye and Linda Nyquist. 1977. "The Female Register: An Empirical Study of Lakoff's Hypotheses." *Language and Society* 6(3): 313–322.

Cullen, Deborah L., and Gaye Luna. 1993. "Women Mentoring in Academe: Addressing the Gender Gap in Higher Education." *Gender and Education* 5(2): 125–137.

Currie, Jan, Bev Thiele, and Patricia Harris. 2002. *Gendered Universities in Globalized Economies*. Lanham, MD.: Lexington Books

Daniels, Ronald J. 2015. "A Generation at Risk: Young Investigators and the Future of the Biomedical Workforce." *Proceedings of the National Academy of Sciences* 112(2): 313–318.

Dasgupta, Nilanjana. 2011. "Ingroup Experts and Peers as Social Vaccines Who Inoculate the Self-Concept: The Stereotype Inoculation Model." *Psychological Inquiry* 22(4): 231–246.

Dean, Donna J., and Janet B. Koster. 2013. *Equitable Solutions for Retaining a Robust STEM Workforce: Beyond Best Practices*. New York: Academic Press.

Desai, Sreedhari D., Dolly Chugh, and Arthur Brief. 2012. "Marriage Structure and Resistance to the Gender Revolution in the Workplace." Retrieved on March 1, 2015 (http://c.ymcdn.com/sites/www.newonline.org/resource/resmgr/research/marriageandgenderdiversity.pdf).

De Welde, Kristine, and Andi Stepnick (eds.) 2014. *Disrupting the Culture of Silence*. Sterling, VA: Stylus.

Dhanaraj, Charles, Marjorie A. Lyles, H. Kevin Steensma, and Laszlo Tihanyi. 2004. "Managing Tacit and Explicit Knowledge Transfer in IJVs: The Role of Relational Embeddedness and the Impact on Performance." *Journal of International Business Studies* 35(5): 428–442.

Dreyfus, Stuart E. 2004. "The Five-Stage Model of Adult Skill Acquisition." *Bulletin of Science, Technology and Society* 24(3): 177–181.

Eaton, Susan C. 1999. "Surprising Opportunities: Gender and the Structure of Work in Biotechnology Firms." *Annals of the New York Academy of Sciences* 869(1): 175–188.

Ecklund, Elaine H., Anne E. Lincoln, and Cassandra Tansey. 2012. "Gender Segregation in Elite Academic Science." *Gender and Society* 26(5): 693–717.

Edwards, Paul N. 1990. "The Army and the Microworld: Computers and the Future of Gender Identity." *Signs: Journal of Women in Culture and Society* 16: 102–127.

Ehrenberg, Ronald G., and Michael J. Rizzo. 2003. *Who Bears the Growing Cost of Science at Universities?* Cambridge, MA: National Bureau of Economic Research.

Ellemers, Naomi, Henriette Van den Heuvel, Dick de Gilder, Anne Maass, and Alessandra Bonvini. 2004. "The Underrepresentation of Women in Science:

Differential Commitment or the Queen Bee Syndrome?" *British Journal of Social Psychology* 43: 315–38.

Emerson, Robert M., Rachel I. Fretz, and Linda L. Shaw. 1995. *Writing Ethnographic Fieldnotes*. Chicago: University of Chicago Press.

Engel, Beverly. 2001. *The Power of Apology: Healing Steps to Transform All Your Relationships*. New York: Wiley.

Ensmenger, Nathan. 2010. "Making Programming Masculine." In *Gender Codes: Why Women are Leaving Computing*, edited by T. J. Misa. New York: John Wiley and Sons.

Ericsson, K. Anders. 2006. "An Introduction to the Cambridge Handbook of Expertise and Expert Performance: Its Development, Organization, & Content." In *The Cambridge Handbook of Expertise and Expert Performance*, edited by K. A. Ericsson, N. Charness, P. Feltovich, and R. R. Hoffman. Cambridge: Cambridge University Press.

Ernst and Young. 2014. "Beyond Borders: Unlocking Value—Biotechnology Industry Report 2014." *Ernst and Young*. Retrieved March 5, 2015 (http://www.ey.com/gl/en/industries/life-sciences).

Espinosa, Lorelle L. 2011. "Pipelines and Pathways: Women of Color in Undergraduate STEM Majors and the College Experiences that Contribute to Persistence." *Harvard Educational Review* 81(2): 209–241.

Espiritu, Yen Le. 1997. *Asian American Women and Men: Labor, Laws and Love*. Thousand Oaks, CA: Sage Publications.

Esteban-Marquillas, J. M. 1972. "A Reinterpretation of Shift-share Analysis." *Regional and Urban Economics* 2(3): 249–261.

Etzkowitz, Harry, Carol Kemelgor, and Brian Uzzi. 2000. *Athena Unbound: The Advancement of Women in Science and Technology*. Cambridge: Cambridge University Press.

Evans, Robert. 2008. "The Sociology of Expertise: The Distribution of Social Fluency." *Sociology Compass* 2(1): 281–298.

Fernandez, Roberto M., and M. Lourdes Sosa. 2005. "Gendering the Job: Networks and Recruitment at a Call Center." *American Journal of Sociology* 111(3): 859–904.

Ferreira, Maria. 2003. "Gender Issues Related to Graduate Student Attrition in Two Science Departments." *International Journal of Science Education* 25(8): 969–989.

Fields, Barbara J. 1990. "Slavery, Race and Ideology in the United States of America." *New Left Review* 181: 95–118.

Finn, Michael G. 2014. "Stay Rates of Foreign Doctorate Recipients from U.S. Universities, 2011." Science Education Programs, Oak Ridge Institute for Science and Education. Retrieved March 5, 2015. http://orise.orau.gov/files/sep/stay-rates-foreign-doctorate-recipients-2011.pdf

Fiske, Susan T. 1998. "Stereotyping, Prejudice, and Discrimination." In *The Handbook of Social Psychology*, vol. 15, edited by D. T. Gilbert, S. T. Fiske, and G. Lindzey. New York: McGraw-Hill.

Foster-Fishman, Pennie G., and Dannelle D. Stevens. 2002. "Outreach in a New Light: Documenting the Scholarship of Application." In *Tenure in the Sacred Grove: Issues and Strategies for Women and Minority Faculty*, edited J. E. Cooper and D. D. Stevens. Albany, NY: State University of New York Press.

Fox, Mary Frank. 2001. "Women, Science, and Academia: Graduate Education and Careers." *Gender and Society* 15(5): 654–666.

Fox, Mary Frank. 2003. "Gender, Faculty, and Doctoral Education in Science and Engineering." In *Equal Rites, Unequal Outcomes: Women in American Research Universities*, edited by L. Hornig. New York: Kluwer Academic/Plenum Publishers.

Fox, Mary Frank. 2005. "Gender, Family Characteristics, and Publication Productivity among Scientists." *Social Studies of Science* 35(1): 131–150.

Fox, Mary F. 2010. "Women and Men Faculty in Academic Science and Engineering: Social-Organizational Indicators and Implications." *American Behavioral Scientist* 53: 997–1012.

Fox, Mary Frank. 2015. "Gender and Clarity of Evaluation Among Academic Scientists in Research Universities." *Science, Technology, and Human Values* 40(4): 487–515.

Fox, Mary Frank, and Carol Colatrella. 2006. "Participation, Performance, and Advancement of Women in Academic Science and Engineering: What Is at Issue and Why." *Journal of Technology Transfer* 31: 377–86.

Fox, Mary Frank, and Catherine A. Faver. 1984. "Independence and Cooperation in Research: The Motivations and Costs of Collaboration." *The Journal of Higher Education* 55 (3): 347–359.

Fox, Mary Frank, and Sushanta Mohapatra. 2007. "Social-organizational Characteristics of Work and Publication Productivity among Academic Scientists in Doctoral-granting Departments." *The Journal of Higher Education* 78(5): 542–571.

Fox, Mary Frank, Gerhard Sonnert, and Irina Nikiforova. 2009. "Successful Programs for Undergraduate Women in Science and Engineering: *Adapting* versus *Adopting* the Institutional Environment." *Research in Higher Education* 50: 333–353.

Fox, Mary Frank, Gerhard Sonnert, and Irina Nikiforova. 2011. "Programs for Undergraduate Women in Science and Engineering: Issues, Problems, and Solutions." *Gender and Society* 25: 589–615.

Fox, Mary Frank, and Wenbin Xiao. 2013. "Perceived Chances for Promotion Among Women Associate Professors in Computing: Individual, Departmental, and Entrepreneurial Factors." *Journal of Technology Transfer* 38: 135–152.

Fox, Kristin M., Catherine White Berheide, Kimberly Frederick, and Brenda Johnson. 2010. "Adapting Mentoring Programs to the Liberal Arts College Environment." In *Mentoring Strategies to Facilitate the Advancement of Women Faculty*, edited by K. Karukstis, B. Gourley, M. Rossi, and L. Wright. Washington, D.C.: American Chemical Society.

Frehill, Lisa, and J. McGarth Cohoon. 2015. "Gender and Computing." In *Advancing Women in Science: An International Perspective*, edited by W. Pearson, L. Frehill, and C. McNeely. New York: Springer.

Frehill, Lisa M., Sorina Vlaicu, and Kathrin Zippel. 2010. "International Scientific Collaboration: Findings from a Survey of NSF Principal Investigators." In Report for National Science Foundation, OISE 0936970.

Frehill, Lisa M., and Kathrin S. Zippel. 2011. "Gender and International Collaborations of Academic Scientists and Engineers: Findings from the Survey of Doctorate Recipients, 2006." *Journal of the Washington Academy of Sciences* 97(1): 49–69.

Frome, Pamela M., Corinne J. Alfeld, Jacquelynne S. Eccles, and Bonnie L. Barber. 2006. "Why Don't They Want a Male-Dominated Job? An Investigation of Young Women Who Changed their Occupational Aspirations." *Educational Research and Evaluation* 12(4): 359–372.

Frome, Pamela M., and Jacquelynne S. Eccles. 1998. "Parent's Influence on Children's Achievement-Related Perceptions." *Journal of Personality and Social Psychology* 74(2): 435–452.

Gappa, Judith M., Ann E. Austin, and Andrea G. Trice. 2007. *Rethinking Faculty Work: Higher Education's Strategic Imperative.* San Francisco: Jossey-Bass.

Garrison, Howard H., and Susan A. Gerbi. 1998. "Education and Employment Patterns of US PhD's in the Biomedical Sciences." *The FASEB Journal* 12(2): 139–48.

Garrison, Howard H., Bethany Drehman, and Elisabeth Campbell. 2014. "NIH Research Funding Trends: FY1995–2014." FASEB PowerPoint. Retrieved March 5, 2015 (www.faseb.org/Portals/2/PDFs/opa/2015/NIH Grant Slideshow.pptx).

Garrison, Howard H., and Elisabeth Campbell. 2015. "Education and Employment of Biological and Medical Scientists 2015, Data from National Surveys." FASEB PowerPoint. Retrieved March 5, 2015 (http://www.faseb.org/Policy-and-Government-Affairs/Data-Compilations/NIH-Research-Funding-Trends.aspx).

Geisler, Cheryl, Debbie Kaminski, and Robyn A. Berkley. 2007. "The 13+ Club: An Index for Understanding, Documenting, and Resisting Patterns of Non-Promotion to Full Professor." *NWSA Journal* 19(3): 145–162.

Gibons, Ann. 2014. "Sexual Harassment is Common in Scientific Fieldwork." Retrieved on March 1, 2015 (http://news.sciencemag.org/scientific-community/2014/07/sexual-harassment-common-scientific-fieldwork).

Glenn, Evelyn Nakano. 2002. *Unequal Freedom: How Race and Gender Shaped American Citizenship and Labor.* Cambridge, MA: Harvard University Press.

Goffman, Erving. 1959. *The Presentation of Self in Everyday Life.* New York: Doubleday.

Gómez, Laura. E. 2007. *Manifest Destinies: The Making of the Mexican American Race.* New York: New York University Press.

Good, Catherine, Joshua Aronson, and Jayne Ann Harder. 2008. "Problems in the Pipeline: Stereotype Threat and Women's Achievement in High-level Math Courses." *Journal of Applied Developmental Psychology* 29(1): 17–28.

Good, Catherine, Anne Rattan, and Carol Dweck. 2012. "Why Do Women Opt Out? Sense of Belonging and Women's Representation in Mathematics." *Journal of Personality and Social Psychology* 102(4): 700–717.

Gorman, Elizabeth H. 2005. "Gender Stereotypes, Same-Gender Preferences, and Organizational Variation in the Hiring of Women: Evidence from Law Firms." *American Sociological Review* 70(4): 702–728.

Goulden, Marc, Mary Ann Mason, and Karie Frasch. 2011. "Keeping Women in the Scientific Pipeline." *Annals of the American Academy of Political and Social Science* 638: 141–162.

Government Accountability Office (GAO). 2011. "H-1B VISA PROGRAM: Reforms Are Needed to Minimize the Risks and Costs of Current Program." January 14. Retrieved on March 1, 2015 (http://www.gao.gov/products/GAO-11-26).

Graham, Lindsey O., and Charles E. Schumer. 2010. "The Right Way to Mend Immigration." *Washington Post*, March, 19.

Grahn, Joyce. 1981. "General College Job Satisfaction Survey, University of Minnesota. Summer 1980." *General College Studies* 16(1): 1980–1981.

Griffith, Amanda L. 2010. "Persistence of Women and Minorities in STEM Field Majors: Is It the School that Matters?" *Economics of Education Review* 29(6): 911–922.

Gruer, Denise, and Tracy Camp. 1998. "Investigating the Incredible Shrinking Pipeline for Women in Computer Science." Final Report (Project 9812016) to the National Science Foundation.

Gunter, Ramona, and Amy Stambach. 2003. "As Balancing Act and As Game: How Women and Men Science Faculty Experience the Promotion Process." *Gender Issues* 21(1): 24–42.

Haag, Pamela. 2005. "Is Collegiality Code for Hating Ethnic, Racial, and Female Faculty at Tenure Time?" *The Education Digest* 15: 57–62.

Hackett, Gail, Donna Esposito, and M. Sean O'Halloran. 1989. "The Relationship of Role Model Influences to the Career Salience and Educational Plans of College Women." *Journal of Vocational Behavior* 35: 164–180.

Hagedorn, Linda S. 2000. "Conceptualizing Faculty Job Satisfaction: Components, Theories, and Outcomes." *New Directions for Institutional Research* 2000(105): 5–20.

Haigh, Thomas. 2010. "Masculinity and the Machine Man." In *Gender Codes: Why Women are Leaving Computing*, edited by T. J. Misa. New York: John Wiley and Sons.

Hall, Roberta M., and Bernice R. Sandler. 1982. *The Classroom Climate: A Chilly One for Women? The Project on the Status of Education of Women.* Washington, DC: The Association of American Colleges.

Hanson, Sandra. 1996. *Lost Talent: Women in the Sciences.* Philadelphia, PA: Temple University Press.

Hanson, Sandra L., Maryellen Schaub, and David P. Baker. 1996. "Gender Stratification in the Science Pipeline: A Comparative Analysis of Seven Countries." *Gender and Society* 10(3): 271–290.

Harding, Sandra. 1991. *Whose Science? Whose Knowledge?: Thinking from Women's Lives.* Ithaca, NY: Cornell University Press.

Hargens, Lowell, and J. Scott Long. 2002. "Demographic Inertia and Women's Representation Among Faculty in Higher Education." *Journal of Higher Education* 73: 494–517.

Hayes, Caroline Clark. 2010. "Gender Codes: Prospects for Change." In *Gender Codes: Why Women are Leaving Computing*, edited by T. J. Misra. New York: John Wiley.

Haythornthwaite, Caroline. 2006. "Learning and Knowledge Networks in Interdisciplinary." *Journal of the American Society for Information Science* 57(8): 1079–1092.

Heimeriks, Gaston, and Ron Boschma. 2013. "The Path- and Place-Dependent Nature of Scientific Knowledge Production in Biotech 1986–2008." *Journal of Economic Geography* (Online First): 1–26.

Henry, Patrick Justin. 2011. "The Role of Group-Based Status in Job Satisfaction: Workplace Respect Matters More for the Stigmatized." *Social Justice Research* 24(3): 231–238.

Herzberg, Frederick, Bernard Mausner, and Barbara Bloch Snyderman. 1959. *The Motivation to Work*, 2nd edition. New York: John Wiley and Sons.

Hess, Cynthia, Barbara Gault, and Youngmin Yi. 2013. *Accelerating Change for Women of Color Faculty in STEM: Policy, Action, and Collaboration*. Institute for Women's Policy Research. Retrieved March 1, 2015 (http://www.iwpr.org/publications/pubs/accelerating-change-for-women-faculty-of-color-in-stem-policy-action-and-collaboration/).

Hill, Beverley, Judith Secker, and Fay Davidson. 2014. "Achievement Relative to Opportunity: Career Hijacks in the Academy." In *Gender Transformation in the Academy*, vol. 19, *Advances in Gender Research*, edited by V. Demos, C. W. Berheide, and M. T. Segal. Bingley, UK: Emerald Publishing Group Limited.

Hill, Catherine, Christianne Corbett, and Andresse St. Rose. 2010. *Why So Few? Women in Science, Technology, Engineering, and Mathematics*. Washington, DC: American Association of University Women.

Hirshfield, Laura E., and Tiffany D. Joseph. 2012. "'We Need a Woman. We Need a Black Woman': Gender, Race & Identity Taxation in the Academy." *Gender and Education* 24(2): 213–227.

Hirshfield, Laura E. 2011. *Authority, Expertise, and Impression Management: Gendered Professionalization of Chemists in the Academy*. PhD dissertation, University of Michigan.

Hirshfield, Laura E. 2014. "'She's Not Good with Crying': The Effects of Gender Expectations on Graduate Students' Assessments of Their Principal Investigators." *Gender and Education* 26(6): 601–617.

Hirshfield, Laura E. Forthcoming. "'I Don't Know Everything, But Ethan Would Know': Interactional Style, Expertise, and the Cultural Mismatch for Women Scientists." *NASPA Journal about Women in Higher Education*.

Hirshfield, Laura E. 2010. "'She Won't Make Me Feel Dumb': Identity Threat in a Male-Dominated Discipline." *International Journal of Gender, Science and Technology* 2(1): 5– 24.

Hirshman, Charles, and Morrison G. Wong. 1981. "Trends in Socioeconomic Achievement among Immigrant and Native-Born Asian-Americans, 1960–1976." *The Sociological Quarterly* 22(4): 495–514.

Ho, Colin, and Jay W. Jackson. 2001. "Attitudes toward Asian Americans: Theory and Measurement." *Journal of Applied Social Psychology* 31(8): 1553–1581.

Hogan, Alice, Kathrin S. Zippel, Lisa M. Frehill, and Laura Kramer. 2010. Report of the International Workshop on International Research Collaboration. Washington, DC: National Science Foundation.

Hohman, James, and Michael LaFaive. 2009. "The Michigan Economic Development Corporation: A Review and Analysis." Mackinac Center. Retrieved March 17, 2015 (http://www.mackinac.org/10896).

Holleran, Shannon E., Jessica Whitehead, Toni Schmader, and Matthuas R. Mehl. 2011. "Talking Shop and Shooting the Breeze: A Study of Workplace Conversation and Job Disengagement Among STEM Faculty." *Social Psychological and Personality Science* 2(1): 65–71.

Holmes, Mary Anne. 2014. "Advancing Women in Oceanography: How NSF's ADVANCE Program Promotes Gender Equity in Academia." *Oceanography* 27(4): 30–38.

Holmes, Mary Anne, Suzanne O'Connell, Connie Frey, and Lois Ongley. 2008. "Gender Imbalance in US Geoscience Academia." *Nature Geoscience* 1(2): 79–82.

Hsiehchen, David, Magdalena Espinoza, and Antony Hsieh. 2015. "Multinational Teams and Diseconomies of Scale in Collaborative Research." *Science Advances* 1(8)1–9.

Huber, Mary Taylor. 2002. "Faculty Evaluation and the Development of Academic Careers." *New Directions for Institutional Research* 114: 73–83.

Hur, Hyungjo, Navid Ghaffarzadegan, and Joshua Hawley. 2015. "Effects of Government Spending on Research Workforce Development: Evidence from Biomedical Postdoctoral Researchers" *PLoS One* 10(5): e0124928.

Ibarra, Herminia. 1992. "Homophily and Differential Returns: Sex Differences in Network Structure and Access in an Advertising Firm." *Administrative Science Quarterly* 37(3): 422.

Ignatiev, Noel. 1995. *How The Irish Became White*. New York: Routledge.

Jackson, Judy. 2004. "The Story Is Not in the Numbers: Academic Socialization and Diversifying the Faculty." *NWSA Journal* 16(1): 172–185.

Jacoby, Sally, and Patrick Gonzales. 1991. "The Constitution of Expert-Novice in Scientific Discourse." *Issues in Applied Linguistics* 2(2): 149–181.

Jagacinski, Carolyn M., William K. LeBold, and Gavriel Salvendy. 1988. "Gender Differences in Persistence in Computer-related Fields." *Journal of Educational Computing Research* 4(2): 185–202.

Joens, Heike. 2007. "Transnational Mobility and the Spaces of Knowledge Production: A Comparison of Global Patterns, Motivations and Collaborations in Different Academic Fields." *Social Geography* 2: 97–114.

Jöns, Heike. 2009. "'Brain Circulation' and Transnational Knowledge Networks: Studying Long-term Effects of Academic Mobility to Germany, 1954–2000." *Global Networks: A Journal of Transnational Affairs* 9(3): 315–338.

Johnson, Angela, Jaweer Brown, Heidi Carlone, and Azita K. Cuevas. 2011. "Authoring Identity Amidst the Treacherous Terrain of Science: A Multiracial Feminist Examination of the Journeys of Three Women of Color in Science." *Journal of Research in Science Teaching* 48(4): 339–366.

Johnson, Dawn Rene. 2007. "Sense of Belonging Among Women of Color in Science, Technology, Engineering, and Math Majors: Investigating the Contributions of Campus Racial Climate Perceptions and Other College." PhD dissertation, Department of Counseling and Personnel Services, University of Maryland.

Johnson, Jean M. 1993. *Human Resources for Science and Technology the Asian Region.* Washington, D.C.: National Science Foundation.

Johnson, Judith A. 2013. "Brief History of NIH Funding: Fact Sheet." Washington, DC: Congressional Research Service.

Johnsrud, Linda K. 1995. "Women in Graduate Education: Reviewing the Past, Looking to the Future." *New Directions for Student Services* 72: 69–80.

Johnsrud, Linda K. 2002. "Measuring the Quality of Faculty and Administrative Worklife: Implications for College and University Campuses." *Research in Higher Education* 43(3): 379–395.

Jordan, C. Greer, and Diana Bilimoria. 2007. "Creating a Productive and Inclusive Academic Work Environment." In *Transforming Science and Engineering: Advancing Academic Women* edited by A. Stewart, J. Malley, and D. LaVaque-Manty. Ann Arbor, MT: The University of Michigan Press.

Joseph, Joretta. 2012. "From One Culture to Another: Years One and Two of Graduate School for African American Women in the STEM Fields." *International Journal of Doctoral Studies* 7: 125–142.

Joseph, Tiffany D., and Laura E. Hirshfield. 2011. "'Why Don't You Get Somebody New to Do It?' Race and Cultural Taxation in the Academy." *Ethnic and Racial Studies* 34(1): 121–141.

Justin-Johnson, Carolyn. 2004. *Good Fit or Chilly Climate: An Exploration of the Persistence Experiences of African-American Women Graduates of Predominantly White College Science.* PhD dissertation, Department of Educational Leadership, University of New Orleans.

Kachchaf, Rachel, Lily Ko, Apriel Hodari, and Maria Ong. 2015. "Career-life Balance for Women of Color: Experiences in Science and Engineering Academia." *Journal of Diversity in Higher Education* 8(3): 175–191.

Kannankutty, Nirmala, and Keith R. Wilkinson. 1999. *SESTAT: A Tool for Studying Scientists and Engineers in the United States.* Arlington, VA: National Science Foundation.

Kanter, Rosabeth Moss. 1977. *Men and Women of the Corporation.* New York: Basic Books.

Karp, David A., Lynda Lytle Holmstrom, and Paul S. Gray. 1998. "Leaving Home for College: Expectations for Selective Reconstruction of Self." *Symbolic Interaction* 21(3): 253–276.

Kasumovic, Michael M., and Jeffrey H. Kuznekoff. 2015. "Insights into Sexism: Male Status and Performance Moderates Female-Directed Hostile and Amicable Behaviour." *PloS One*, 10(7): p.e0131613.

Katz, Sandra, David Allbritton, John Aronis, Christine Wilson, and Mary Lou Soffa. 2006. "Gender, Achievement, and Persistence in an Undergraduate Computer Science Program." *SIGMIS Database* 37(4): 42–57.

Keller, Evelyn Fox. 1985. *Reflections on Gender and Science*. New Haven, CT: Yale University Press.

Kelly, Kimberly, and Linda Grant. 2012. "Penalties and Premiums: The Impact of Gender, Marriage, and Parenthood, on Faculty Salaries in SEM and non-SEM Fields." *Social Studies of Science*, 0306312712457111.

Kennelly, Ivy. 1999. "That Single Mother Element: How White Employers Typify Black Women." *Gender and Society* 13(2): 168–192.

Khare, Manorama M., and Linda Owens. 2006. *Faculty Work Climate Survey*. University of Illinois at Chicago. Retrieved October 16, 2008 (www.uic.edu/depts/oaa/faculty/climatesurvey.html).

Kilty, Keith M. 2002. "Race, Immigration, and Public Policy: The Case of Asian Americans." *Journal of Poverty* 6(4): 23–41.

Kling, Kristen C., Janet Shibley Hyde, Carolin J. Showers, and Brenda N. Buswell. 1999. "Gender Differences in Self-esteem: A Meta-analysis." *Psychological Bulletin* 125(4): 475–500.

Kmec, Julie A., Shanyuan Foo, and Amy S. Wharton. 2014. "The Influence of Departmental Culture on Academic Parents' Pro-Work Behaviors." In *Disrupting the Culture of Silence* edited by K. De Welde and A. Stepnick. Sterling, VA: Stylus.

Knorr-Cetina, Karin. 1981. *The Manufacture of Knowledge: An Essay on the Constructivist and Contextual Nature of Science*. Oxford: Pergamon Press.

Ko, Lily T., Rachel R. Kachchaf, Apriel K. Hodari, and Maria Ong. 2014. "Agency of Women of Color in Physics and Astronomy: Strategies for Persistence and Success." *Journal of Women and Minorities in Science and Engineering* (20)2: 171–195.

Kuck, Valerie J. 2001. "Refuting the Leaky Pipeline Hypothesis." *Perspective* 79(47): 71–73.

Kuck, Valerie J., Cecilia H. Marzabadi, Janine P. Buckner, and Susan A. Nolan. 2007. "A Review and Study on Graduate Training and Academic Hiring of Chemists." *Journal of Chemical Education* 84(2): 277–284.

Kulis, Stephen, Diane Sciotte, and Shawn Collins. 2002. "More Than a Pipeline Problem: Labor Supply Constraints and Gender Stratification Across Academic Science Disciplines." *Research in Higher Education* 43: 657–691.

LaFaive, Michael, and James Hohman. 2009. *The Michigan Economic Development Corporation: A Review and Analysis*. Mackinac Center. Retrieved on March 17, 2015 (http://www.mackinac.org/10932).

Lagesen, Vivian. 2006. "The Woman Problem in Computer Science." In *Encyclopedia of Gender and Information Technology*, edited by E. M. Trauth. Hershey, PA: Idea Group Reference.

Lagesen, Vivian. 2007. "The Strength in Numbers: Strategies to Include Women Into Computer Science." *Social Studies of Science* 37: 67–92.

Lambert, Eric G., Nancy Lynne Hogan, and Shannon M. Barton. 2001. "The Impact of Job Satisfaction on Turnover Intent: A Test of a Structural Measurement Model Using a National Sample of Workers." *The Social Science Journal* 38(2): 233–250.

Larivière, Vincent, Chaoqun Ni, Yves Gingras, Blaise Cronin, and Cassidy R. Sugimoto. 2013. "Global Gender Disparities in Science." *Nature* 504(7479): 211–213.

Larson, Magali L. 1979. "The Rise of Professionalism." *Pediatrics* 63(3): 490.

Leaper, Campbell, and Rachael D. Robnett. 2011. "Women Are More Likely Than Men to Use Tentative Language, Aren't They? A Meta-Analysis Testing for Gender Differences and Moderators." *Psychology of Women Quarterly* 35(1): 129–142.

Lee, Marlene. 2014. "Shift-Share Analysis of Growth in U.S. Biomedical Postdoctoral Employment in Research Education Institutions." *Population Reference Bureau*. Retrieved March 5, 2015 (http://www.prb.org/publications/articles/2014/us-biomedical-postdoctoral-employment.aspx).

Leemann, Regula Julia. 2010. "Gender Inequalties in Transnational Academic Mobility and the Ideal Type of an Academic Entrepreneur." *Discourse: Studies in the Cultural Politics of Education* 31(5): 605–625.

Levy, Amir, and Uri Merry. 1986. *Organizational Transformation: Approaches, Strategies, Theories*. New York: Praeger.

Lieberson, Stanley. 1980. *A Piece of the Pie: Blacks and White Immigrants Since 1880*. Berkeley: University of California Press.

Lincoln, Anne E. 2010. "The Shifting Supply of Men and Women to Occupations: Feminization in Veterinary Education." *Social Forces* 88(5): 1969–1998.

Lindberg, Sara M., Janet Shibley Hyde, and Jennifer L. Petersen. 2010. "New Trends in Gender and Mathematics Performance: A Meta-Analysis." *Psychological Bulletin* 136(6): 1123–1135.

Long, J. Scott, Paul D. Allison, and Robert McGinnis. 1979. "Entrance into the Academic Career." *American Sociological Review* 44(5): 816–830.

Long, J. Scott, Paul Allison, and Robert McGinnis. 1993. "Rank Advancement in Academic Careers: Sex Differences and the Effects of Productivity." *American Sociological Review* 58: 703–722.

Lowell, B. Lindsay. 2013. "Skilled Immigration Policy in the United States: Does Policy Admit 'Enough' Skilled." In *Wanted and Welcome? Policies for Highly Skilled Immigrants in Comparative Perspective*, edited by T. Triadafilopous. New York: Springer.

Lubitow, Amy, and Kathrin Zippel. 2014. "Strategies of Academic Parents to Manage Work-Life Conflict in Research Abroad." In *Advances in Gender Research*, edited by M. Segal, C. Berheide, and V. Demos. Bingley, UK: Emerald Books.

Luke, Carmen. 2001. *Globalization and Women in Aacademia: North/West-South/East, Sociocultural, Political, and Historical Studies in Education*. Mahwah, NJ: L. Erlbaum Associates.

Lundeberg, Mary A., Paul W. Fox, and Judith Puncochar. 1994. "Highly Confident But Wrong: Gender Differences and Similarities in Confidence Judgments." *Journal of Educational Psychology* 86(1): 114–121.

Lyman, Stanford M. 2000. "The 'Yellow Peril' Mystique: Origins and Vicissitudes of Racist Discourse." *International Journal of Politics, Culture and Society* 13(4): 683–747.

MacLachlan, Anne J. 2006. "The Graduate Experience of Women in STEM and How It Could Be Improved." In *Removing Barriers: Women in Academic Science, Technology, Engineering, and Mathematics*, edited by J. M. Bystydzienski and S. R. Bird. Bloomington, IN: Indiana University Press.

Mahaffy, Kimberly A. 2004. "Girls' Low Self-Esteem: How Is It Related to Socioeconomic Achievement?" *Gender and Society* 18(3): 309–327.

Malcom, Lindsey E., and Shirley M. Malcom. 2011. "The Double Bind: The Next Generation." *Harvard Educational Review* 81(2): 162–172.

Malcom, Shirley M., Paula Hall, and Janet Brown. 1976. *The Double Bind: The Price of Being a Minority Woman in Science*. Washington, D.C.: American Association for the Advancement of Science.

Malcom, Shirley M., and Lindsey E. Malcom-Piqueux. 2013. "Critical Mass Revisited Learning Lessons From Research on Diversity in STEM Fields." *Educational Researcher* 42(3): 176–178.

Maldonado, Marta Maria. 2009. "'It is Their Nature to Do Menial Labour': The Racialization of 'Latino/a Workers' by Agricultural Employers." *Ethnic and Racial Studies* 32(6): 1017–1036.

Major, Brenda, and Laurie T. O'Brien. 2005. "The Social Psychology of Stigma." *Annual Review of Psychology* 56: 393–421.

Maranto, Cheryl L., and Andrea E. C. Griffin. 2011. "The Antecedents of a 'Chilly Climate' for Women Faculty in Higher Education." *Human Relations* 64(2): 139–159.

Margolis, Jane, and Allan Fisher. 2003. *Unlocking the Clubhouse: Women in Computing*. Cambridge, MA: The MIT Press.

Martinez, Alina, Carter Epstein, Amanda Parsad, and Karla Whittaker. 2012a. "Emerging International Researchers: Findings from the Evaluation of the East Asia and Pacific Summer Institutes Program." Retrieved on March 21, 2015 (https://www.nsf.gov/od/oise/tokyo/reports/EAPSI-Report-Final-Full-4–23–12.pdf).

Martinez, Alina, Carter Epstein, Amanda Parsad, and Karla Whittaker. 2012b. "Evaluation of NSF's International Research Fellowship Program: Final Report." Retrieved on March 21, 2015 (http://abtassociates.com/AbtAssociates/files/58/581035b4–c55a-40b9–bd09–98b23cb59321.pdf).

Massey, Douglas S. 2007. *Categorically Unequal: The American Stratification System*. New York: Russell Sage Foundation.

Mathews, Kiernan R. 2014. "Perspectives on Midcareer Faculty and Advice for Supporting Them." Cambridge, MA: The Collaborative on Academic Careers in Higher Education. Retrieved on March 1, 2015 (http://scholar.harvard.edu/files/kmathews/files/coache_mathews_midcareerfaculty_20140721.pdf).

Matloff, Norman. 2013. "Are Foreign Students the 'Best and the Brightest'? Data and Implications for Immigration Policy." *Economic Policy Institute*, February 28. Retrieved January 7, 2016 (http://www.epi.org/publication/bp356-foreign-students-best-brightest-immigration-policy/).

Matthews, Kristin R., Kara M. Calhoun, Nathan Lo, and Vivian Ho. 2010. "The Aging of Biomedical Research in the United States." *PLoS One* 6(12): E29738.

McArdle, Elaine. 2008. "The Freedom to Say 'No.'" Retrieved on March 1, 2015 (http://www.boston.com/bostonglobe/ideas/articles/2008/05/18/thefreedomtosayno/?page=4).

McIlwee, Judith, and J. Gregg Robinson. 1992. *Women in Engineering: Gender, Power, and Workplace Culture*. Albany, NY: State University of New York Press.

McIntyre, Alice. 2008. *Participatory Action Research*. Los Angeles, CA: Sage Publications.

McPherson, Miller, Lynn Smith-Lovin, and James M. Cook. 2001. "Birds of a Feather: Homophily in Social Networks." *Annual Review of Sociology* 27(1): 415–444.

McQuaid, Jim, Laurel Smith-Doerr, and Daniel J. Monti Jr. 2010. "Expanding Entrepreneurship: Female and Foreign-born Founders of New England Biotechnology Firms." *American Behavioral Scientist* 53(7): 1045–1063.

McTigue, Tricia, Kevin Stainback, and Donald Tomaskovic-Devey. 2009. "An Organizational Approach to Understanding Sex and Race Segregation in US Workplaces." *Social Forces* 87(3): 1499–1527.

Medina, Karen. 2011. "Arriving as Pregnant Tourists, Leaving With American Babies." *New York Times*. March 28. Retrieved November 25, 2013 (http://www.nytimes.com/2011/03/29/us/29babies.html?pagewanted=1&_r=1).

Mieg, Harald A. 2006. "Social and Sociological Factors in the Development of Expertise." In *The Cambridge Handbook of Expertise and Expert Performance*, edited by K. A. Ericsson, N. Charness, P. J. Feltovich, and R. R. Hoffman. Cambridge: Cambridge University Press.

Miller, Jennifer M., and Maryann P. Feldman. 2014. "The Sorcerer's Postdoc Apprentice: Uncertain Funding and Contingent Highly Skilled Labour." *Cambridge Journal of Regions, Economy, and Society* 7(2): 289–305.

Mintz, Beth, and Daniel H. Krymkowski. 2010. "The Intersection of Race/Ethnicity and Gender in Occupational Segregation." *International Journal of Sociology* 40(4): 31–58.

Misa, Thomas J. 2010. "Gender Codes: Defining the Problem." In *Gender Codes: Why Women are Leaving Computing*, edited by T. J. Misa, 3–23. Hoboken, NJ: John Wiley and Sons.

Misra, Joya, Jennifer Lundquist, Elissa Dahlberg Holmes, and Stephanie Agiomavritis. 2011. "The Ivory Ceiling of Service Work." *Academe* 97(1): 22–26.

Misra, Joya, Jennifer H. Lundquist, and Abby Templer. 2012. "Gender, Work Time, and Care Responsibilities Among Faculty." *Sociological Forum* 27(2): 300–323.

MIT (Massachusetts Institute of Technology). 1999. "A Study on the Status of Women Faculty in Science at MIT." The MIT Faculty Newsletter. Retrieved on March 1, 2015 (http://web.mit.edu/fnl/women/women.pdf).

Monroe Kristen, Saba Ozyurt, Ted Wrigley, and Amy Alexander. 2008. "Gender Equality in Academia: Bad News from the Trenches and Some Possible Solutions." *Perspectives Politics* 6(2): 215–233.

Moody, JoAnn. 2012. *Faculty Diversity: Removing the Barriers*. New York: Routledge.

Moss, Philip, and Chris Tilly. 2001. *Stories Employers Tell: Race, Skill, and Hiring in America*. New York: Russell Sage Foundation.

Moss-Racusin, Corrine. A., John F. Dovidio, Victoria L. Brescoll, Mark J. Graham, and Jo Handelsman. 2012. "Science Faculty's Subtle Gender Biases Favor Male Students." *Proceedings of the National Academy of Sciences* 109(41): 16474–16479.

Moss-Racusin, Corinne A., and Laurie A. Rudman. 2010. "Disruptions in Women's Self- Promotion: The Backlash Avoidance Model." *Psychology of Women Quarterly* 34(2): 186–202.

National Academy of Sciences. 2007. *Rising Above the Gathering Storm: Energizing and Employing America for a Brighter Economic Future*. Washington, D.C.: National Academies Press.

National Academy of Sciences. 2010. *Rising Above the Gathering Storm, Revisited: Rapidly Approaching Category 5*. Washington, D.C.: The National Academies Press.

National Academy of Sciences. 2011. *Expanding Underrepresented Minority Participation: America's Science and Technology Talent at the Crossroads*. Washington, D.C.: National Academies Press.

National Academy of Sciences, Committee on Maximizing the Potential of Women in Academic Science and Engineering. 2007. *Beyond Bias and Barriers: Fulfilling the Potential of Women in Academic Science and Engineering*. Washington, D.C.: The National Academies Press.

National Institutes of Health. n.d. "NIH—Office of Budget—Appropriations History by Institute/Center (1938 to Present)." *National Institutes of Health: Office of Budget*. Retrieved March 21, 2015 (http://officeofbudget.od.nih.gov/approp_hist.html).

National Institutes of Health. 2012. "NIH Research Project Grant Program (R01)." *NIH Research Project Grant Program (R01)*. Retrieved March 20, 2015 (http://grants.nih.gov/grants/funding/r01.htm).

National Institutes of Health. 2014a. "NIH Data Book." *Research Portfolio Online Reporting Tools*. Retrieved March 20, 2015 (http://report.nih.gov/nihdatabook/index.aspx).

National Institutes of Health. 2014b. "Table #218: Success Rates Of NIH R01 Equivalent and Research Project Grants Applications, Fiscal Years 1970–2014." Retrieved March 21, 2015 (www.reports.nih.gov).

National Institutes of Health. 2015. "Kirschstein-NRSA Stipend Levels." Retrieved March 5, 2015 (era.nih.gov/files/nrsa_stipend_history.xlsx).

National Research Council. 2000. *Enhancing the Postdoctoral Experience for Scientists and Engineers. A Guide for Postdoctoral Scholars, Advisers, Institutions, Funding Organizations and Disciplinary Societies.* Washington, D.C.: National Academy Press.

National Research Council. 2005a. *Bridges to Independence Fostering the Independence of New Investigators in Biomedical Research.* Washington, D.C.: National Academies Press.

National Research Council. 2005b. *Policy Implications of International Graduate Students and Postdoctoral Scholars in the United States.* Washington, D.C.: National Academies Press.

National Research Council. 2010. *Gender Differences at Critical Transitions in the Careers of Science, Engineering, and Mathematics Faculty.* Washington, D.C.: National Academies Press.

National Research Council. 2011. *Research Training in the Biomedical, Behavioral, and Clinical Research Sciences.* Washington, D.C.: National Academies Press.

National Research Council. 2014. *The Postdoctoral Experience Revisited.* Washington, D.C.: National Academies Press.

National Science Board. 2008. *Science and Engineering Indicators, 2008: Volume 2, Appendix Tables (NSF 08–01A).* Arlington, VA: National Science Foundation.

National Science Board. 2014. *Science and Engineering Indicators 2014 (NSB 14–01).* Arlington, VA: National Science Foundation.

National Science Foundation. 1993. *Human Resources for Science & Technology: The Asian Region (NSF 93–303).* Arlington, VA: National Science Foundation.

National Science Foundation. 2009. "Survey of Graduate Students and Postdoctorates in Science and Engineering." Retrieved March 1, 2015 (http://www.nsf.gov/statistics/srvygradpostdoc/).

National Science Foundation, National Center for Science and Engineering Statistics. 2013. *Women, Minorities, and Persons with Disabilities in Science and Engineering: 2013.* Special Report NSF 13–304. Arlington, VA. Retrieved May 1, 2013 (http://www.nsf.gov/statistics/wmpd/).

National Science Foundation, National Center for Science and Engineering Statistics. 2015. *Women, Minorities, and Persons with Disabilities in Science and Engineering: 2015.* Special Report NSF 15–311. Arlington, VA. Retrieved March 27, 2015 (http://www.nsf.gov/statistics/wmpd/).

National Science Foundation, Science Resources Statistics. 2008. *Thirty-Three Years of Women in S&E Faculty Positions (NSF-08–308).* Arlington, VA: National Science Foundation.

National Science and Technology Council. 2013. *Federal Science, Technology, Engineering, and Mathematics (STEM) Education 5–Year Strategic Plan.* Washington, D.C.: Executive Office of the President.

Neckerman, Kathryn M., and Joleen Kirschenman. 1991. "Hiring Strategies, Racial Bias, and Inner-City Workers." *Social Problems* 38(4): 433–447.

Nelson, Lori J., and Joel Cooper. 1997. "Gender Differences in Children's Reactions to Success and Failure with Computers." *Computers in Human Behavior* 13(2): 247–267.

Newbold, K. Bruce. 2002. "Refugees into Immigrants: Assessing the Adjustment of Southeast Asian Refugees in the U.S., 1975–1990." *Canadian Studies in Population* 29(1): 151–171.

Ngai, Mae. 2004. *Impossible Subjects: Illegal Aliens and the Making of Modern America.* Princeton, NJ: Princeton University Press.

Niemann, Yolanda Flores, and John F. Dovidio. 1998. "Relationship of Solo Status, Academic Rank, and Perceived Distinctiveness to Job Satisfaction of Racial/ethnic Minorities." *Journal of Applied Psychology* 83(1): 55–71.

Nonaka, Ikujiro, Ryoko Toyama, and Akiya Nagata. 2000. "A Firm as a Knowledge-creating Entity: A New Perspective on the Theory of the Firm." *Industrial and Corporate Change* 9(1): 1–20.

Nutt, Paul C., and Robert W. Backoff. 1997. "Organizational Transformation." *Journal of Management Inquiry* 6(3): 235–254.

O'Laughlin, Elizabeth M., and Lisa G. Bischoff. 2005. "Balancing Parenthood and Academia Work/F,amily Stress as Influenced by Gender and Tenure Status." *Journal of Family Issues* 26(1): 79–106.

Olsen, Deborah, Sue A. Maple and Frances K. Stage. 1995. "Women and Minority Faculty Job Satisfaction: Professional Role Interests, Professional Satisfactions, and Institutional Fit." *The Journal of Higher Education* 66(3): 267–293.

O'Meara, KerryAnn. 2014. "Half-Way Out: How Requiring Outside Offers to Raise Salaries Influences Faculty Retention and Organizational Commitment." *Research in Higher Education* 56(3): 279–298.

Ong, Maria. 2005. "Body Projects of Young Women of Color in Physics: Intersections of Gender, Race, and Science." *Social Problems* 52(4): 593–617.

Ong, Maria. 2011. "The Status of Women of Color in Computer Science." *Communications of the ACM* 54(7): 32–34.

Ong, Maria, Carol Wright, Lorelle L. Espinosa, and Gary Orfield. 2011. "Inside the Double Bind: A Synthesis of Empirical Research on Undergraduate and Graduate Women of Color in Science, Technology, Engineering, and Mathematics." *Harvard Educational Review* 81(2): 172–208.

Oshagbemi, Titus. 1997. "The Influence of Rank on the Job Satisfaction of Organizational Members." *Journal of Managerial Psychology* 12(8): 511–519.

Oshagbemi, Titus. 2000. "Gender Differences in the Job Satisfaction of University Teachers." *Women in Management Review* 15(7): 331–343.

Paek, Hye J., and Hemant Shah. 2003. "Racial Ideology, Model Minorities, and the "'Not-So-Silent Partner': Stereotyping of Asian Americans in U.S. Magazine Advertising." *Howard Journal of Communications* 14(4): 225–243.

Page, Scott E. 2007. *The Difference: How the Power of Diversity Creates Better Groups, Firms, Schools, and Societies.* Princeton, NJ: Princeton University Press.

Park, Lora E., Ariana F. Young, Jordan T. Troisi, and Rebecca T. Pinkus. 2011. "Effects of Everyday Romantic Goal Pursuits on Women's Attitudes Towards Math and Science." *Personality and Social Psychology Bulletin* 37(9): 1259–1273.

Park, Shelley M. 1996. "Research, Teaching, and Service: Why Shouldn't Women's Work Count?" *Journal of Higher Education* 67(1): 46–84.

Pearson, Willie, and Alan Fechter. 1994. *Who Will Do Science? Educating the Next Generation.* Baltimore, MD: Johns Hopkins University Press.

Perna, Laura W. 2001. "Sex and Race Differences in Faculty Tenure and Promotion." *Research in Higher Education* 42(5): 541–567.

Pinker, Susan. 2008. *The Sexual Paradox: Extreme Men, Gifted Women and the Real Gender Gap.* Toronto, Canada: Random House.

Polanyi, Michael. 1966. *The Tacit Dimension.* Garden City, NY: Doubleday and Company, Inc.

Porter, Stephen R. 2007. "A Closer Look at Faculty Service: What Affects Participation on Committees?" *The Journal of Higher Education* 78(5): 523–541.

Powell, Walter, and Karisa Spellman. 2004. "The Knowledge Economy." *Annual Review of Sociology* 30: 199–220.

Preston, Anne Elizabeth. 2004. *Leaving Science: Occupational Exit from Scientific Careers.* New York: Russell Sage Foundation.

Probert, Belinda. 2005. "'I Just Couldn't Fit In': Gender and Unequal Outcomes in Academic Careers." *Gender, Work, and Organization* 12(1): 50–72.

Pyke, Karen. 2011. "Service and Gender Inequity among Faculty." *PS: Political Science and Politics* 44(1): 85–87.

Rabinowitz, Vita C., and Virginia Valian. 2007. "Beyond Mentoring: A Sponsorship Program to Improve Women's Success." In *Transforming Science and Engineering: Advancing Academic Women*, edited by A. Stewart, J. Malley, and D. LaVaque-Manty. Ann Arbor, MI: University of Michigan Press

Rajgopal, Shoba Sharad. 2010. "'The Daughter of Fu Manchu': The Pedagogy of Deconstructing the Representation of Asian Women in Film and Fiction." *Meridians: Feminism, Race, Transnationalism* 10(2): 141–162.

Regets, Mark. 2007. "Research Issues in the International Migration of Highly Skilled Workers: A Perspective with Data from the United States." Working Paper, Science Resource Statistics, National Science Foundation.

Reskin, Barbara F., 2000. "The Proximate Causes of Employment Discrimination." *Contemporary Sociology* 29(2): 319–328.

Reskin, Barbara. 2003. "Including Mechanisms in Our Models Ascriptive Inequality." *American Sociological Review* 68: 1–21.

Reskin, Barbara F. and Patricia A. Roos. 1990. *Job Queues, Gender Queues: Explaining Women's Inroads into Male Occupations.* Philadelphia, PA: Temple University Press.

Reyes, Marie-Elena. 2011. "Unique Challenges for Women of Color in STEM Transferring from Community Colleges to Universities." *Harvard Educational Review* 81(2): 241–262.

Rhoton, Laura. 2011. "Distancing as a Gendered Barrier: Understanding Women Scientists' Gender Practices." *Gender and Society* 25(6): 696–716.

Rice, R. Eugene, Mary Deane Sorcenelli, and Ann Austin. 2000. *Heading New Voices: Academic Careers for a New Generation.* Washington, D.C.: American Association for Higher Education.

Richardson, Matthew. 2013. "A Funding Profile of the NIH." *Research Trends*. Retrieved March 20, 2015 (http://www.researchtrends.com/issue-34-september-2013/a-funding-profile-of-the-nih/).

Ridgeway, Cecilia L. 2011. *Framed by Gender: How Gender Persists in the Modern World*. Oxford: Oxford University Press.

Riegle-Crumb, Catherine, and Melissa Humphries. 2012. "Exploring Bias in Math Teachers' Perceptions of Students' Ability by Gender and Race/Ethnicity." *Gender and Society* 26(2): 290–322.

Riegle-Crumb, Catherine, and Barbara King. 2010. "Questioning a White Male Advantage in STEM: Examining Disparities in College Major by Gender and Race/Ethnicity." *Educational Researcher* 39: 656–664.

Riessman, Catherine Kohler. 2004. "Narrative Analysis." In *Encyclopedia of Social Science Research Methods*, edited by M. S. Lewis-Beck, A. E. Bryman, and T. F. Liao. London and Newbury Park, CA: Sage Publications.

Riffle, Rebecca, Tamera Schneider, Amy Hillard, Emily Polander, Sarah Jackson, Peggy DesAutels, and Michele Wheatly. 2013. "A Mixed Methods Study of Gender, STEM Department Climate, and Workplace Outcomes." *Journal of Women and Minorities in Science and Engineering* 19(3): 227–243.

Riger, Stephanie, Joseph P. Stokes, Sheela Raja, and Megan Sullivan. 1997. "Measuring Perceptions of the Work Environment for Female Faculty." *The Review of Higher Education* 21(1): 63–78.

Risman, Barbara. 2004. "Gender as Social Structure: Theory Wrestling with Activism." *Gender and Society* 18(4): 429–450.

Romero, Mary. 1988. "Sisterhood and Domestic Service: Race, Class and Gender in the Mistress-Maid Relationship." *Humanity and Society* 12(4): 318–346.

Roos, Patricia A., and Mary L. Gatta. 2009. "Gender (In)equity in the Academy: Subtle Mechanisms and the Production of Inequality." *Research in Social Stratification and Mobility* 27: 177–200.

Roth, Louise Marie. 2004. "The Social Psychology of Tokenism: Status and Homophily Processes on Wall Street." *Sociological Perspectives* 47(2): 189–214.

Roth, Wendy, and Gerhard Sonnert. 2011. "The Costs and Benefits of 'Red Tape': Anti-Bureaucratic Structure and Gender Inequity in a Science Research Organization." *Social Studies of Science* 41: 385–409.

Rosenbloom, Joshua L., Ronald A. Ash, Brandon Dupont, and LeAnne Coder. 2008. "Why Are There so Few Women in Information Technology? Assessing the Role of Personality in Career Choices." *Journal of Economic Psychology* 29(4): 543–554.

Rosser, Sue Vilhauer. 2004. *The Science Glass Ceiling: Academic Women Scientists and the Struggle to Succeed*. New York: Routledge.

Rosser, Sue V. 2014. "Senior Compared to Junior Women Academic Scientists: Similar or Different Needs?" In *Gender Transformation in the Academy*, (vol. 19, *Advances in Gender Research*), edited by V. Demos, C. W. Berheide, and M. T. Segal. Bingley, UK: Emerald Publishing Group Limited.

Ruble, Racheal A., and Yan B. Zhang. 2013. "Stereotypes of Chinese International Students Held By Americans." *International Journal of Intercultural Relations* 37(2): 202–211.

Sabharwal, Meghna, and Elizabeth A. Corley. 2009. "Faculty Job Satisfaction across Gender and Discipline." *The Social Science Journal* 46(3): 539–556.

Sakamoto, Arthur, and Hyeyoung Woo. 2007. "The Socioeconomic Attainments of Second-Generation Cambodian, Hmong, Laotian, and Vietnamese Americans." *Sociological Inquiry* 77(1): 44–75

Samble, Jennifer N. 2008. "Female Faculty: Challenges and Choices in the United States and Beyond." *New Directions for Higher Education* 143: 55–62.

Sánchez, George. J. 1995. *Becoming Mexican American: Ethnicity, Culture, and Identity in Chicano Los Angeles, 1900–1945.* New York: Oxford University Press.

Schneider, Beth E. 1987. "Graduate Women, Sexual Harassment, and University Policy." *The Journal of Higher Education* 58(1): 46–65.

Schumann, Katrina, and Michael Ross. 2010. "Why Women Apologize More Than Men: Gender Differences in Thresholds for Perceiving Offensive Behavior." *Psychological Science* 21(11): 1649–1655.

Shanteau, James. 1988. "Psychological Characteristics of Expert Decision Makers." *Acta Psychologica* 68: 203–215.

Seigel, Roberta. 1996. *Ambition and Accommodation.* Chicago: University of Chicago Press.

Seldin, Peter. 1984. *Changing Practices in Faculty Evaluation.* San Francisco: Jossey-Bass.

Settles, Isis H., Lilia M. Cortina, Abigail J. Stewart, and Janet Malley. 2007. "Voice Matters: Buffering the Impact of a Negative Climate for Women in Science." *Psychology of Women Quarterly* 31(3): 270–281.

Sharpe, Norean Radke, and Gerhard Sonnert. 1999. "Proportions of Women Faculty and Students in the Mathematical Sciences: A Trend Analysis by Institutional Group." *Journal of Women and Minorities in Science and Engineering* 3: 17–27.

Shaw, Allison K., and Daniel Stanton. 2012. "Leaks in the Pipeline: Separating Demographic Inertia From Ongoing Gender Differences in Academia." *Proceedings of the Royal Society B: Biological Sciences* 279(1743): 3736–3741.

Sheridan, Jennifer T., Eva Fine, Christine Maidl Pribbenow, Jo Handelsman, and Molly Carnes. 2010. "Searching for Excellence & Diversity: Increasing the Hiring of Women Faculty at one Academic Medical Center." *Academic Medicine* 85(6): 999–1007.

Shih, Johanna. 2002. "'. . .Yeah, I Could Hire this One, But I Know It's Gonna be a Problem': How Race, Nativity and Gender Affect Employers' Perceptions of the Manageability of Job Seekers." *Ethnic and Racial Studies* 25(1): 99–119.

Smith-Doerr, Laurel. 2004. *Women's Work: Gender Equality vs. Hierarchy in the Life Sciences.* Boulder, CO: Lynne Rienner Publishers.

Smith-Doerr, Laurel. 2006. "Stuck in the Middle: Doctoral Education Ranking and Career Outcomes for Life Scientists." *Bulletin of Science, Technology and Society* 26(3): 243–245.

Solórzano, Daniel, Miguel Ceja, and Tara Yosso. 2000. "Critical Race Theory, Racial Microaggressions, and Campus Racial Climate: The Experiences of African American College Students." *The Journal of Negro Education* 69(1): 60–73.

Solórzano, Daniel G., and Octavio Villalpando. 1998. "Critical Race Theory, Marginality, and the Experience of Students of Color in Higher Education." In *The Sociology of Education: Emerging Perspectives*, edited by C. A. Torres and T. R. Mitchell. Albany, NY: State University of New York Press.

Sonnert, Gerhard, Mary Frank Fox, and Kristen Adkins. 2007. "Undergraduate Women in Science and Engineering: Effects of Faculty, Fields, and Institutions Over Time." *Social Science Quarterly* 88: 1333–1356.

Sonnert, Gerhard, and Gerald Holton. 1995. *Gender Differences in Science Careers.* New Brunswick, NJ: Rutgers University Press.

Stainback, Kevin, and Donald Tomaskovic-Devey. 2012. *Documenting Desegregation: Racial and Gender Segregation in the Private-Sector Since the Civil Rights Act.* New York: Russell Sage Foundation.

Stake, Joyce, and Margaret Noonan. 1985. "The Influence of Teacher Models on the Career Confidence and Motivation of College Students." *Sex Roles* 12(9/10): 1023–1031.

Steinpreis, Rhea E., Katie A. Anders, and Dawn Ritzke. 1999. "The Impact of Gender on the Review of the Curricula Vitae of Job Applicants and Tenure Candidates: A National Empirical Study." *Sex Roles* 41(7/8): 509–528.

Stephan, Paula E. 2012. *How Economics Shapes Science.* Cambridge, MA: Harvard University Press.

Stephan, Paula E., and Sharon G. Levin. 1992. *Striking the Mother Lode in Science: The Importance of Age, Place, and Time.* New York: Oxford University Press.

Stephan, Paula, and Jennifer Ma. 2005. "The Increased Frequency and Duration of the Postdoctorate Career Stage." *American Economic Review* 95(2): 71–75.

Stewart, Abigail J., Danielle La Vaque-Manty, and Janet E. Malley. 2004. "Recruiting Female Faculty Members in Science and Engineering: Preliminary Evaluation of One Intervention Model." *Journal of Women and Minorities in Science and Engineering* 10(4): 361–375.

Stewart, Abigail, Janet E. Malley, and Danielle LaVaque-Manty. 2007. *Transforming Science and Engineering: Advancing Academic Women.* Ann Arbor, MI: University of Michigan Press.

Stout, Jane G., Nilanjana Dasgupta, Matthew Hunsinger, and Melissa A. McManus. 2010. "STEMing the Tide: Using Ingroup Experts to Inoculate Women's Self-Concept in Science, Technology, Engineering, and Mathematics (STEM)." *Journal of Personality and Social Psychology* 100(2): 255–270.

Strage, Amy, and Joan Merdinger. 2015. "Professional Growth and Renewal for Mid-Career Faculty." *The Journal of Faculty Development* 29(1): 41–50.

Strenta, A. Christopher, Rogers Elliott, Russell Adair, Michael Matier, and Jannah Scott. 1994. "Choosing and Leaving Science in Highly Selective Institutions." *Research in Higher Education* 35(5): 513–547.

Su, Rong, James Rounds, and Patrick Armstrong. 2009. "Men and Things, Women and People: A Meta-Analysis of Sex Differences in Interests." *Psychological Bulletin* 135(6): 859–884.

Tack, Martha W., and Carol L Patitu. 1992. *Faculty Job Satisfaction: Women and Minorities in Peril (ASHE-ERIC Higher Education Report No. 4)*. Publications Department, ASHE-ERIC Higher Education Reports, The George Washington University: Washington, D.C.

Tajfel, Henri, and John Turner. 1979. "An Integrative Theory of Intergroup Conflict." In *The Social Psychology of Intergroup Relations*, edited by W. G. Austin and S. Worchel. Monterey, CA: Brooks/Cole.

Takaki, Ronald. 1989. *Strangers From a Different Shore: A History of Asian Americans*. Boston: Little, Brown and Company.

Takaki, Ronald. 1993. *A Different Mirror: A History of Multicultural America*. Boston: Back Bay Books.

Teitelbaum, Michael S. 2014. *Falling Behind? Boom, Bust, and the Global Race for Scientific Talent*. Princeton, NJ: Princeton University Press.

Terosky, Aimee LaPointe, KerryAnn O'Meara, and Corbin M. Campbell. 2014. "Enabling Possibility: Women Associate Professors' Sense of Agency in Career Advancement." *Journal of Diversity in Higher Education* 7(1): 58–76.

Thoman, Dustin, and Paul White. 2008. "Variations of Gender–Math Stereotype Content Affect Women's Vulnerability to Stereotype Threat." *Sex Roles* 58: 702–712.

Thon, Jonathan N. 2014. "Nothing To Lose: Why Early Career Scientists Make Ideal Entrepreneurs." *Trends in Biochemical Sciences* 39(12): 571–73.

Thorne, Barrie. 1993. *Gender Play: Girls and Boys in School*. New Brunswick, NJ: Rutgers University Press.

Tilly, Charles. 1999. *Durable Inequality*. Berkeley: University of California Press.

Timberlake, Jeffrey M., Junia Howell, Amy Baumann Grau, and Rhys H. Williams. 2015. "Who 'They' Are Matters: Immigrant Stereotypes and Assessments of the Impact of Immigration." *The Sociological Quarterly* 56(2): 267–299.

Toutkoushian, Robert K., and Valerie Martin Conley. 2005. "Progress For Women in Academe, Yet Inequities Persist: Evidence from NSOPF: 99." *Research in Higher Education* 46(1): 1–28.

Tripp, Aili Mari. 2002. "Combining Intercontinental Parenting and Research: Dilemmas and Strategies for Women." *Signs* 27(3): 793–811.

Trix, Frances, and Carolyn Psenka. 2003. "Exploring the Color of Glass: Letters of Recommendation for Female and Male Medical Faculty." *Discourse and Society* 14(2): 191–220.

Trower, Cathy Ann. 2012. *Success on the Tenure Track: Five Keys to Faculty Job Satisfaction*. Baltimore: Johns Hopkins University Press.

Trower, Cathy Ann, and Jared L. Bleak. 2004. *Study of New Scholars. Institutional Type: Statistical Report*. Harvard Graduate School of Education, Cambridge, MA. Retrieved on March 1, 2015 (http://www.kuleuven.be/studentenadministratie/diversiteit/publicaties/Gender-statistical-report.pdf).

Tsui, Anne S., and Charles A. O'Reilly. 1989. "Beyond Simple Demographic Effects: the Importance of Relational Demography in Superior-Subordinate Dyads." *Academy of Management Journal* 32(2): 402–423.

Uhly, Katrina, Laura Visser, and Kathrin Zippel. 2015. "Gendered Patterns in International Research Collaborations in Academia." *Studies in Higher Education*: 1–23.

Valian, Virginia. 1998. *Why So Slow? The Advancement of Women.* Cambridge, MA: MIT Press.

Van den Brink, Marieke, and Yvonne Benschop. 2012. "Slaying the Seven-Headed Dragon: The Quest for Gender Change in Academia." *Gender, Work and Organization* 19(1): 71–92.

Varma, Roli. 2007. "Women in Computing: The Role of Geek Culture." *Science as Culture* 16(4): 359–376.

Varma, Roli. 2010. "Why So Few Women Enroll in Computing? Gender and Ethnic Diferences in Students' Perception." *Computer Science Education* 20(4): 301–316.

Vilorio, Dennis. 2014. "STEM 101: Intro to Tomorrow's Jobs." *Occupational Outlook Quarterly*, Spring 2014. Washington, D.C.: Bureau of Labor Statistics.

Wagner, David G., and Joseph Berger. 1997. "Gender and Interpersonal Task Behaviors: Status Expectation Accounts." *Sociological Perspectives* 40(1): 1–32.

Wajcman, Judy. 1991. *Feminism Confronts Technology.* University Park, PA: Pennsylvania State Press.

Waldinger, Roger D., and Michael I. Lichter. 2003. *How the Other Half Works: Immigration and the Social Organization of Labor.* Berkeley, CA: University of California Press.

Waldinger, Roger, Nelson Lim, and David Cort. 2007. "Bad Jobs, Good Jobs, No Jobs? The Employment Experience of the Mexican American Second Generation." *Journal of Ethnic and Migration Studies* 33(1): 1–35.

Wasem, Ruth Ellen. 2012. "Immigration of Foreign Nationals with Science, Technology, Engineering, and Mathematics (STEM) Degrees." Congressional Research Service, 7–5700. Retrieved on March 1, 2015 (https://www.fas.org/sgp/crs/misc/R42530.pdf).

Watanabe, Megumi, and Christina D. Falci. 2014. "A Demands and Resources Approach to Understanding Faculty Turnover Intentions due to Work-Family Balance." *Journal of Family Issues.* Online First. 1–23.

Weeden, Kim A. 2002. "Why Do Some Occupations Pay More Than Others? Social Closure and Earnings Inequality in the United States." *American Journal of Sociology* 108(1): 55–101.

Wegner, Daniel M. 1986. "Transactive Memory: A Contemporary Analysis of the Group Mind." In *Theories of Group Behavior*, edited by B. Mullen and G. R. Goethals. New York: Springer-Verlag.

Wenneras, Christine, and Agnes Wold. 1997. "Nepotism and Sexism in Peer-Review." *Nature* 387: 341–343.

West, Candace, and Don Zimmerman. 1987. "Doing Gender." *Gender and Society* 1(2): 125–151.

West, Martha S., and John W. Curtis. 2006. *AAUP Faculty Gender Equity Indicators 2006*. Retrieved August 15, 2011 (http://www.aaup.org/NR/rdonlyres/63396944–44BE-4ABA-9815–5792D93856F1/0/AAUPGenderEquityIndicators2006.pdf).

Whitman, Neal, and Elaine Weiss. 1982. *Faculty Evaluation: The Use of Explicit Criteria for Promotion, Retention, and Tenure*. AAHE-ERIC Higher Education Research Report. Washington, D.C.: American Association for Higher Education.

Wiest, Lynda R. 1999. "Addressing the Needs of Graduate Women." *Contemporary Education* 70(2): 30–33.

Williams, Christine. 1992. "The Glass Escalator: Hidden Advantages for Men in the 'Female' Professions." *Social Problems* 39(3): 253–267.

Williams, Joan C. 2000. *Unbending Gender*. Oxford: Oxford University Press.

Williams, Joan C., Katherine W. Phillips, and Erika V. Hall. 2014. "Double Jeopardy: Gender Bias Against Women of Color." *Work Life Law: UC Hastings College of Law*. Retrieved on March 1, 2015 (http://www.uchastings.edu/news/articles/2015/01/double-jeopardy-report.pdf).

Williams, Rick L. 2000. "A Note on Robust Variance Estimation for Cluster-Correlated Data." *Biometrics* 56: 645–646.

Wilson, Fiona, and Donald Beaton. 1993. "The Theory and Practice of Appraisal." *Higher Education Quarterly* 47: 163–189.

Winkler, Larry Dean. 1982. *Job Satisfaction of University Faculty in the United States*. PhD dissertation, University of Nebraska-Lincoln. Paper AAI8217565. Retrieved on March 1, 2015 (http://digitalcommons.unl.edu/dissertations/AAI8217565).

Wischnevsky, J. Daniel, and Fariborz Damanpour. 2006. "Organizational Transformation and Performance: An Examination of Three Perspectives." *Journal of Management Issues* 28: 104–128.

Wolf-Wendel, Lisa Ellen, and Kelly Ward. 2006. "Academic Life and Motherhood: Variations by Institutional Type." *Higher Education* 52(3): 487–521.

Wolf-Wendel, Lisa Ellen, and Kelly Ward. 2013. "Work and Family Integration for Faculty: Recommendations for Chairs." *The Department Chair* 23(4): 1–3.

Wolfinger, Nicholas, Mary Ann Mason, and Marc Goulden. 2008. "Problems in the Pipeline: Gender, Marriage, and Fertility in the Ivory Tower." *Journal of Higher Education* 79: 388–405.

Wonch Hill, Patricia, Mary Anne Holmen, and Julia McQuillan. 2014. "The New STEM Faculty Profile: Balancing Family and Dual Careers." In *Gender Transformation in the Academy*, vol. 19, *Advances in Gender Research*, edited by V. Demos, C. W. Berheide, M. T. Segal. Bingley, UK: Emerald Group Publishing Limited.

Wooten, Melissa E., and Enobong H. Branch. 2012. "Defining Appropriate Labor: Race, Gender, and Idealization of Black Women in Domestic Service." *Race, Gender and Class*. 19(3): 292–308.

Wroblewski, Angela. 2014. "Gender Bias in Appointment Procedures for Full Professors: Challenges to Changing Traditional and Seemingly Gender Neutral Practices." In *Gender Transformation in the Academy*, vol. 19, *Advances in Gender*

Research edited by V. Demos, C. W. Berheide, and M. T. Segal. Bingley, UK: Emerald Publishing Group Limited.

Wu, Lilian, and Wei Jing. 2011. "Asian Women in STEM Careers: An Invisible Minority in a Double Bind." *Issues in Science and Technology* 28(1): 82–87.

Xie, Yu and Kimberlee Shauman. 1997. "Modeling the Sex-typing of Occupational Choice Influences of Occupational Structure." *Sociological Methods and Research* 26(2): 233–261.

Xie, Yu, and Kimberlee A. Shauman. 2003. *Women in Science: Career Processes and Outcomes.* Cambridge, MA: Harvard University Press.

Xie, Yu, and Kimberlee A. Shauman. 2004. "Immigrant Scientists/Engineers." *Social Forces* 82(4): 194–206.

Xu, Yonghong Jade. 2008. "Gender Disparity in STEM Disciplines: A Study of Faculty Attrition and Turnover Intentions." *Research in Higher Education* 49: 607–624.

Yeager, David Scott, and Carol S. Dweck. 2012. "Mindsets That Promote Resilience: When Students Believe That Personal Characteristics Can Be Developed." *Educational Psychologist* 47(4): 302–314.

Yen, Joyce W., Kate Quinn, Coleen Carrigan, Elizabeth Litzler, and Eve A. Riskin. 2007. "The ADVANCE Mentoring-for-Leadership Lunch Series for Women Faculty in STEM at the University of Washington." *Journal of Women and Minorities in Science and Engineering* 13(3): 191–206.

Yosso, Tara. J., William A. Smith, Miguel Ceja, and Daniel G. Solórzano. 2009. "Critical Race Theory, Racial Microaggressions, and Campus Racial Climate for Latina/o Undergraduates." *Harvard Educational Review* 79(4): 659–691.

Zamora, Emilio. 1993. *The World of the Mexican Worker in Texas.* College Station: Texas A&M Press.

Zhou Ying and J. Fredericks Volkwein. 2004. "Examining the Influences on Faculty Departure Intentions: A Comparison of Tenured versus Non-tenured Faculty at Research Universities Using NSOPF-99." *Research in Higher Education* 45(2): 139–176.

Zhou, Min. 2009. *Contemporary Chinese America: Immigration, Ethnicity, and Community Transformation.* Philadelphia: Temple University Press.

Zippel, Kathrin. 2011. "How Gender Neutral are State Policies on Science and International Mobility of Academics?" *Sociologica* 5(1): 1–17.

Zippel, Kathrin. Forthcoming. *Passport to Global Science: Academic Women Navigate International Collaborations.* Palo Alto, CA: Stanford University Press.

Index

About the Contributors

Sharla Alegria is a PhD candidate in the Department of Sociology at the University of Massachusetts-Amherst. Her dissertation examines how and why women remain underrepresented in the computing workforce despite support from both the private and public sectors to increase women's participation. She focuses on the interplay between race, gender, and migration in the development of the tech workforce and the experiences of tech workers to shed new light, not just on women's representation, but more broadly on how gender, race, and migration together shape opportunities for technical workers in the United States.

Mindy Anderson-Knott is the director of evaluation and development for the Social and Behavioral Sciences Research Consortium at the University of Nebraska-Lincoln. She was the internal evaluator on the ADVANCE-Nebraska NSF grant, and continues to evaluate projects on a wide variety of topics, many of which address gender and race inequities.

Catherine White Berheide is professor of sociology at Skidmore College and was principal investigator for the College's National Science Foundation ADVANCE PAID grant. Her research focuses on gender, work, and occupations as well as the relationship between work and family. She has published several books, numerous articles, book chapters, and other publications on these and related topics. Her most recent book, which she co-edited, *Gender Transformation in the Academy* (vol. 19 *Advances in Gender Research*, Emerald Publishing Group, 2014), also contains a chapter on promotion to full professor that she co-authored.

Enobong Hannah Branch is an associate professor of sociology and director of diversity advancement for the College of Social and Behavioral Sciences at University of Massachusetts-Amherst. She is also the past co-chair of the Social Science Advisory Board of the National Center for Women in Information Technology. Her research interests are in race, racism, and inequality; intersectional theory; work and occupations; and diversity in science. She is the author of *Opportunity Denied: Limiting Black Women to Devalued Work* (2011) as well as several journal articles.

Mary Frank Fox is an ADVANCE Professor in the School of Public Policy and co-director of the Center for the Study of Women, Science, and Technology at Georgia Institute of Technology. Her research focuses upon gender, science, and academia and has introduced and established ways in which the participation and performance of women and men reflect and are affected by social and organizational features of science and academia. Her publications appear in over fifty different scholarly and scientific journals, books, and collections.

Lisa M. Frehill is acting director of analytics at Energetics Technology Center currently serving as an Organizational Evaluation and Assessment researcher at the U.S. National Science Foundation (NSF). Since 1991, her research has focused on gender, science, and technology, with an emphasis on human capital issues within the international context. She was one of the first principal investigators/program directors of the NSF ADVANCE: Institutional Transformation program while an Associate Professor of Sociology at New Mexico State University. A research methodologist, her extensive knowledge of human resources data and evaluation expertise have been instrumental in change efforts at more than two dozen U.S. and international universities as well as many government agencies and non-governmental organizations. She co-edited the volume *Advancing Women in Science: An International Perspective* (Springer, 2015) with Willie Pearson Jr. and Connie L. McNeely.

Rachel A. Gordon is a professor of sociology and Faculty Fellow of the Honors College at the University of Illinois at Chicago and a professor at the Institute of Government and Public Affairs (IGPA) at the University of Illinois. Her research broadly aims to measure and model the contexts of children and families' lives, often using longitudinal datasets. She regularly engages with audiences beyond academia in order to both increase the relevance of her research for public decision making and to share the results of her own as well as her colleagues' research with policymakers, practitioners, journalists, and the public.

Patricia Wonch Hill is a research assistant professor in the Department of Sociology at the University of Nebraska-Lincoln. She conducts both applied and basic research that focuses on understanding how people use science to make decisions about their health and how science informs their opinions about health policy. Hill is particularly passionate about broadening participation in science, technology, engineering, and math (STEM), and much of her applied work involves creating and evaluating programs to increase STEM participation for both adults and youth who belong to historically underrepresented groups.

Laura E. Hirshfield is an assistant professor in the Department of Medical Education and Sociology at the University of Illinois at Chicago. Her research focuses on cultural/identity taxation or the "hidden labor" expected of women and numeric minorities in the workplace, specifically in the academy. Another area of focus is on gender in medical and STEM disciplines and how authority and expertise are established and portrayed in scientific settings.

Apriel K. Hodari is a principal investigator at Eureka Scientific, Inc., and serves as co-leader (with Maria Ong) of the Beyond the Double Bind projects, investigating the lived experiences of women of color in science, technology, engineering, and mathematics (STEM). She is an expert in STEM education research, STEM educational equity and workforce diversity, and the culture of STEM disciplines. Her work appears in over one hundred research and policy publications.

Mary Anne Holmes is a professor of practice (emerita) in the Department of Earth and Atmospheric Sciences, former director of the NSF-funded

ADVANCE-Nebraska at University of Nebraska-Lincoln, and former AD-VANCE Program Officer at the National Science Foundation (NSF). She is a past president of the Association for Women Geoscientists and a fellow of the Association for Women in Science. She is currently doing research on strategies to overcome barriers to the advancement of geoscience women in academia and is editor of *Women in the Geosciences: Practical, Positive Practices towards Parity* (Wiley, 2015).

Kathryn Kline is an assistant researcher at the National Regulatory Research Institute where she focuses on grid modernization, consumer experience, and infrastructure development issues. She is a recent graduate of the School of Public Policy at the Georgia Institute of Technology where she earned her master's degree. Her research interests include science, gender, and innovation policy.

Lily T. Ko is a research associate at Technical Educational Research Centers, Inc. (TERC), a STEM education research organization in Cambridge, Massachusetts. Via multiple NSF-funded projects led by Drs. Mia Ong and Apriel Hodari, she has advanced research on the success factors of women of color in STEM with the goal of broadening participation and increasing diversity. She is a strong proponent of connecting research to practitioners and policymakers.

Julia McQuillan is professor and chair of the Department of Sociology at the University of Nebraska. She has collaborated on multiple articles on the social dimensions of fertility and infertility using the longitudinal National Survey of Fertility Barriers, which she helped to create. She was the co-principal investigator on the ADVANCE-Nebraska NSF grant and helped lead research-based efforts to recruit, retain, and promote women in STEM at the University of Nebraska. She is currently co-investigator on an NIH Science Education Partnership Award called "Biology of Human," a project that involves a multi-disciplinary team that is using a longitudinal, network study of middle school youth, social inequality, and science identities to create ways to increase science engagement among middle school–aged youth.

Maria (Mia) Ong is a senior research scientist and Evaluator at the Technical Educational Research Centers, Inc. (TERC), a STEM education research organization in Cambridge, Massachusetts. Her research focuses on girls and women of color in education and careers in STEM. Her work has appeared in reports to U.S. Congress and to the U.S. Supreme Court, as well as in several journals.

Cassaundra Rodriguez is a PhD candidate in the Department of Sociology at the University of Massachusetts-Amherst. Her research interests include race, gender, immigration, social inequality, and labor.

Laurel Smith-Doerr is a professor of sociology and director of the Institute for Social Science Research at the University of Massachusetts-Amherst. Her research focuses on collaboration, implications of different organizational forms for women's equity in science, gendering of scientific networks and scientists' approaches to social and ethical responsibilities, and tensions in the institutionalization of science policy. She is the author of *Women's Work: Gender Equity v. Hierarchy in the Life Sciences* (Lynne Rienner, 2004).

Timothy Sacco is a PhD student in the Department of Sociology at the University of Massachusetts-Amherst. His research interests include science and technology studies, organizations, and culture. He focuses on interdisciplinarity, research collaboration, and commercialization in academic science.

Angela Stoutenburgh received her master's degree in gender and women's Studies at the University of Arizona. Her graduate research focused on the production of student indebtedness through discourse. She participated as a research assistant in the National Science Foundation–funded project "The Social Organization of Collaboration in the Chemical Sciences" (PIs Laurel Smith-Doerr and Jennifer Croissant).

Margaret L. Usdansky is a research associate professor in the Department of Child and Family Studies and director of the Academic Integrity Office at Syracuse University. Her research interests are in the areas of families, early childhood and parenting, higher education, and the transition to adulthood, particularly college and career.

Kathrin Zippel is an associate professor in the Department of Sociology and Anthropology at Northeastern University. Her research focuses on gender and globalization of academia including the mobility of academics and international research collaborations. Her research interests also include gender equality politics in higher education. She was the co-principal investigator on the ADVANCE-Northeastern NSF grant. She is the author of *The Politics of Sexual Harassment: A Comparative Study of the United States, the European Union, and Germany* (Cambridge University Press, 2006).